D1230031

The Spirits of Crossbones Graveyard

A PLAN of the CITYS of LONDON, WESTMINSTER and Borough of SOUTHWARK; with the new Additional Buildings Anno 172
A New Map of
LONDON
RIVER THAMES
Artillery Ground
St. James's Park
Lambeth
A Scale of Half a Mile

The Spirits of Crossbones Graveyard

TIME, RITUAL, AND SEXUAL COMMERCE IN LONDON

Sondra L. Hausner

INDIANA UNIVERSITY PRESS

BLOOMINGTON & INDIANAPOLIS

This book is a publication of

Indiana University Press
Office of Scholarly Publishing
Herman B Wells Library 350
1320 East 10th Street
Bloomington, Indiana 47405 USA

iupress.indiana.edu

The paper used in this publication meets the minimum requirements of the American National Standard for Information Sciences—Permanence of Paper for Printed Library Materials, ANSI Z39.48–1992.

Manufactured in the United States of America

Cataloging information is available from the Library of Congress.

ISBN 978-0-253-02124-3 (cloth)
ISBN 978-0-253-02136-6 (paperback)
ISBN 978-0-253-02147-2 (ebook)

1 2 3 4 5 21 20 19 18 17 16

For Ion

Ion Alexis Will (December 10, 1941–December 26, 2010)

A ROYAL PALACE

HENRY BOLINGBROKE Can no man tell me of my unthrifty son?
'Tis full three months since I did see him last;
If any plague hang over us, 'tis he.
I would to God, my lords, he might be found:
Inquire at London, 'mongst the taverns there,
For there, they say, he daily doth frequent,
With unrestrained loose companions,
Even such, they say, as stand in narrow lanes,
And beat our watch, and rob our passengers;
Which he, young wanton and effeminate boy,
Takes on the point of honour to support
So dissolute a crew.

HENRY PERCY My lord, some two days since I saw the prince,
And told him of those triumphs held at Oxford.

HENRY BOLINGBROKE And what said the gallant?

HENRY PERCY His answer was, he would unto the stews,
And from the common'st creature pluck a glove,
And wear it as a favour; and with that
He would unhorse the lustiest challenger.

HENRY BOLINGBROKE As dissolute as desperate; yet through both
I see some sparks of better hope, which elder years
May happily bring forth.

William Shakespeare, *Richard II* (1595–1596)

CONTENTS

ACKNOWLEDGMENTS

This project did not start as a book, but as the 2010 Barbara E. Ward Memorial Lecture, which I gave under the title of "Ritual Redemption in London's Economy of Love" at the invitation of Oxford's Institute for Gender Studies, and I remain grateful to Peggy Morgan and Maria Jaschok for thinking of me at the time. Rather than stopping there, it became a book at the encouragement of my institution, the Faculty of Theology—now the Faculty of Theology and Religion—at the University of Oxford, and particularly the rallying of my senior colleagues, including Sarah Foot, Paul Joyce (whose visit to the ritual with me was memorable), George Pattison, Guy Stroumsa, and Johannes Zachhuber, all of whom were willing and delighted to have an anthropologist visit the habits of English history.

But it is no mean task to undertake a historical investigation when one's colleagues are the best historians in the trade. Mark Edwards has been a constant source of intellectual support and inexhaustible knowledge, and a dear friend throughout. Diarmaid MacCulloch encouraged me to work in the thick of Reformation history when he knew full well I was a novice; his scholarship is an inspiration. Sarah Apetrei offered kind and helpful commentary. The historians of St. Peter's College, Oxford—most especially experts in the medieval histories of gender, Henrietta Leyser and Caroline Barron—gave me a green light and an encouraging push, and graciously introduced me to the larger world of medieval scholarship. Martha Carlin took considerable care to teach me something of Southwark in the Middle Ages. More than the usual scholarly caveat, any errors in this text are mine alone.

I have relied on long-standing academic mentorship as well as recent collegiality: I am lucky to have had mentorship and training on gender and sexuality early on in academic life, and the inspiration of anthropologist and theorist Carole Vance, as well as the friendship of Diane di Mauro, influence me still. The late professor A. Thomas Kirsch trained me as an anthropologist of religion, and I am honored to follow in his footsteps in this fulfilling profession. Since 2007, the Institute of Social and Cultural Anthropology at Oxford has been a disciplinary intellectual home.

St. Peter's College has been a support in many ways, specifically the women's empowerment network that comprised Hanneke Grootenboer, Abigail Williams, Claire Williams, and myself. This book would not have seen the light of day—nor any of us the joy of being together at Oxford—without our sisterhood. The St. Peter's College Library patiently extended my long list of borrowed books on women's histories in England time and time again—and Janet Foot and David Johnson insisted that they wanted to see the finished product in a way that kept me going. My students at St. Peter's and at other Colleges across the University cannot know how much they helped me think through the layered terrain of ritual thought and action.

Women friends in Oxford and in London have been the most sustaining part of the last five years, during which this book was conceived, researched, written, and rewritten: Jocelyn Alexander, Bridget Anderson, Rutvica Andrijasevic, Julie Archambault, Elizabeth Frood, Clare Harris, Hélène Neveu Kringelbach, Emily Paddon, and Isabel Shutes—all wonderful scholars in their own right but, more importantly, wonderful friends—made the complex worlds of gender theory and academic life rich and fruitful. In addition, many dear ones have supported me along the way, and accompanied me to the ritual on which this book is based: Ben Eaton (who also gave me remedial history lessons); the late Lindsay Friedman; my mother and sister, Nancy and Ellen Hausner; and the memory of my father, Bernard Hausner. On the other side of the Atlantic, I am lucky to have Greta Austin, church historian and close friend. Most importantly, John Constable-Crow supported the writing of this book and the investigations it elicited: it was a treat to have him hear an early reading and disagree with parts. John and his flock have welcomed me with open arms, for which I owe much thanks.

Early versions of chapter 4, under the name "Gender, Resistance, and the Origins of English Transnationalism (1558–Present)," were given in 2014 at the Radical Anthropology Group in London, the Religious History Seminar in Oxford, and the Wednesday Club at Christ Church. My thanks go to convenors and open-minded audiences both, who received the argument with some curiosity but also genuine interest in the combined contours of cultural history and social theory. The Humanities Division at Oxford supported the project throughout, including with a John Fell Fund grant in 2011 to enable writing at what turned out to be an early stage. The wondrous Bodleian Libraries never disappointed, and the Southwark Local History Library gave me a taste of what it was to be a practicing historian.

A project of temporal complexity goes through many phases of its own. The last stages of writing took place during a visiting appointment at the University of Tübingen in 2015, where the book as a whole was presented to the Department of Social and Cultural Anthropology; my thanks go to Roland Hardenberg for that generous invitation. Final editing took place at the gracious home of Sophia Preza and Ira Schepetin in Woodstock, New York, with the support of many New York City friends and family members. At Indiana University Press, three anonymous readers kept me true both to the ethos of the project and to the discipline of anthropology, and Rebecca Tolen remained a steadfast support and superb editor. Darja Malcolm-Clarke was an exceptionally patient and kind project manager.

The book is dedicated to Ion Will, known to me since early life as Wicked Uncle Ion, who inspired me to end up at Oxford, much as he insisted that I attend the ritual in the first place. He was sure John and I would have a lot to say to each other. He did not live to see the book come to fruition, but he knew it was in process and that it would be for him. He was an inspiration to see the world with mischievous eyes, never to take anything for granted, and to commune with the spirits who had been around the block—and listen to what they might have to say.

The Spirits of Crossbones Graveyard

John Crow

Introduction

SET AND SETTING

So keep on playing those mind games together
Doing the ritual dance in the sun
Millions of mind guerrillas
Putting their soul power to the karmic wheel
Keep on playing those mind games together
Raising the spirit of peace and love

John Lennon, "Mind Games" (1973)

On November 23, 1996, a London playwright and performer by the name of John Constable had a shamanic vision. In it, a totemic Goose appeared to tell him her tale. She was the spirit of a particular Goose, one who hailed from the jurisdiction of Winchester. In fact, she identified as a Winchester Goose, argot for a medieval prostitute. She and her fellow Winchester Geese had been sex workers in what were called "stews" (or "stewes") or brothels—or, in later colloquial accounts, "nunneries"[1]—on London's South Bank, in what is now the Borough of Southwark, a mere five hundred years ago.

It is impossible to establish exactly when these Southwark stews were first set up, but we know they operated at least from the late fourteenth century to the mid-sixteenth century. Prostitution in the area very likely preceded this date, however, and we know from court documents intending to bring offenders to trial that it continued long after. Sex work, lest we forget, is the world's oldest profession, and places on the periphery—where Southwark once was—are likely to be the host locations for the perennial trade of love for money, whether or not that exchange is considered a sin.

Whether such a transaction is more sinful than most is the subject of much debate in many places and among many populations. The halls of academe and the churches of England are some of the places where people have pondered whether prostitution should be legal or illegal, supported or barred—and whether the women who sell sex should be pitied or protected, kept down or bolstered up. Religious institutions throughout history and across the world have had to negotiate the ineffable power of sexual attraction and desire—and the resultant place of sex work in society—no matter how much emphasis they also place on moral sexual standards, or on the importance of family, kinship, and marital relations within the home.

The Winchester Goose did not appear to John in order to argue that her trade was sacred, as prostitution might be cast in some religious contexts. She was simply asking for respect: since it had not been accorded her in her own lifetime or era, might she be recognized now, in the twenty-first century? A historical injustice, she claimed, had been done: she and her fellow Geese were not illegal sex workers or trafficked women, but prostitutes who worked under the jurisdiction of the church—under the aegis of none other than the Bishop of Winchester, to be precise, who, it is said by her shamanic advocate, "issued her license." And yet, when she died, as she inevitably would, she was buried in "unconsecrated ground," as an outcast, to become a pile of bones in an unmarked graveyard a stone's throw from the parish church, or what is now Southwark Cathedral. She may have been licensed by the bishop, but she was denied her funereal rights, which is to say her funeral rites. She was buried in what John calls "a paupers' burial ground," along with orphans and other destitute members of her class—anyone without money, connections, or status—"without," as John says, "a Christian burial."

The medieval church clearly acknowledged the realities of prostitution, not only in the iconic figure of Mary Magdalene, but as an inevitable eruption of all the social, physical, and emotional dimensions of a dense, thriving urban location. Although much debated in early Christian doctrine and law, prostitution in pre-Reformation Europe was largely seen as a necessary outlet for human passions. The church "licensed" the women who would later come to be called Winchester Geese to practice, and also put a number of rules in place to ensure their integrity. (Some of these medieval ordinances might provide models for sex worker advocates today: brothel owners were not allowed to prevent prostitutes from moving freely, for example, so no one would have been caged in, or prevented from leaving brothel premises of her own volition.) But prostitutes' graves were separated from the church's proper cemeteries, their contemporary lobbyists tell us, and in death, their status as the lowest of the low and the poorest of the poor was confirmed.

Going South of the River Thames

The River Thames is famed as a glorious, winding artery through the south of England, forming the central visual course of contemporary London's landscape. It was not always so: for centuries, the Thames was a place of refuse, its banks a smelly border lining the capital city. And yet city life thrived: a neighborhood known as Bankside, just south of the River Thames, is where Shakespeare first staged his plays at the Globe Theatre in the late sixteenth century. As glamorous as the Globe may sound to early-twenty-first-century tourists, open-air theaters were not particularly respectable institutions, faring little better in public reputation than the stews that had been located a few blocks away just fifty years before Shakespeare started producing plays in the area.

Southwark is—and always has been, arguably, at least since the Norman invasion if not earlier—notably diverse nationally, ethnically, and economically. A place of immigration and considerable poverty (at least in patches) through the sixteenth century, and even into the present (although efforts to clean it up intensified once the Reformation began in earnest), the dense area of the Borough near the River Thames was basically considered a slum for a millennium. Southwark was as urban as the City of London, but the river conveniently—geographically—separated its less reputable goings-on from the center of what would soon become the British Empire.

Beginning in the late fourteenth century, the Tudor monarchs tried to rid Southwark of its "vagabonds" and its "rogues"; in the late 1500s, Queen Elizabeth I insisted that the area be evacuated and closed when a cholera epidemic broke out. Close to a century later, in 1642, under the reign of Charles I, the Globe was shut again, in response to the English Civil War, the renewed war of the Reformation, when Puritan sentiment could no longer accept such bawdry public displays in the city (or a king who married a Catholic; Charles's efforts to subdue the population backfired, and he was beheaded in 1649). In early modern England, theaters—like their predecessors, the brothels of Bankside—were bawdy, tawdry places where human emotion and raucous behavior might be put on display, or even unleashed—an unbecoming prospect in a cultural setting dominated by a powerful Protestant ethos.

Through the centuries, Southwark was a receptive society, easier to penetrate than London proper. Arguments for culture should not depend on geography, and yet all these activities arguably derived from Southwark's position: close to but just outside of London, the Borough was a place where immigrants landed, waiting to get into the big city—and it was a convenient location to which the famous capital could outsource its more practical human needs. Goods and people both had to travel through Southwark to get to the city; it was (and remains) the location of prominent bridges that crossed into London proper. South of the river, Southwark was just far enough from the City of London, where, by contrast, the noble matters of government and commerce had to be buffered. Southwark—"the Borough," pronounced "the burra"—thus became what anthropologists today might call a border crossing, or what sociologists might call a host society for migrant workers, including prostitutes in the medieval period. Many of these visitors to England—traders, merchants, entertainers, travelers—provided rowdy entertainment that the city's inhabitants, eager to let off steam, could not legally find in their own local areas. Luckily, Southwark was just a boat ride away.

For close to a thousand years then (and possibly longer, if we consider that Saxons arrived and fought on these banks in the ninth and tenth centuries), Southwark was known as the seedy side of town, where questionable or seemingly "low-life" activities—taverns, stews, bear-baiting, street theater—were exiled across the river from the City of London. Bankside was the area with "the poorest streets of London," as John Constable puts it, "as chronicled by the Reformation historian John Stow and recounted by the nineteenth-century English writer Charles Dickens." It was an urban periphery, where most everyone in pre-Reformation and Elizabethan England struggled to make a buck.

This history appears to be undisputed. Even the contemporary London Borough of Southwark confirms that the "red-light district and theatres became established in Southwark because the City of London was sufficiently powerful to exclude them from the area it administered and the weaker, or more tolerant, jurisdiction . . . allowed them to settle" (Reilly and Marshall 2001:19). Unlike many public campaigns that insist that illicit histories were respectable in their way, Southwark apparently revels in its nefarious past: it may have been "weak" in comparison to London, but so too was it "tolerant" of these necessary pastimes.

Boasting a countercultural history does not protect a central location from developers, however. The Southwark Council may claim its red-light past proudly, but the Borough—and it is still called that, as an homage to its renegade history—is no longer what nineteenth-century demographers might have called a Malthusian tableau. Since the completion of the Shard, Europe's tallest building, in 2012, Southwark has consolidated its reputation as one of the most up-and-coming parts of the great city. Just around the corner, Borough Market, which claims to be a thousand years old and London's oldest produce market, was refurbished over the course of a decade; the multimillion-pound project is now a major international tourist attraction. In 2013, a two-bedroom apartment or flat cost more than half a million pounds: being just south of the Thames means that Southwark is now at the heart of contemporary central London.

Although it has gradually become part of the City of London (a process that spanned many centuries, concluding only in the mid-twentieth), Southwark has never minded its riotous history and is not about to start apologizing for it: who could begrudge an affinity with Shakespeare? Arguably the greatest writer in the English language plied his trade on these very streets, seedy though they may have been. All that human passion served great ends for art, and for humanity. Southwark's underclass history is long, but it is productive, and contemporary activists do not want that truth forgotten.

The Ritual

Today, to commemorate the outcast dead, a somewhat ragged group of self-identified misfits meet at their graveside, at 7:00 PM on the dot, on the twenty-third of every month. Now named the Crossbones Graveyard, it really is an unmarked burial site: the yew trees found in church cemeteries throughout England are nowhere in sight. Normally, in fact, all that is visible is a metal gate covered with ribbons and lace—mementoes placed there during the monthly ritual that John began after his vision. The graveyard is also a contested building site: in 2002 it was meant to become a parking garage or carpark, but John successfully lobbied the Southwark Council to prevent its construction. For years, a cramped garden and a small Madonna-like statue were all that were visible behind the gate; a large wooden wall cordoned off the neighboring area, which had been bought by developers. Over the summer of 2014, work on the site behind the gate had to begin, but by that time John and his fellow advocates had raised enough of a ruckus in the neighborhood to make the corporation that owned the property, Transport for London, move the shrine-like fence two hundred yards down the street so that it could retain its local presence.

John's vision has enabled the gradual restoration of not only this small shrined area itself, but, in his rendering, a long-overdue respect for the Winchester Geese as central to the cultural life of Bankside. Building support slowly but surely, John and his partner, Katy Nicholls, have held a ritual every month since 2004: "Someone has always been there . . . maybe only two or three people, but we've kept it going." Every month, rain or shine, summer or winter, you know where they will be. By word of mouth, however, the location is not necessarily easy to find: to a newcomer, the area is a maze of alleyways near the now popular Borough Market. One landmark is a long-standing pub across the street, the Boot and Flogger, a family business that sells a red wine known simply as "French No. 1" by the bottle. The site is on a side street evocatively named Redcross Way; a small alley, it is in the *London A to Z*, and luckily, it is well marked once you find it. And once you've been there the first time, it's easy to spot: in keeping with the artistic character of the once radical neighborhood, dozens of multicolored lights mark the tunnel that turns into Redcross Way, as if to encircle the gates. You can see it from a distance, and they give the entrance to the alley a psychedelic effect, as if you are entering Oz.

The ritual itself is a simple affair. Incense is already lit when John chimes two Tibetan cymbals together to begin the ritual, "bringing us into silence." It is not precisely timed, but the gathering rarely lasts longer than forty minutes or an hour. "Spirits of the dead! Spirits of the living!" John incants, inviting these souls and spirits into "the space." He welcomes the group (of the living), however large or small it may be on a particular twenty-third. And then he begins to orate. He tells the tale of his vision. He sings a song or two from his play, *The Southwark Mysteries.* He invites others to tell a story that needs to be told; sometimes people take him up on it. On some occasions, others sing, or recite poetry. All are invited to speak about what moves them, or what is on their minds and relevant to this intimate (if open-air) space. We are given the opportunity to cite the names of those we've loved and lost. John reports on community efforts to protect the Memorial Gates and to create a Crossbones Garden, which would be a community memorial garden of renewal; he updates us with responses the council or the mayor's office may have sent. He explains again why we are here: to acknowledge those aspects of ourselves that need redemption; to include those of us who are more akin to social outcasts; and to form a community when we might have none. It is an ecumenical event, based on presence, narrative, and a sense of social justice.

Tied to the Memorial Gates—just a municipal fence that has been transformed into a public shrine—are hundreds of mementoes of mourning and remembrance: lace, costume jewelry, notes, poems, baubles, ribbons, and pearls. "Girly things! This is a women's graveyard!" reminds John. Each month, we are invited to tie a bauble or a ribbon onto these gates; in case we don't have one of our own to offer, we are handed a red or a white ribbon to affix to the railings, as part of the ritual to create and re-create these gates of memory, and as a contemporary testament to the spirits that lie unmarked within. The group might light candles or stand in silence. In some senses, it is deferential: we do as we are told by our charismatic leader as if he is our guide. Half a millennium after the fact, John has created a graveyard for women who had none, using it as a platform to mobilize a local community of outcasts, and we sense the potential of the action.

After twenty minutes of free variation—songs, poems, testimonies to recently lost loved ones, and an intermittent sermon of sorts from John, who usually wears a long, wizard-like, blue velvet robe and a chunky salmon-colored cross—a short chant for the prostitutes of old is offered by everyone standing at the gates, who turn to face the graveyard. In the manner of an English poem that might have been inscribed in a schoolgirl's journal, we repeat three times:

Here lay your hearts
Your flowers
Your book of hours

Your fingers
Your thumbs
Your miss-you-mums

Here hang your hopes
Your dreams
Your might-have-beens

Your locks
Your keys
Your mysteries.

Then we encircle the group with a pouring of gin—an alcohol that, John explains, has given poor women solace for centuries. Sometimes it doesn't quite work, or there isn't quite enough, but in principle everyone has a communal, commensal swig as it goes around. On some occasions, individuals offer each other a slug from their personal flasks, in the spirit of generosity—sometimes with whisky instead of gin.

Whichever twenty-third it is, the ritual begins with the chimes, includes an incantation to the spirits within, and ends with a chant to the Goose:

Goose, may you never be hungry!
Goose, may you never be thirsty!
Goose, may your spirit fly free!

Throughout the proceedings, we are reminded of John's vision and his purpose, namely to establish solidarity with women who did not have enough status to be buried with ritual. And he does his best to evoke for us the legacy of this location, or what it must have been like in poor, dense sixteenth-century Bankside, south of the River Thames and outside the City of London, where all manner of illicit acts could happen freely.

The Gathering

There is not much that is illicit in the contemporary rendering or performance of our exclusion, although we might get a bit rowdy at times. There may be a reference to the Brazilian psychotropic drug ayahuasca, but this is hardly a gathering of explicit radicalism: it is no séance, orgy, or even a drumming circle. And yet, mild as it is, it is clear that many of the gathered have seen difficult patches in the course of their lives, involving sex, drugs, or money—or all three. Those who flock to these gates have seen or participated in illicit behaviors and know what it means to be on the margins of society, of their own or others' volition; that much is sure. Thus is John able to gather, month after month, participants who understand and wish to reclaim the experience of being outcast or peripheral. Six hundred years after their deaths, in early twenty-first-century London, sex workers in unmarked graves finally get their funeral, among contemporary urban dwellers, some of whom, through choice, circumstance, or both, find themselves at the same place on the social totem pole—the bottom, struggling with illness, or joblessness, or a lack of stability, or perhaps simply an adventurous spirit—as those whom they memorialize.

Usually about thirty to forty people gather on any given occasion, and the mood varies in accordance with the weather and the crowd. The point of ritual anywhere in the world—and in any tradition—is that it will stick to the form, and thereby be of a recognizable structure (Humphrey and Laidlaw 1994). But there will be a slightly different constellation of actors and circumstances at each enactment, and the event will thus vary every time (Hausner 2007). It is not formulaic, but rather haphazard—and a little random, as befits a group of former hippies. Seasonal variation is encouraged: depending on the month, we might dance, or hear the tale of Isis (in July), or St. George (in April). On December 23, 2009, for example, we followed the forty-minute ritual with Christmas carols. John wished us "good tide and the yule . . . and, if you wish, Diwali and Hanukkah. Any pagans here?" In case there were, he had to clarify: "we'll be doing the orthodox versions [of the carols] tonight. If pagans are uncomfortable, please don't feel you have to go along with it!"

As the shamanic master of ceremonies, John is a brilliant orator and performer, easily charismatic enough to keep even the most cynical well within his thrall. But that doesn't mean that his flock is unduly obedient. On this night, aided by a little wine, some of the carolers got a little bawdy themselves, replacing classic verses of "The Twelve Days of Christmas" with erotic wish lists of their own, or inserting foul language just because the syllabic rhythm of the song allowed it. Sensing that things were dissolving into drunken caroling, John protested, "Hey, we're still in ritual here! Later you can do your pickups!" (It was an unsuccessful plea, however: by the end of the ritual, two participants proclaimed themselves soulmates.)

A few months later, on February 23, 2010, we repaired to the nearby Wheatsheaf pub after the proceedings, where a self-identified shaman visiting from Sheffield, wearing turquoise, feathers, and holding a large staff, introduced himself. He passed around his staff, so that others could feel its power, and he generously distributed handfuls of white sage. He used to spend time in Stonehenge, he reported, where, two winter solstices ago, a Druid came to visit. We are in the thick of the New Age movement, verging on the absolutely kooky, but all are welcome here. John simply says: "It's great to have people on pilgrimage." Along with the Sheffield shaman, we are joined at the pub by hippies, activists, artists, travelers, sex workers, former sex workers, performers, drug users—self-identified outcasts of all shapes and sizes. Whether they chose their current lifestyles or not, or desired a status of alterity or not, they are drawn to John's call on behalf of the downtrodden.

Unlike most communities that are the subject of an ethnography, no one is a member of this one. It is as loose a social gathering as they come: you can show up or not; you can plan to attend or happen upon it; and you can stay for a part of the proceedings or the whole. The Friends of Crossbones, as they are sometimes known in their political formation, is a reminder of how the contours of a community can ebb and flow: there is no fixed boundary around the people who participate. This group, such as it is, takes its inclusive message seriously: everyone is welcome, and to come or go as they please. "Once we even forgave Margaret Thatcher at this ritual!" John recalls, showing how open-spirited we are.

Most attendees are British, but international visitors are welcome; it is a notably multiracial, multigenerational, and genuinely ecumenical assembly. Some participants are regular stalwarts and old friends of John; others are newcomers, friends of friends, or even passersby. Most are like-minded artists or psychedelic explorers. One long-standing participant spent twenty years traveling outside of Britain and found he needed a countercultural world in South London to return to when he moved back to England and into a council flat in Camberwell. Another man, a former sex worker and a lobbyist for sex workers' rights, attended assiduously until he married and moved to Wales. One devoted woman participant, who called in to a well-known Radio 4 BBC program to discuss her experiences on air, identified as a survivor of child sexual abuse. Many South London poets, songwriters, and musicians make the event a regular stop on their schedules. Fittingly, a sizeable majority of the participants on most occasions are local residents—sometimes people who live in the flats across the street watch from their upper-floor windows—but the gathering is also listed on relevant websites easily accessed from all over the world, such as that of the International Union of Sex Workers, and anyone visiting London with an interest in the subject may show up.[2] Some people travel a good distance to be able to attend.

What we know about ritual is that it is a good way to establish a continuity of community over time. By telling us that now, in the present, we are connected to people from the late 1300s, John not only shows us how fluid the boundaries of this community must be, but also offers up our history: "We are united in mind and in intention—we are part of a continuum." And we don't need to arrange a time to meet, or find out if the group is going to be performing the ritual this time around, or "remember if it's the third Thursday or the fourth Thursday of the month": it's the twenty-third at 7:00 PM, and all—bar none—are welcome. There is, John argues, a freedom in this fixity: the meetings on the twenty-third are a self-conscious use of ritual to establish a community, or social network, of friends and partners—which is in turn unfixed—among fellow outcasts in urban London, who explicitly join together through conscious remembrance of an analogous community that extends backward in time.

The Context

One major ethnographic question in the anthropological study of religion is whether ritual more effectively integrates societies—the socially cohesive function of ritual (van Gennep 1960 [1909]; Durkheim 1995 [1912]); Turner 1969)—or solidifies their differentiation, which is the resistant aspect of ritual (Lincoln 1987; Kertzer 1988). Here in Southwark, we see very clearly the former use of ritual, that is, as a means to forge community and consolidation where there might otherwise be fragmentation, diffusion, or solitude. John has created a countercultural society, a ritual time and place where people on the periphery of mainstream social worlds—self-identified outcasts, in this context—may find others who feel they do not fit or who otherwise would feel they do not have a community to belong to. This consolidation of a social order (even if, as in this case, it is not a mainstream one) is a classic function of a ritual event.

But this gathering is not only about consolidation: it is also a ritual that precisely contradicts a major cultural institution—the church—at the same time as it opposes the wider, mainstream society that engenders that institution. And if this ritual is able to do both at one time—consolidate its own group as well as challenge on its own terms the larger social frame from which it deviates—we must press further: what is the relationship between the challenging minority and the supposedly mainstream majority? That is, in what instances and in what ways—and for what reasons—might the social challenge posed by an activist or countercultural group be usefully integrated by the center itself? This possibility would suggest that social or ritual consolidation can take place in a kind of accordion effect, first within a social movement and against the mainstream, and then, as the opportunity arises or the occasion necessitates, between the periphery and its formerly oppositional center, which find a way to act together as a revitalized, integrated social unit of their own, sometimes in opposition to a larger center still.

That there is a social critique built into the performance of some rituals—and it does seem like there is a challenge contained in this one—is well documented. The Ncwala ceremony in Swaziland, southern Africa, first documented by Hilda Kuper (1947) in the 1930s, gave rise to a host of articles on "rituals of rebellion": much as rituals can serve the purpose of social cohesion, they can also provide the opportunity for social uprising, or a rejection of—or public statement against—the mainstream social order. Bruce Lincoln returned to the Ncwala ritual in 1987 to argue that if we look at the particular place and time, we can understand both whom the particular ritual may be enacted against—the British colonial regime, for example, in this instance—and whose power it consolidates: the royal clan, in the case of Swaziland.

Moving east to the region of South Asia, Richard Burghart (1983) taught us that an analyst's perspective—whether we see people as in or out of a group—will depend upon which fold in the accordion of social relations we focus on, in relation to which fold in the accordion from which we speak. Take ascetics, for instance—the most socially marginal or countercultural people in South Asian society (and arguably elsewhere, although they may be integrated to varied degrees in different contexts): viewed from the vantage point of the mainstream, ascetics are outside the social group. But viewed from their own perspective, they occupy a known social milieu, whereby ascetic orders are as carefully delineated from one another as householder ones are; the sense of communal belonging and hierarchy that ascetic life is ostensibly meant to evade are nonetheless re-created all over again.

In all these cases, there is an awareness among self-consciously oppositional groups that to resist the mainstream will require creating an intentionally separate society: to be an outcast—and to appropriate or inhabit that status with dignity—one cannot be "in." The same ritual of consolidation for one group will mean an articulated difference from—and reaction to or defiance against—another group. Ritual proclaims alterity even as it consolidates community.

Sometimes these two positions are considered alternatives: either we are part of the mainstream or dominant ideology, or we are subalterns, subordinate, acknowledging but actively resistant to the majority stance, practice, political position, or point of view. The present case, however, shows us precisely how ritual may both integrate and resist at one and the same time, and at multiple levels. Ritual may be potentially useful for the internal integration of the periphery—with an event or an act of consolidation, those on the margins need not be so dispersed—even as it serves to mobilize a consciousness of outsiderhood. Once you belong to a collective of outsiders, you know who you are and can act from that conscious stance, appropriating the status as you see fit. Indeed, from this position, the invitation to join the mainstream, might it be forthcoming, could well be declined: there is power in the margins, as Mary Douglas (1966) so saliently reminds us.

For this reason, the mainstream may precisely wish to integrate what it views as a sectarian or separatist group: a thorn in the side is a bothersome nuisance, and it is often better to assimilate such opposition. A reframing of the larger social whole may thus be the result of what might be experienced as an oscillation between these two seemingly contradictory but in truth coexistent aspects of ritual, namely integration and opposition. And indeed, if a consolidated result—a larger or more expansive social order that includes the thorn rather than excludes or tries to pluck it out—is the effect of a ritual of resistance, the oppositional movement will, to some degree at least, have achieved its end.

The Crossbones Graveyard gatherings are about finding and establishing a sense of community, particularly for those who are self-consciously not integrated into mainstream social orders. Thus, the ritual facilitates social coherence through reminding us of social incoherence: "Even the wretched of the earth are capable of receiving something called grace," incants John. He continues, reading from his own play:

> By the grace of Lady Mary Overie,
> and the tarts who tested positive for HIV . . .
> Let them see the shining eyes of our goddess of mercy.

This ritual is a public performance of defiance, an insistence that dominant institutions acknowledge illness, poverty, and circumstance. It is not a call for the socially marginal periphery to join the mainstream, but rather an entreaty that the center respectfully regard its own periphery as a place of dignity.

Even as we resist a mainstream mentality of ignorance and inequality, we still have to behave as citizens of London. Two of our number—known as our brave "Goose Samurai"—wear the fluorescent yellow jackets of highway marshals to make sure the rest of us don't step past the painted yellow lines on the road, where we would be interfering with motor traffic on Redcross Way. "Get behind the yellow lines!" John yells, health- and safety-conscious shaman that he is. And when he sees us hesitate because it means we have to squish up against the gates still closer together, he admonishes us to get cozy: "It's intimate! We're communing with dead prostitutes here!"

Whatever other dimensions ritual may encompass, we know it to assert at least these two—the capacity to integrate and the capacity to resist—in its ability jointly to maintain and to shift the social order. This shifting may be either forward or backward in time; one point of ritual is to muddy this distinction as well. London's economy of love has lasted a long, long time, and what John Constable shows us, month after month, is how a temporal continuum of ritual can erase six hundred years in a single oration. The same issues, he argues, are salient today: there will always be outcasts. The question is how they are received.

Since the early 1980s, feminist intellectual circles have debated the extent to which agency may be involved in sex work, or the degree to which prostitutes may elect—or must be forced into—such a profession. How and in which cases is it possible to choose to sell sex? However varied the feminist positions on sex work may be, there appears to be an analytic and social agreement that prostitutes, whether their profession is chosen or not, tend to find themselves on the bottom of the social totem pole. The Winchester Goose is an icon of exclusion, and her ritual at the Crossbones Graveyard is offered as a memorial to those whom everyone knew stood outside the social order, although they may well have sustained it.

In this construction we find a solidarity with the outcast—the sex workers of old—and also a subtle critique of the church or mainstream society writ large, for not seeing their protections through, or, shall we say, for not putting their money where their mouth was. Prostitutes were held in a double bind by the Church of England: they were pitied on one hand, but denigrated on the other. At the Crossbones Graveyard, everyone, by contrast, is welcome in self-consciously equal measure. It's a "simple and inclusive ritual," John explains, "not a doctrine. Even fundamentalists are welcome here!" His is a downright refusal to make a hierarchy based on ideology of any kind. This position can be interpreted as a consolidating, insider position, whereby he is willing to demonstrate publicly the ability to include and incorporate, or as an activist, outsider one, whereby, in the shadows of the Southwark Cathedral, he and his fellow outcasts are banging on the seemingly closed doors, asking to be let in.

Ritual Action: Symbol and Meaning

With such a focus on inclusion, the cultural analyst must ask: is it really sexuality that is at stake in this public performance of social resistance? What is the underlying focus of John's ritual, from the perspective of cultural consciousness? This is the question for the anthropologist: what are the subterranean currents of culture, historically and in the present, that have led to the display of activist sentiments as they presently appear? In the case at hand, or in the performance of this particular ritual—that seemingly universal expression of human conduct—what does it mean to be countercultural in the London of the early twenty-first century?

Let us expand our view somewhat from the narrative of the ritual itself, in order to interrogate its larger context. In contemporary London—as indeed in most urban centers of the world, for which London may be held as a global icon—relations of capital, or the world of international corporate finance, mark the city in every corner; they are perhaps especially visible in this one. Having been an area of dense poverty for so many centuries, Southwark is now home to the highest building in Europe, the Shard, a glamorous structure consistently spoken of in superlative tones, which was paid for primarily by the banks of the state of Qatar. Unsurprisingly, skyrocketing property prices have accompanied Southwark's newly built skyscraper: enormous local and foreign property deals in the millions and billions of pounds are now regularly announced in the area. Migrant sex workers caused some outrage in medieval Southwark, and migrant workers are still a political thorn in the side of contemporary Europe, but foreign capital, disembodied as it is, apparently is nowhere a problem.

National banks are not the only foreign sources of finance to pour into Southwark since the turn of the millennium: on the popular—and at least embodied—side of the spectrum, the South Bank in London is home to such world-renowned institutions as the Tate Modern, built in 2000 (by 2001 it was "the most popular modern art museum in the world and the third most popular tourist attraction in Britain")[3] and the London Eye, constructed in 2001, as well as a skateboarding and open-air market area. It has become, over the past few decades, one of the prime tourist destinations in the world. (Thus the skateboarders are soon to be moved out, it is reported.) This part of Southwark is an example of global gentrification to the highest degree: a place where people for centuries struggled to create urban livelihoods has now become a center of capital relations.

It is this pivotal question of commerce that marks the current—and arguably the past—cultural modality of Bankside. But our priorities have shifted: where we used to have to work out financial arrangements in order to enable or facilitate human relations, now we have to work out social arrangements in order to enable or facilitate financial relations. Things have been turned on their head, such that global capital markets have trumped social relationships. And it is this mode of capital relations—which is about the consumption of London goods and the ownership of London property, with its swollen global market value—and its unquestioned domination in Southwark, in London, and in the world, that is being challenged by our ritualists, who insist rather on presence. They have refused to let corporate London tear up a history of bodily exchange, demanding in its stead a memorial garden, where material nature will organically live on. Twenty-first-century modes of transaction—where bodies, sensuality, people, and human interaction are less important or ranked lower than markets, profit, and capital—are what is being questioned by the symbolic reference to sex work in our ritual: medieval corporeal exchange relations are held up against postmodern corporate exchange relations.

But let us not move too quickly into our anthropological tale. The sociologist Emile Durkheim (1995 [1912]) tells us that before we have ritual action, we have to have a totem, or an icon or deity—often an animal—with whom we can identify. The Goose, clearly, is our first totem. The medieval sex worker—known in colloquial parlance as the Winchester Goose, although it is debated when this appellation became a popular reference—is our preeminent symbol. She was a woman whose exchange for capital happened in the most embodied sense imaginable. She was, in some ways, supported in this endeavor, since she provided a service that even the church had to acknowledge served a human purpose. But in offering such a service, she was seen as sullied, and so, while she might have been useful in some measure, she could not be an integral part of the social order. Her way of earning money was put to good use, then, but it also separated her from her own personhood, ironically: by using her body for her livelihood—by offering her bodily capital, if we wish to call it that—she relegated her person to the junk heap of society.

Now, in the capital relations of the twenty-first century, we have taken this equation to its logical conclusion: the farther away one's body is from a tangibly commercial transaction, the higher one has traveled on the totem pole, it would seem. Both cash and bodies are passé in contemporary financial worlds: it is better to be signing mergers in a corporate boardroom. And in that spirit, for this ritual, we have a second totem: John Constable's shamanic doppelgänger, John Crow, who is in charge of bringing us back to the time when, by contrast, relations of capital exchange were precisely embodied. It is the Crow who can tell us the story of the Goose—two sides of the same coin—in such a way that we understand her relevance to the medieval streets of London and also to the present. We have two totems, and together they move us back and forth between the London of old and the London of today: the Goose is the subject of John Constable's visionary unveiling, while the Crow is the shaman himself.

Ritual Performance: Art and Activism

On April 23, 2010, as usual, there was a small group at the Memorial Gates: committed participants meet in rain and shine, and in numbers impressive and not. In addition, however, and no longer in the shadows, the tale of the Goose and the Crow was being publicly performed nearby, in none other than the Southwark Cathedral. John's account of his shamanic vision and the history it uncovers is the centerpiece of our monthly ritual; an artist through and through, John has also written that story in the form of a temporally appropriate medieval mystery play, *The Southwark Mysteries.* On this evening—April 23, known everywhere in England as St. George's Day and celebrated as Shakespeare's birth and death day—the play was performed with the participation of the whole community, the choir made up of a hundred local schoolchildren, and the warm support of the diocese, which enthusiastically promoted the performance inside the Cathedral.

If the point of the ritual is to find alliance with the social outcast within us, through the symbol of the unmemorialized medieval sex worker, how was that story now to be told inside the chapel of the Anglican church? It was not a move of direct challenge: in addition to the dean and chapter of Southwark Cathedral in the Diocese of Southwark, the Southwark Council supported the production, as did London South Bank University, eleven local businesses, and the Big Lottery Fund. The play may have been produced as a countercultural event, but it was accepted and promoted by those institutions that stood to come under its critique.

Still, although shocking in moments—the play is about sexuality and sex work in the context of the church, and there is not a lot that is held back—it was easy to see why the Cathedral accepted and supported the production. The time-splicing narrative depicts the arrival of the Goose into John Crow's life, her affair with Jesus, and Jesus's subsequent victory over Satan. If Christ is ultimately victorious, a little lewdness on the side only speaks to the truth of the human condition. Indeed, the Christian church—Anglican and other—is well known for acknowledging the exigencies of human desire; such is its power, and it is part of the tale John tells. It is the social repercussions of that acknowledgment that he wishes to expose, and to press upon his audience—and Southwark, having itself been the geographical underdog of the city, is more than happy to participate in that proclamation.

Indeed, this was South London at its proudest. The play was sold out all three nights of its performance, with people clamoring at the door. The manager of the Cathedral's bookshop said she might sneak in the back. Was it unusual for a cathedral to put on a play that was inspired by the spirit of a sex worker? She said, "Yes, it's quite unconventional," but, invoking the spirit of the place that has remained in a relationship of opposition with the center (meaning London, or north of the river) for centuries, it was also "very Southwark." The Cathedral only dates from 1905, and still has the sense of the parish church it was for the four centuries before that: "You can feel it's a living church," she offered, "not a monument. It's ours: people feel very possessive about it." Everyone should be able to belong, she suggested: this inclusiveness is the principle of sanctuary, embodied in a Southwark that refuses to exclude, since it is a place of alterity itself.

Already we start to see the layered social processes at work, and the way different identifications play themselves out with the accordion effect: Southwark Cathedral presents itself as the heart of a more liberal and inclusive diocese, in comparison to those that identify with the center of the Anglican establishment. In this larger context, Southwark proudly positions its social theology against the mainstream, as does the ritual of Crossbones. The fundamental ideology of inclusiveness among John Crow's flock and that of the Southwark Diocese thus converge here, such that there need be no further resistance. Insofar as the Cathedral publicly identifies as a progressive force on its own terms, John's ritual may solidly align with it, even though the larger institution of the Anglican church is that which he seemingly opposes.

Ritual Oscillation: Politics and Presence

This ritual is not entirely about social exclusion, then, but also about the possibility of social inclusion or, more accurately, about the perpetual oscillation between the two. The capacity of ritual to accommodate—indeed to produce—a social alternation between integration and rebellion should be familiar to scholars of Edmund Leach, who wrote of an oscillatory social pattern between "autocratic" and "democratic" political orders among the Kachin of Burma (Leach 1954; Kirsch 1973:1). A. Thomas Kirsch, who also worked in Southeast Asia (in Isaan, the northeastern area of Thailand), while in the main agreeing with Leach, showed how these oscillatory patterns can be—indeed should be—found in religious models as well. Rather than seeking "political power," some groups are more explicitly seeking "ritual efficacy," "potency," or "enhanced ritual status" (Kirsch 1973:3). Kirsch (along with Charles Keyes and Clifford Geertz) was a committed Weberian: while he agreed with his fellow Parsonians that politics, economics, and religion are never that far apart, he reminds us that, in some instances, the religious trumps the political; it is not always the other way around. Most often, they even each other out, the one standing in for the other.

To make a "distinction between purely 'secular' acts and statuses and purely 'sacred' acts and statuses" is thus to misunderstand badly the way Southeast Asian cultures—and maybe cultures everywhere—work (Kirsch 1973:16). Both Leach and Kirsch insist that an "equilibrium" model of social relations is seriously flawed, and they show us how societies, cultures, political systems, and religions are all in constant flux (Kirsch 1973:1). History happens in emergent phases; ideologies are never static, because people never are. Barbara Ward (1966) suggests that people in every culture have multiple "conscious models" that we juggle depending on the context—from one that focuses on our immediate environment to a nationalist ideology to an awareness of other groups that, along with our own, are supposed to constitute the whole, "as if it made no difference whether they might be called sacred or secular" (at least in the case of Chinese theater in Ward [1979:34]). We may even be aware of these multiple ideologies working all at once, and perhaps even the fluid way in which we subscribe to one or to another, sometimes at the same time.

The human capacity to reflect upon and be conscious of such multiple models is underestimated in our current understandings of ritual, and this book aims to right that balance, at least in a social scientific paradigm. Ritual precisely enables such cognitive oscillation, between presence and reflection, and between the present and times past or future. We might understand this experienced oscillation as that between being transported beyond thought altogether (as in Durkheimian collective effervescence, for example), on one hand, and a self-conscious mindfulness whereby we view ourselves as specks in the larger contexts of history and community, on the other.

Ritual inspires a clearer perspective on selfhood in its insistence on being aware of the present. Not only do we experience what is taking place in our immediate surroundings through what is sometimes described as heightened consciousness, but, by making our stories relative to others in history or society—by placing ourselves in context—ritual narrative can also bring about the very clear (but also very quotidian) consciousness that our personal narratives are but a few among many. We tend to assume that being swept up in the moment is the power of ritual, and that the point of ritual action is to set us apart from our everyday lives. But equally important, and also encoded in the performance of ritual, is the consciousness that our everyday lives parallel others' everyday lives. The heightened awareness engendered by ritual activity can push us in either direction, or both. What ritual does is bring us to ourselves as we act: it enables our consciousness of the present. We take stock: we note where—and who—we are.

Critically, then, the generative capacity of ritual boils down to its ability to encompass both time-as-fresh and time-as-repeated—linear and cyclical—all at once. (We are brought back to Leach [1961], who knew that time is the fundamental way a society articulates itself, politically and ritually.) Anthropologically speaking, ritual oscillation appears to reflect what we might think of as an innate or natural human tendency to juggle multiple temporal frames. Humans engaged in ritual may consciously move between not only linear time (this particular ritual or event) and cyclical time (the ritual's history and longevity), but also between synchrony and diachrony—or the experience engendered by this moment in time in the former, and the consciousness of experience over time in the latter—at both individual and collective levels. That is, ritual contains both the experience and also the self-consciousness of that experience, the myth and the history. Thus it is that ritual encompasses time, such that it resolves into the present.

Following these temporal considerations, an oscillation between the self-as-liminal (synchronic) and the self-as-reflective (diachronic, in both the linear and cyclical senses) may give rise to both the assimilative and the rebellious capacities of ritual. These layers of consciousness and self-consciousness—myth and history, if you will—are what John means when, during the ritual, he reminds us that its purpose is to "remember ourselves." His ritual is an occasion that encompasses the most antinomian or unthinkable in "normal" or "respectable" society: there is no outside. It is an event designed for "settling the score between you and the outer part of yourself," the time and the place where we come to terms with the "outcast part of ourselves." It is an integrative move, even in rebellion. It leaves us no choice but to face who we are, now.

Redemption may lie in the completion of temporal cycles, or in the repeated swings of the pendulum, such that the possibility of being able to come back around again offers open-endedness in the face of duality, opposition, and hierarchy. The accordion of social process may have to recalibrate its folds with a fresh performance. Perhaps redemption is simply renewal: if the telling of myth and the performing of ritual reflect the oscillation between experiencing something new and experiencing something anew, redemption—like ritual—might be the state of being renewed, the possibility that we might consciously start again, even if our histories began long, long ago.

Structure of the Text: The Process of History

This book is a case study that shows how the telling of history—or, indeed, myth—is an act of agency that can be designed to produce particular social ends. History is constructed and reconstructed; alliances in that set of told tales will shift, and may shift again, depending on who tells the tales, and the ends or aims those tellers wish to effect. The history described firsthand in this book is a brief and recent one, namely that of a ritual that takes place in contemporary London. But the history of which this ritual tells invokes a much longer stretch of time—past, present, and future—and speaks to all England, Europe, and the world.

The processes described in this book show how history is deployed in the production of culture. By linking artistic endeavors with social movements, this ritual questions the role of religious institutions in a political society, using the negotiation of human sexuality as a frame to position different actors as in the moral right or wrong. These processes are one manifestation of what might be seen as the universal negotiation of cultural dominance and cultural alterity: gender, religion, and hierarchy, broadly speaking, all play a role in the display of cultural contests as a given society makes its way in the world.

The story of this ritual may best be told through its own oscillation, one that moves back and forth between ethnography and history, with a healthy dose of mythic timelessness that resolves, inevitably, into the present. The body of the book has five chapters that oscillate between the temporal frames of the contemporary ritual and the historical tale the ritual wishes to lay bare. Broadly speaking, the historical sections of the book are designed to shed light on the ways in which the histories of gender and sexuality—and church and nation—in early modern England are used to contemporary ends: history, here, is not a fixed series of facts but a continually evolving set of narratives that together conspire to create who we are in the present.

Chapter 1 sets up the twin theoretical bases for the discussion, detailing the predominant theories in the anthropology of religion and ritual, first, and exploring the construction of sexuality for monetary exchange as a charged practice for social worlds, second, with which the rest of the book engages. It reviews the canonical debates about prostitution in medieval Christian Europe, and sets them alongside contemporary political discussions (as well as feminist scholarship and theory) about sex work. The issues may change in temporal focus, but they circle around the same themes, regardless of the century in which they emerge.

Chapter 2 moves backward in time, to medieval London, a period for which we have ample evidence of the stews in Southwark, including legal ordinances from the Winchester estate that mandated the treatment of prostitutes. Sex workers were clearly viewed as at the bottom of the social order at this point in history as in most, but in pre-Reformation Southwark, as in the rest of Europe, they were accommodated and seen as deserving of protections nonetheless. While not exactly incorporating sex workers into respectable society, the matter-of-fact way in which the Bishop of Winchester's manor handled the relations between the brothel owners who were its tenants and the prostitutes who rented individual rooms from them stands as a clear-eyed document about where abuses may lie and how best to guard against them.

Chapter 3 returns to the present, to consider explicitly how the strange ambivalence that surrounded the medieval stews and the prostitutes who worked there—permission and protection, on one hand,

and denigration and shame, on the other—is socially manipulated in the context of contemporary London. As a kind of shamanic healing, the tale of the Winchester Geese is told again and again, as a reminder, a demonstration, and a forum for social unity and diversity all in one. By presenting the ritual to a receptive South London audience, or group of participants, John Crow, the shaman, exposes local history as the ground of contemporary action. The ritual may not be dramatic, but it brings our focus to the present, through our continuities with the past. Some stories—like sexual intimacy and the complications that arise when cash enters the equation—really can be universally told.

Chapter 4 moves back to the past, and continues the analysis of sexuality as it moves symbolically through the sixteenth century. During the English Reformation, and after the Bankside brothels are closed in 1546, how is sexuality constructed? Queen Elizabeth I—the so-called Virgin Queen—ascends to the throne in 1558. As a monarch who never marries, she puts the consolidation of the Protestant nation above the goal of producing an heir; or rather, the Church of England, along with the nation that she rules, becomes her heir. In the context of her reign and her Supreme Governorship of the church, chastity and purity become the most resonant qualities not only of women's sexuality during this period of Protestant reform, but of the church itself. More explicitly still, capital, or the form of monetary exchange surrounding object relations, becomes focused on goods—rather than on women or families—in Elizabeth's multiple international markets and burgeoning trade expansionism. Here we have the beginnings of commodity capitalism abroad, paralleling the suppression of sexual exchange in England.

Prostitution was pushed underground and subjected to a new moral order that could not abide by the exchange of sex for money after the mid-sixteenth century, but places carry their legacies. The brothel as a public institution may have been outlawed, but Southwark retained its fame as a location of bawdy, sexual women and thus its position as a place of alterity. In the mid-sixteenth century, however, instead of a place of prostitution, Southwark becomes a place of performance. Chapter 5 details the history of alterity in Southwark, first in theater, and then in terms of the contemporary life of its Cathedral, where John

Constable's play was performed. Finally, the possibility that the performance of ritual is where its power lies, through its capacity to effect a public symbolic shift, is considered as the locus of social change.

In every period of human history, social worlds—and the public constructions of their histories—are products of the categories of the human mind. Ritual may be an opportunity to put those categories on full display, or at least to remind us what the most salient categories are for our culture and in our time. What we find through an analysis of our countercultural group of outcasts on the South Bank is that sex work, the nation, memorialization, and the construction not only of alterity but also of history are symbolic frames that are always manipulable, on their own and in relation to each other; in this case, they are consciously manipulated with political intent. These elements may be the terms of identification in every period of English religious life. Here they are being toyed with explicitly, so as to redirect our collective thinking about the construction of our culture—the ways we view our history, religion, commerce, and sexuality—today.

Coda: The Past in the Present

Although anthropology may be able to look beneath the surface for the historical and contemporary currents that constitute the cultural worlds being described, we would do well to remember that the dynamics of social worlds are often deeply understood by the participants themselves: their narratives are the starting point for any ethnographic study, much as synchrony and diachrony are two points on the spectrum of experience as well as on the spectrum of analysis. While much may be revealed by the outsider looking in, a great deal more may be said from the inside looking out. People sometimes choose—consciously or not—the worlds to which they wish to belong, or with which they wish to affiliate. The ideologies, practices, and identifications of the human groups that people construct are not static over time: the sets of relations they have with the larger world shift perpetually, in accordion fashion. Individuals and groups both respond to and constitute the discursive and practical universes in which they operate.

This is one way to understand what Weber (1976 [1930]) meant when he described history as a charismatic process, or a dynamic set of events that is underscored by a particular set of cultural logics that also change with time, and that may be precisely tweaked by an inspired individual agent. Weber shows how the way we view the world grounds our actions in it: whole new systems may emerge as unintended—and even contradictory—consequences of those behaviors that logically emerge from the perspectives we ideologically uphold. This book hopes to go further still, suggesting that because the narration of history will itself have material implications, it will very likely be mobilized so as to realize those impacts. Even if entire cultural systems can arise out of contradictory ideologies (as in the case of capitalism arising out of Calvinism in the Weberian analysis), people can also be tellingly aware of the ways in which their actions have effects. Our analysis must take place, then, on at least two levels: we may ask what happened in the past, but we must also interrogate what people in the present say happened in the past—and how it still affects them today, such that, after Ricoeur (1984 [1983]) and Hobsbawm and Ranger (1983), we understand the stakes of the present through the terms of the narration of the past. We need to understand how people today talk about what happened to people in history, in order to make a claim for themselves in the present.

Whom we align with to get the job done—the best alliances to enable particular (or even general) outcomes and the kind of charismatic individuals that are needed to set off the spark and get the movement moving—are further elements of this tale. It is in part a story of unlikely allegiances and uncommon alliances in the past and in the present: it was the bishop and the brothel owner in the past (although elaborate financial and even legal terms grounded these negotiations); it is the outcast and the church in the present (a theologically sound partnership that also reflects the contested state of secularity in England). Who is central and who is peripheral in this narrative? From where does one stand to formulate the analysis? What authority does the church in Southwark have, such that to position oneself in alignment with it, or in opposition to it, would matter, and to whom? How does a countercultural resistance to a received church theology feature in the negotiating of shared ideologies that are both expressly global and explicitly pluralist—and what are the different stakes of these positions? Where, exactly, do the lines of identity fall—or, if we accept that these markers are themselves multiple and shifting, how do we assess who belongs where?

Part of the approach of this book is to understand the terms of cultural discourse at the most public level. Such is the study of symbols, as Clifford Geertz (1973) seminally explained to us. Those terms are contested, of course, but the dominant (or even hegemonic, to some) worlds that we by definition take for granted as the ground of culture also constitute the very terrain from which we may most productively act—as social mobilizers, or intellectual critics, or both. Southwark's alterity is a self-conscious one, and its identity as such may be deployed to its best advantage by whomsoever may claim it. To be peripheral is to have a certain kind of power—of the unruly and potentially dangerous (and therefore extremely effective) kind—and is therefore a status that may provide access to useful resources. Marginality is thus not only an inevitable aspect of the hierarchical social world; sometimes, with the benefit of hindsight—and in the sense of representation, at least—it is a position that might be worth seeking out because of the material and ritual benefits it may, ironically, provide.

So this is the story of unusual bedfellows, literally and figuratively. The women in this book are either hookers or queens (Bennett 2002), and they figure in the margins of society, at its nadir and at its zenith, respectively. But they engender the story as much as the center does, for in their access to all of human passion, in the case of the prostitute—or, ironically, in a public resistance to passion, in the case of the Reformation queen—they bracket the story of England and its church. They are neither the tellers of the tale nor the sole creators of it, but it could not be told—nor could it have happened—without them. Interestingly, and not coincidentally as far as the resonance of contemporary symbolic structures go, it is about women that the contemporary Church of England launched its latest debate, in the vitriolic dispute over whether women might become bishops or not. As this book was being completed in the summer of 2014, this latest question was finally resolved in favor of letting women accede to one of the highest positions in the church. The feminist movement is, thankfully, alive and well.

This book tries to answer two questions, then, in the spirit of the contemporary anthropology of religion. First, what explains the perennial presence of ritual as a human phenomenon—even (and sometimes even more markedly) in a so-called secular society? And second, what are the underlying dynamics of this particular, contemporary London ritual, as understood through the historical and cultural exigencies of England? These two questions—the general and the particular, or the theoretical and the case—together form the oscillating backbone of the book, moving back and forth through history to trace the long-term processes of culture, and meaning, in the making. This is a contemporary story in the guise of a historical one: in what follows we lay out the cultural symbolics of a long stretch of London's material life. Through the frame of symbols and actions that emerges from and in turn sustains the set of malleable but enduring human relationships in multiple forms—bodily, monetary, virtual, and ritual—on a southern bend of the Thames, we tell a story of old.

The Myth of the Goose

1 ❁ The Myth of the Winchester Goose

Take away prostitutes, and what evils would ensue.

St. Augustine, *On Order* (386 CE)

Mythic reality is a strange and ethereal one, one of those few places in the human social universe unconstrained by the limits of time. Whether we embrace the functionalism of the Polish British field-worker Bronislaw Malinowski or the structuralism of the great French theorist Claude Lévi-Strauss, myth is eternal, as it is designed to be. Its source and its power are both attributable to that particular, enduring capacity of myth to transcend time: mythic narrative creates, sustains, and maneuvers the very origin of our existence. We use the stories of our beginnings to recount—to ourselves and our kin—how it is we see the passage of time, not least the way we understand what is happening to us now, at the time of our telling.

Anthropologists adore myths, for they constitute a body of ready-made stories that give us an easy, inviting route into the way a group narrates itself. For Malinowski (1948 [1925]), myth was famously analogous to a tribe's "charter," or rulebook, or even constitution, of how a culture lived its morality. In this functionalist interpretation of myth, if one wants to know how people think they should behave, one need only consult a culture's myths: they inscribe a set of moral ideals by which a culture's inhabitants know they should live. For Lévi-Strauss (1963), myth bespoke the very structure of the human mind, constituting the formless but somehow architectural web upon which consciousness builds itself. For Mircea Eliade (1954), myth was an *axis mundi*, the pole around which a nation tells its tales, anchoring its fleet to cosmic truth.

For the tellers themselves, myths recount—or even create—the story of being, otherwise a perennial mystery. As such, they have an unchanging or constant quality, even as they speak to all the variations and exigencies of contemporary life. It is in this paradox—the eternality of myth alongside its changeability and seemingly endless variation—that mythical narratives have come to be seen as the cornerstone of religious cultures across the world and throughout history.

Even our tiny, unnamed tribe, gathering rain or shine by the gates of Crossbones Graveyard, repeats and reveres its origin myth: the tale of its brief history is an integral part of its ritual actions. Every time we participate in this ritual, we hear how a Goose appeared in the life of a contemporary London artist named John Constable (not the Romantic English painter of the same name), also known as John Crow, one night early in the twenty-first century. This particular Goose, in her interaction with our Crow, was an inspirational totem: she led John to the site, he recounts to us, that would subsequently be identified as a historic graveyard, where the bones of 148 skeletons would be excavated in the process of preparing the land for an extension of one of London's underground lines (the Jubilee Line, to be precise). The story of the Winchester Goose—the totemic spirit who came to visit the storytelling shaman—came streaming out of the present-day poet: overnight he wrote a play that would in due course be performed at the Southwark Cathedral, the locus of worship in his neighborhood, and an important site in the Church of England's diocese of the same name.

This artistic act was not an insignificant achievement (nor exactly an anti-establishment one) on the part of an iconoclastic rebel poet in South London. But the good graces of the Cathedral are not to be relied upon in an everyday sense: the whole point of the ritual is to remind us how powerful institutions (even if—or perhaps especially if—they are subordinate to still more commanding interests) have a way of asserting their dominance when it suits them. An index of the inevitably hierarchical structure of social orders, this ritual is most comfortable in the open air, in front of its self-created memorial altar, not inside the Cathedral itself.

And so, as we know, every month since it happened, John holds a ritual in honor of the shamanic vision that brought him to the Crossbones Graveyard on Redcross Way. John's ritual points out—explicitly—how the Church of England distinguished between different kinds of dead: some people, those who had enough money or were connected to family members who could pay, were buried in the church graveyard; others were buried outside, down the road, in unmarked graves. This story, orated by Constable's shamanic alter ego, John Crow, is the origin myth of this particular social group, and we gather to hear it on each twenty-third.

It is not particularly effervescent—we are a small gaggle of fairly tame counterculturalists on a side street in central London—but it is our ritual. Often wearing a blue robe that could equally be a terry cloth bathrobe (or, in British parlance, a dressing gown) or a wizard's cloak, with a large amber rosary around his neck, John Crow performs on a ritual stage as he tells us of his vision—the dreamlike, shamanic awakening that brought him, and now us, to this location in the first place—and also of the activist vision into which he would translate that clarion call from the spirits of Southwark. His hope is that, through the telling of this story over time, we may gradually reveal the social hierarchies within our societies and thereby act to undo them: through their exposure in ritual, those structures that determine who's in and who's out—in every society, in every period, and even within ourselves—are weakened. This is a ritual about the past, but it is performed for the benefit of the future, and for the sake of the site, namely the memorial garden that he hopes we can create for the community of Bankside, as well as for "all humanity."

As we have seen, the ritual opens by invoking the spirits of the dead (and equating them with us, the "spirits of the living"), and closes with a release, or an incantation to the totem ("Goose! May your spirit fly free!"), and a literal circle of gin, poured around us, a group huddled by a graveyard, and down our gullets too. Human societies need solace, John Crow explains, and gin was an alcohol that was cheap enough to be the balm of many: "It was mother's comfort, and mother's ruin." This ritual, and the telling of this particular myth, is also a source of solace; it offers a gathering of like-minded people who care about memorialization, and who need a place to come every now and again for some open-hearted human contact.

The Early Canonical Position on Harlotry

Like gin, sexual congress has the capacity to be a comfort, or a ruin. Thus have theologians, lawyers, policy makers, intellectuals, and emancipators wrestled with the nuts and bolts of the practices of sexuality—that which our species needs in order to survive, and one of the greatest sources of pleasure in the human repertory—over the centuries. A deep and powerful urge, sexual desire has also gotten human beings into a great deal of trouble, and most if not all religious systems in the world have set about trying to harness, deflate, direct, or subdue its sometimes overwhelming charge. For all the conundrums it causes, sexuality cannot be simply outlawed; it must be managed.

Historically variable as the meanings of money and sexuality will always be, what is it about the concatenation of these two spheres that brings about such seemingly universal cultural debate and reprobation—involving theological institutions, criminal courts, moral codes, and legal manifestos, not to mention welfare, rehabilitation, and reintegration systems? Is there something about this heightened realm of sensual, bodily experience that so definitely places it into an arena of human cognition and action that is separate from a society's standard rules governing labor transactions or exchange? Certainly, human bodily sense is increasingly understood as the very ground of our perception and consciousness of the world (Csordas 1994; Stoller 1989; Schaefer 2015).[1] That bodies can know (and that such knowledge is a form of power) is undisputed: it is whether this form of knowledge—experience—may be trusted, denigrated, or put to use that is so culturally and historically debated.

Every culture in the world has had to wrestle with the sticky issue of the profitable use value of the body's sensory experience that is at stake in the exchange of sexual congress for financial gain. Arguably embedded in the bramble thicket of prostitution are not only the questions of what to do about sex outside of marriage, or for reasons other than procreation, but also the very kernel at the heart of the matter (cf. Žižek 1989), namely what to do about human desire. From here matters get only more complicated, in the establishment of the nitty-gritty juridical requirements that both shape and govern collective institutions and societies: where should those who might offer sex for money live? How should they be integrated into society if they give up their trade—or if they don't? What is a society meant to do with children that are conceived of morally anathema unions? What should happen if a prostitute falls in love with someone who is not her client—or, thornier still, if a client should fall in love with her? Who is responsible for making these decisions, and how should they be regulated: how should moral rigor be balanced with social care, of both society at large and the necessarily marginal worlds whose bodily labor—sexual and otherwise—may support its steady functioning?

Our ritual's invocation of a double standard on the part of the medieval bishopric in Southwark speaks to a long history of explicit debate in the Christian church around the ethical troubles with sexual conduct. Much detailed consideration regarding permission and permissiveness around sexuality, the nature of lust (and, to a certain degree, the nature of money offered for it), the appropriate handling of agents involved in facilitating sexual transactions, and the moral status withheld from sex workers, among others, characterizes the discussions of the early and late medieval canonists. The constellation of dense moral complexity around the exchange of sensual experience outside of monogamous couplehood—an institution designed to contain human lust in the first place—is made trickier still by the element of monetary exchange, which throws into relief the question of who is paying for what, and who is to be held accountable (quite literally) for the seepage of human sexual activity outside morally recognizable (or at least tolerable) norms. Both elements—the unmanageability of promiscuity and the financial exchange around sexual acts—were deeply problematic for medieval thinkers, for whom they were inextricably linked.

In the fourth century, St. Jerome wrote: "A whore [*meretrix*] is one who is available for the lust of many men" (cited in Brundage 1989 [1976]:81). This phraseology is not kind nor full of praise, exactly—*meretrix* is not a neutral appellation in the Latin, but rather carries a derogatory note—and yet St. Jerome's definition does not carry the suggestion of depraved criminality that prostitution begins to garner after the Reformation. What is clear here, in the first instance, is that promiscuity is one root of the sin: sexuality is too unruly a set of actions—and the emotions it can trigger too delicate to dabble in—for people to express outside of a singular marital union. At the same time, even the church knows that monogamy is not an assured state of affairs among humans, for a whole host of emotional and physical reasons. The core of the trouble is that humans are lustful, and sometimes couples do not work, or a particular coupling is not sufficient, or lust or emotion needs to be taken elsewhere, for more reasons than we can count under the sun.

St. Jerome is not alone in his attempt to offer a somewhat balanced assessment of the practice of providing extra or surplus sexuality, as it were; perhaps the most frequently quoted theologian on the subject of prostitution is St. Augustine, also writing in the fourth century, who proclaims, "If you remove harlots from society, you will disrupt everything because of lust" (cited in Brundage 1987:106; an alternative translation in Karras [1989:100] reads: "Remove prostitutes from human affairs and you will destroy everything with lust"). In short, there is no doubt that prostitution is sinful, but society, in its fallen nature, needs it; in the early church, as Brundage explains, "prostitution was an evil, but an evil that was necessary for the preservation of the social structure and the orderly conduct of civic life" (1987:106). This canonical position is the ground of much of what is to follow in Christian thought: it is "the classical Christian rationale for a policy of practical toleration toward prostitution" (1987:106). The Bishop of Winchester did not have to look far for theological justification in order to accept tithes from brothel owners on the estate.

Indeed, many subsequent theologians used Augustine's logic. In the thirteenth century, Aquinas goes further with the metaphor, suggesting in *Opuscula Philosophica* that sex work is "like a sewer in a palace. Take away the sewer, and you will fill the palace with pollution. . . . Take away prostitutes from the world and you will fill it with sodomy" (cited in Wunderli 1981:96). Here, too, there is a moral, and even a theological, way to permit prostitutes to work in a socially upright order, insofar as prostitution is acknowledged as a necessary sin. Human lust, problematic though it is, is a "natural lust" (Aquinas cited in Wunderli 1981:83) in this interpretation of human nature, and prostitution—at least in some forms—allows for its containment. (It should be noted, however, that this position does not condone pleasure, even within a marital union: Aquinas argued that "a man who had intercourse with his wife solely for enjoyment was treating her as if she were a whore" [Brundage 1987:448], that is, presumably, as a woman who facilitates the base urges of a man.) Read through these early Christian theological dictums, permitting prostitution is the most morally appropriate direction the church can take, for it allows a singular outlet for sexual sin. The alternative would be far worse.

This seeming canonical consensus about the dubious but ultimately convincing worth of an institution based on sinful acts does not cut short the contestations around sex work, which goes well beyond the crimes of adultery and fornication (both of which are sex outside of marital unions, but neither involves financial transaction). Through the centuries, canonical lawyers and theologians continue to wrestle with the definitions of prostitution by trying to find the precise location of the immorality inherent in sex work. Anticipating Aquinas, who was worried about the effects on families and children when parents were not monogamous, Gratian's twelfth-century *Decretum* asserts that the defining quality of prostitution was promiscuity (Brundage 1989 [1976]:81). Apart from the obvious questions about legitimate inheritance that are embedded in the morass of having multiple sexual partners—one of the material repercussions of promiscuity—were emotional complications. In the thirteenth century Cardinal Hostiensis suggests that with the public availability of whoredom or harlotry came notoriety, already a negative trait, and by the fourteenth century, Joannes Andrea argues that with a notoriously multiple sexual stance comes deception—an emotional corollary of promiscuity—and the possibility or indeed likelihood that men would be duped by a sex worker's feigned emotional availability, itself a crime in the lawmaking of Cardinal Cajetan. (These canonists' emphases on multiple partners and public display draw from Roman law, which—in contrast to the rules in the manor of Winchester—assumed that prostitutes would live in brothels.)

Here, with the worry on deception, we see the role of clients—and indeed the role of men (for male prostitutes do not seem to appear in these canonists' discussions, which are much more focused on subduing the natural lust of women)—enter the picture. The notion that a prostitute's true crime lies in the way her clients feel about her and their intimate interactions suggests that prostitution, in these canonical descriptions, may be as problematic for the way men are implicated in the problem of women's lustful nature as for the acting on lust itself. If women are seen as lustful creatures to begin with, which seems to be the case in medieval canonry (and arguably throughout history), prostitution is really no surprise to the canonists. (Brundage cites the frequent gloss on sex work as "an evil use of a bad thing" [1989 [1976]:85]—although it could as easily be seen, through the grudging acceptance Augustine and Aquinas endorse, as the good, or reasonable, use of an evil thing: prostitutes were already expendable.)

The aspect of sex work that is really "evil" here is not the sadly natural state of a woman's multiple and active sexuality: it is the fact that men are shown up as willing to pay for it. It turns out they are as lustful as women are, in some cases, and worse, in being exposed as such, the gender dynamic whereby men are upright citizens able to hold their own and women are libidinous creatures who must learn to be moral and virtuous, is turned on its head. Men are as desirous of sexual congress and intimacy as women are, apparently, as evidenced by their willingness to pay. And women, using their own lustful natures anyway, get to benefit from men's desires—indeed, they can transform this whole state of affairs into a livelihood if need be.

This understanding of the cultural analytic is not intended to suggest that all sex workers enjoy or manipulate or feel that they benefit from these interactions, nor that they are invariably the ones in control. There is no doubt that throughout history, many or most women who have been prostitutes would rather not have been. And how could it be otherwise: the social shame and the physical dangers alone are such that women might very likely choose alternative professions if they could. But the wound that is being unveiled here is that prostitution suffers social shame for the light it sheds not on women's but on men's sexuality—and, as is so often the case, it is women who have to bear the brunt of that revelation. It is a case of displacement, whereby women are shamed precisely because they are engaging in—will offer—something that men want so much they will join the market. It is the men's shame, in this construction (that is, where sexual desire is itself shameful), but it is the women who are meant and made to feel it, in order that the men do not have to.

The Troubles with Prostitution: Embodiment, Sensuality, and Exchange

While important to historicize—and Ruth Mazo Karras (1996:10) is of course right to point out that "sex for money" meant something different in medieval Southwark than it does today—it is also important to ask why this constellation of issues is of such seemingly universal consternation. Prostitution rubs people in two different directions: some defend and uphold it, and others find it morally anathema—and sometimes both positions are held at the same time. It is rarely if ever viewed as a neutral human action, perhaps because sexuality is so rarely seen that way. And perhaps this is precisely what the trouble is, for the exchange of money is thought to make a purchase neutral, ostensibly reflecting an "objective" or legally mandated value of a good or a service. There is perhaps a fundamental incommensurability between the notion of a financial transaction and the passion of a sexual one.

Indeed, what we see here, in both the heated historical and the contemporary debates, is that the idea of exchange per se in sexuality is not a problem: bodily fluids, emotions, dowries, gene pools, families, kinship, and social relations all are acknowledged to flow between bodies during sexual encounters. Sexuality may be messy and embarrassing in some ideologies and theologies, such that it needs to be kept under strict social controls, lest bodies or emotions become too unruly, but this element is acknowledged and understood as part of human intercourse. It is when money—cold, hard cash—is directly implicated that sexuality becomes a real sin. As Leah Lydia Otis writes of prostitution in medieval France, "Cash plays an essential role in prostitution because of its very impersonality and interchangeability" (1985:154n12).[2] In medieval England, too, "[r]egulation was directed particularly against the money-making aspect of prostitution" (Karras 1996:20). That something so complex could be reduced to a financial exchange suggests the undoing of all the other, comparatively legitimate, forms of exchange: condoned social relations are undermined by the very notion that sexuality may similarly or equivalently be conducted via a transfer of cash, which generally assumes that once a payment is made, a transaction is complete.

It is in the idea that such a form of financial exchange is possible that sexuality in the form of prostitution becomes so charged. That sexuality might somehow be abstracted and commodifiable has implications for all the sanctioned forms of transfer elicited by sexual encounters, which are difficult enough for social worlds to contain. A reaction against prostitution is therefore a kind of public call for the unmitigated value of phenomenological experience, whereby bodily transactions should—must—be kept out of the realm of the market. It is as if the defined nature—the cash value—of the interactions is so anathema to the organic matter that is meant to be exchanged that these two models are simply incommensurable. The idea that there might be a cash-based material benefit (inheritance is complicated enough) from sexuality or sensuality is somehow the final challenge to something that is—or that should be—uncontainable in the best sense. Prostitution in this rendering is at the limit of what is already too difficult to deal with: it is the worst of a bad thing, as Brundage intimates, because it exposes as a heartless manifestation that which is redeemed only because it touches the human heart.

Such an interpretation runs the risk of radically misreading the encounters of sex workers, however: many a human emotion has spilled over into the realm of financial transaction. If an encounter that involves sex for money turns out to reveal not a man's but a woman's heartlessness—consider the many ecclesiastical directives regarding men who wish to marry former harlots—all the worse. In that case, she really has no possibility of redemption, although she might be worthy of social forgiveness if she chooses, willfully or not, to do such heartless work out of desperation. Consider the story of Mary Magdalene, a whore who finds salvation because she repents of her trade and is forgiven by Jesus. It is no longer a sin to have used one's body—or conflated sexuality with cash—in this rendering, for it is the last recourse for livelihood in a world that requires monetary participation.

The choice (even, in some contexts, to suggest that it could be a choice) to exchange bodily sensuality for cash, however, wrongly sullies the boundaries between the commodity market, on one hand, and the world of embodied experience, on the other, no matter that the contemporary world of capital suggests that no commodity or practice should fall outside of market forces. Sexuality is understood in these discourses to be the last bastion of the natural (such that the love and marriage market, in the Western context at least, is now frequently cast as rather about evolutionary forces and its attendant normative forms of desire: here we have a capitalist model for explaining how the market and bodily desire may intersect). For a prostitute to put sex on the market volitionally is a presumptuous act, one by which she would seem to appropriate the job of God.

There is another conflation, however, that must be drawn out here: like sexuality, or femaleness, money is both material and symbolic to the highest degree. Like sex work, the accumulation of capital wealth is charged with meaning—and it comes to carry the highest moral weight in the later Reformation, when England begins to experience national wealth. What we may draw from these cultural transitions is that the salient (and morally charged) forms of exchange in a given context will vary, but the human fact of exchange is constant, as is the necessary oscillation between that which is tangible and that which is represented: these are human symbolic processes. In this story, we move from bodily exchange (prostitution) to monetary exchange (capital) as the object of contention, even as each is implicated in the other. But the focus of cultural concern moves—from the reluctant or resigned accommodation of prostitution in the thirteenth and fourteenth centuries (and earlier), to the growth of commodity capitalism in the sixteenth century, to a slow but palpable resistance to global capital in the twenty-first century—precisely through a reclaiming of the legitimacy of bodily exchange for livelihood, invoking the older history.

Scholarly and Political Debates around Sex Work

In their focus on promiscuity, solicitation, and emotional deception, early Christian, medieval, and early modern debates about sex work look remarkably similar to contemporary ones in some areas, and quite different in others. Arguably the same two features of sex work—promiscuity and financial exchange—are still, with different connotations, those that irk contemporary voices against prostitution. Prostitution has been a source of political wrangling in most societies, including the Christian church, for millennia. Should a person be permitted to participate in a physical act of the most intimate kind, when that relation is established through or grounded in a financial transaction? Does such a transaction strip the act of the intimacy that it can engender? And whose decision is it to make about whether to engage in or permit bodily exchange as livelihood, in ethical terms or in terms of the law of the land? If sex for money is prohibited, whose interests are being protected by those laws—those whose bodies would have engaged in the acts, or those whose moral code is meant to be upheld by juridical (or ecclesiastical or theological) authority? Is it ever legitimate for a state or ecclesiastical body to make decisions about individual experiences of intimacy: when are such laws and policies patronizing, and when are they protective?

This complex web of questions is at the heart of the enduring and perennial debates about sex work in their modern formation. Since the 1970s, with the advent of the contemporary (sometimes called third-wave) feminist movement in the United States and elsewhere, these discussions have become newly salient in the worlds of both activism and scholarship, taking place within a political frame that asks who has control over women's bodies, and what it means to experience bodily sensations in different political, cultural, or social milieux. Feminism itself can occupy any number of positions; it is not a single intellectual, theoretical, or political stance.

Contemporary studies of the social significance of human sexuality use as their starting point the work of Michel Foucault (1980 [1976]), who argued that despite the fundamental bodiliness of sexual experience, society is not absent from the physical encounter. Drawing upon a lofty history of French theoretical work that insists on the social or structural presence in what appears to be individual thought, decision making, bodily sense, or physical stance, Foucault reminds us that not only is the understanding of physicality socially variable, but experience is, too. (Durkheim 1989 [1897] argued the same for suicide at the end of the nineteenth century, as did Mauss 1973 [1935] for walking at the beginning of the twentieth.) It follows, of course: if we understand nature, biology, and the body in a particular, culturally inflected way, our senses and experiences cannot be separated from that consciousness. We act in accordance with what we think we should do, or want, or experience—or perhaps deliberately in contrast to it—or perhaps we find a deviation from a social norm to be erotically charged. Regardless, our physicality takes place against a backdrop—or within the structure—of what resonates in our cultural setting as right, real, normal, or understood. It is in some sense irrelevant whether these are conscious processes or not.

From here, a wealth of studies about the variable histories of human sexuality in the West (the rest of the world was legitimate ground for ethnographic scholarship much earlier) emerged in the late 1980s. Victorian society was explored by Walkowitz (1980); gay society was explored by Weeks (1986) and by Rubin (1994); contemporary adolescent sexuality in the United States was taken up by Thompson (1992). Histories of medieval and early modern European sexuality, including prostitution in France (Otis 1985); women's roles in Germany (Roper 1989); and marriage, family, and sexual mores in England and Europe (Macfarlane 1986; Davis 1995; Mendelson and Crawford 1998), began to constitute a field unto itself. Norms about gender equality, marital and home industry partnerships, and the thorny question of where to fit in "singlewomen" were acknowledged in the contemporary era to have been a significant problem in the historical frame, especially as England moved out of the medieval period and into the modern era (Bennett 1996; McIntosh 2005).

Prostitution (and, relatedly, pornography [see Hunt 1993]) as fields in themselves were a natural outgrowth of these discussions: what did our understanding of the cultural flexibility of sexuality mean for social assumptions about the legitimacy of prostitution, and for the symbolics—and realities—of women's bodies or sexual capacities as objects of transaction? Here the 1980s U.S. feminist movement split starkly down the middle, with one camp insisting that any commodification of women's sexuality—in prostitution, pornography, or other sexually charged or explicit representation—was fundamentally demeaning and exploitative, and would necessarily further denigrate and undermine women. Societies making concerted efforts to improve women's status should thus make illegal any such sexualized representations or professions. The famous extreme of this position, set forward by the feminist lawyer Catharine MacKinnon, suggested that sexuality had become such a basic way of controlling women in social spheres that any act of intercourse was effectively rape (Dworkin 1981). MacKinnon argued that power differentials between men and women were so extreme—even in 1980s Western societies—and that women's understanding and experience of their own sexuality was so steeped in these structures of domination that there was no way to achieve consensual heterosexual relations, let alone an egalitarian encounter facilitated by a financial transaction. Legalizing monetary exchange for any act or representation of sexuality would only exacerbate an already imbalanced power structure: it would legitimate (and even act as an incentive for) women remaining second-class citizens, offering insulting levels of compensation for acts that were by definition degrading (MacKinnon and Dworkin 1997).

This stance was far too extreme—and demeaning in itself—for another wing of American feminism, one that wanted to acknowledge women's power, desire, and claims to pleasure. If women were to achieve power and equal status in society, they needed to be credited with sexual desires of their own, and allowed the possibility of having—as well as contributing to—sexual pleasure in consensual interactions. What forms consensual sexuality might take could not be determined by lawyers, or the state, or any juridical body's interpretation of what constituted appropriate sexuality: indeed, the nature of sexual desire and pleasure means that it must be individually chosen. The suggestion on the part of an outsider or onlooker that a woman who claimed willing participation in a sexual exchange that involved money had been duped or didn't know what was good for her was as patriarchal as a system that told her whom to marry, or that dictated the "legitimate" reasons for sexual intercourse within marriage. Further, the position that women did not know what was in their own best interests had the effect of ensuring that the state, the law, or the church was regarded as the ultimate authority about what was best for women, and which kinds of desire and pleasure were appropriate and beneficial for them, as well as which kinds were not (Vance 1984, 1990). Some writings powerfully attesting to sex work's capacity to give women choices and livelihoods on their own terms were produced by sex workers themselves during this period (Delacoste and Alexander 1987); the links between scholars, activists, and practitioners were necessarily close.

This more complex position of the feminist movement suggests that labor conditions need to be monitored and regulated in the context of national or juridical authority over prostitution (or pornography), and that an outright ban, by contrast, will have a harmful effect. Here we have the classic legalization debate: if we are going to have working prostitutes, let them work in conditions that support them, and ensure that they are protected, not penalized, by the law. There is a realist, or functionalist, element to this position, and it is one that was, apparently, shared by the medieval church: if prostitution is going to exist, better it be practiced in a climate where the social and political worlds acknowledge it, so that prostitutes may work in the best conditions possible. By denying the existence of prostitution—or trying to eradicate it from a particular community, thereby driving it elsewhere, or underground—the very circumstances that inspire the trade will be displaced, or worsened, or both. Anthropological work on sexuality and prostitution globally takes these questions of labor and mobility to their logical conclusion: when sex work, including sex tourism, becomes an operative mode of making money for relatively peripheral communities, ensuring that good labor conditions—including freedom of movement—are in place becomes the most important way to facilitate sex workers' health and resilience (see, for example, Hausner 2005; Kelly 2008; Kempadoo and Doezma 1998; Miller and Vance 2004; Weitzer 2011).

These issues are alive in contemporary London. Indeed, in the case at hand, a number of our ritualists are either sex worker activists or former sex workers or both. And interest and participation in these debates is not limited to marginal rituals on the South Bank: on August 3, 2014, BBC's Radio 4 program *Face the Facts* aired a debate that appeared to parallel exactly these scholarly positions, although in the political and policing spheres rather than the academic ones. Prostitution is not illegal in contemporary England, but soliciting on the street, pimping (soliciting for someone else), and brothels (more than one sex worker under one roof) are. The radio show went back and forth between outspoken opponents, who wanted any evidence of sex work out of their communities once and for all, and advocates involved in the sex work business and not, who argued that the legalization of sex work allowed conditions to be monitored, making it safer and above-board for all those engaged in the practice. Making sex work illegal would only push it underground, and a raid would only move a known concentration of sex workers to a neighboring area. And sometimes, advocates argued, it was safer to have a group of sex workers under one roof; it was more dangerous for a single woman to act on her own, so a brothel, in its current definition, could actually be a protective measure.

Even in contexts where prostitution is legal or quasi-legal, and even where it is accepted in the public sphere, however, as in the case of medieval England and much of medieval Europe (see especially Otis 1985 for France and Roper 1989 for Germany), prostitutes still occupy a second-class (or lower) status. Our ritual uses the narrative of sex workers' rights and blames the church for a seeming hypocrisy: despite their publicly acknowledged use value, prostitutes were not considered upright members of moral society. They were still demeaned and almost always poor: "harlot," "whore," and "hooker" are in no language complimentary. But at the same time, the church understood the exigency of prostitution: it was a way for a woman to make money in desperately poor times, and no effort in the world has been successful at driving prostitution out of society entirely. So although the ritual appears to be blaming the church—the charge is that the Bishop of Winchester and his manor insulted sex workers by refusing to care for a prostitute after her death—we also call for a return to a time when there were actually statutes acknowledging the existence of prostitution and some basic protections in place. Such edicts did exist in fifteenth-century Southwark, despite many centuries of ecclesiastical debates about the moral theology of prostitution, and whether and why such a sinful act could somehow be sanctioned.

The Power of Sexuality: Activist Histories

On August 23, 2014, the 123rd such gathering at the Crossbones Gates, the evening was clear, a distinct early autumnal chill in the air. The summer—warm that year—was winding down; the light that hit the Shard skyscraper—now complete, and even inhabited with its first corporate occupants—rising up behind the gates was almost a sunset, its yellow tones a reminder that the days were already getting shorter, compared to the color of the sky a month earlier. This month, a group of visiting anthropologist activists came to pay homage to the gates. In town for a conference on Brazilian literature and culture, and having heard of the ritual as a commemoration of sex workers, they had contacted John to ask permission to affix the photo of a long-time São Paulo sex worker activist, Gabriele Leite, who had died a year earlier, to the railings. They became the main event of this month's gathering, infusing an internationalist activist flavor into the proceedings (although Amazonian forest rituals are often invoked as an important part of John's repertoire).

This activist tribute to Leite was the cornerstone of the ritual on this occasion, becoming the narrative around which other, spontaneous expressions of hope for the city and solidarity with the outcast were articulated. Those gathered were clearly moved by the visitors' account of Leite's tireless advocacy for prostitutes in Brazil: she had organized, created NGOs, and lobbied the state for sex workers' rights and respect throughout her life and career. To honor her memory, a young representative asked that we participate not in a moment of silence—"she was never silent about prostitutes' rights"—but rather in "a moment of noise," an honor better suited to Leite's refusal to stay quiet in the face of injustice, and a style of tribute that had been spreading among her activist supporters all over the world. "So if you would like to join in, please do, but in this moment of noise, I'm going to scream," the young activist explained.

A memorial focus directed to an individual sex worker activist deviated slightly from the normal ritual practice, which focuses heavily on collective memory. Either way, remembering the dead to honor their work (sex work in particular, but also their presence, their advocacy, their lives) is the heart of the ritual: "Our single greatest purpose is to remember: the dead, the outcast, the living . . . and maybe ourselves," John announced. A monthly mode of practice includes the tying of ribbons, usually red and white, but tonight multicolored, to the gates, and as we did so, John explained the meaning of this action: "Performing this little act of tying a ribbon to the gates connects us to the dead." Although our ritualists resist the idea that they belong to or constitute a religious group, by consciously performing ritual, they align themselves with those actions most obviously associated with religion, namely those communal acts—rituals—that are designed to contain and offer solace for the human emotions and experiences surrounding death and the memorialization of our ancestors, biological, cultural, or, in this case, professional.

A rowdy group of young men trundled by on an urban float, shouting exuberantly. One of our group commented on how the wisdom of the feminine, which our ritual enables, appears to bring out the loud, unaware men of the city, and how this seemingly paradoxical but all too human juxtaposition reminded her of the magic in the world. John joked further: the temporary disruption, he says, is a way of testing us. "How *firmeza* [firmly] are we at these gates? Very *firmeza*, beause we know who we are, living and dead. All the city can pass right through us!" Such positioning outside the city while still within it drives home the point that we occupy a unique position: we are not so much of the city as we are the web or the net that surrounds or weaves through it.

This particular rendering of the ritual was noteworthy for another reason: since July 23, Transport for London (TfL) had moved the Memorial Gates. The space where the gates had stood last month—and for the last decade—was now boarded up (ready for TfL's Jubilee Line extension after all); fifty yards to the north a wall had been broken down to make room for them. With all their mementoes still affixed, the iron railings had been moved intact. In their new location, they looked the same—nothing had been altered—but what was visible behind them was different, and much more beautiful than the building site onto which they used to open. Directly behind the gates was now the nascent Crossbones Garden, long an element of the narrative of John's ritual, and the object of his local activism. Through the metal slats, we could see greenery—trees and shrubs—and a shrine to Lady Mary Magdalene. And the Shard gleamed behind our gathering, as always.

In its almost-the-same-but-still-new location, the form of the ritual was unchanged, and the trope of place did not budge one bit (although the physical referent surely had): "[t]his land was a single women's burial ground," we were told. And yet there was an acknowledgment of the then-present, the current moment in which this particular ritual took place. As he does every month, John tells us of the Goose who came to visit him ("or my alter ego, John Crow"), bringing him to "these gates. . . . No, *these* gates," he corrects himself, remembering that they are in a new location. It was not easy watching them be wrenched from their former spot and moved down the way, "but for the first time we look onto this beautiful guerrilla garden. . . . We can open this space up." He recounts the long battle with TfL: "They said, 'We could destroy these gates—they're ours.' But they didn't. And in fact they spent a lot of money moving them (for their own reasons). But the real thing is the garden that will last forever. We focus here on aspects of ourselves that do last: the connections between us . . . love."

In this brief set of transitions, we see clearly how ritual tends to be understood by the scholarly world of anthropologists and religious studies experts, and why continuity with the dead stands out as the primary reason for ritual: it embodies and embeds our social connections with and memories of the past. Memorialization of the dead (sometimes known as honoring the ancestors in the anthropological literature)—a remembering of our own history—is one of the most important tasks of ritual. But emerging from this performance, we also see another element, namely the making of the present. This is why the study of ritual is so often aligned with the study of performance: it is live; it is real (unlike that which is filmed, screened, or recorded). A theatrical performance, especially like those of John Constable's youthful life in the '60s, is sometimes called a "happening" or a "live show": theater, like ritual, is about creating a situation that is immediate, accessible, present, and spontaneous. "We're a piece of living performance," John reminds us. "We're all about adaptability." There may be a repeated and recognizable form to our monthly gatherings, but we are responsive to the circumstances at hand, the reality that presents itself to us. To dig his heels in against TfL would have been counterproductive; to stop holding the ritual because the gates were in a new place would serve no purpose.

To "remember" sounds like an act that is oriented toward the past, but it is of course also and primarily an action of the present (Ricoeur 1984 [1983]). "This is why we come here," John explains. "It's like Isis who remembers Osiris"—the myth within the myth—"to put his body back together again, or re-member him. We can reconstruct ourselves when things get rocky." Activism—the reconstruction, restructuring, or re-membering of society—by definition takes place in the present. Here, in the context of this ritual as in so many activist or citizen movements, John uses the language—and, consciously, the poetry—of the present to reflect the past. "We don't call ourselves a religion—any religion—so we use poetry and art as our prayer."

Despite an apparent focus on history and memory, the present is the most significant part of this—and all—rituals. A young woman who takes over leading the ritual for a spell asks us "to bring light into all these places in our heart . . . in this moment." On a monthly basis, John asks the Goose to provide "open pathways," so that we may remain responsive and resilient to the circumstances we face. This focus on the "moment" is about making ourselves as we are, or as we wish to be now, thus bringing about the present. We are not just passive recipients of our social worlds, but active makers of them. Ritual, consciously or unconsciously, reminds us of our own participation in the present, and enables us to claim it as the agents we are, even as we acknowledge the circumstances and historical time frame in which we manifestly find ourselves.

Much of this ritual is focused on the past, but the future is also invoked, as when, in one song, we sing about preserving and even nourishing the garden "for future children." Bookended by past and future, time is thus at the heart of what we are doing here, in the telling of mythic origins, invoking the symbols of animals and people, dead and alive, and staying present as we participate in the vigil. As always, the ritual ends with John and his flock shouting into the gates and the garden they give on to (now a different one, but no matter), "Goose, may your spirit fly free! And so she does."

Why does this particular ritual—this live set of events—use the memorialization of sex workers as the way in to the story? What do prostitutes tell us about ourselves and our histories such that, by remembering and linking ourselves to them, we come to create a present that we recognize and value? Sex work, lest we forget, has been around for a very long time, so, for one thing, we are connecting with a phenomenon that is perennial and unchanging, a kind of social relation that is fundamentally and inexorably human. But sex work also touches on that delicate political nexus where the material, bodily actions of human beings resonate powerfully with their public, symbolic weight. It is for this reason that sex work has, along with being the world's oldest profession, been one of the world's oldest sources of activism, scholarship, and political mobilization. Sexuality and the different kinds of exchange networks it implicates are at the heart of human existence.

This complex connection between politics, materiality, sexuality, and symbolism is another unbroken link with the past that John's ritual resurrects, and with which it connects us anew. By using the sex worker as the symbolic cry around which we rally, John reminds us of the age-old debates about the role of the human body, and whether and the extent to which it is socially acceptable—or viable or appropriate—to engage in or permit an exchange relation between sexual intimacy (which is ideally ineffable) and the material benefit that can be derived from money (which is seemingly its opposite). To what extent are our bodies (and women's bodies in particular) ours to do with what we will? Do we damage ourselves or our societies by permitting our or others' bodies to participate in the market of exchange relations? If women accept money for sex, have they become commodities? And is there something about a body that means it must be held above or apart from the commodified exchange relation that now (not, our ritualists imply, then) has become the predominant mode of action in the world?

The implication of our ritualists is that, while the exchange relation between the sexual body and a cash-paying client should not leave the sex worker notched lower on the social hierarchy than anyone else, there was something about using bodies for exchange that was more real, and more present, and more connected to the ways of the world than the modes of exchange in our current global configuration offer. They point us to the hypocrisies of treating sex workers poorly, and in so doing call for social justice—and the rightful recognition of this kind of exchange. The Geese may have done it for money—they may have had to—but in commemorating them, this contemporary flock claims the value of bodily presence as the core model for exchange relations. They bring us back to the realm of bodily relations and experiences as the central aspect of human encounter: not only should sex workers—then and now—be included in society, they should serve as reminders for where we are in our embodied relations with each other and with the world.

History and Myth: The Playwright and the Shaman

Myths, as any stories, are best told with symbolic referents in the real world, so that they touch the hearts, minds, and nerves of their listeners. Often the natural world—locations, animals—serves as the source of myth and legend, but it is always also the canvas of social projection. At Crossbones Graveyard, the myth of our ritual is contained in the story of the Winchester Goose; she is our animal spirit, or our totem, a representation of her namesake, who turns out to have been a real woman, or set of women, otherwise long forgotten. Her symbolic reference acts as an organizing tool.

Myth allows ritual to break things apart, and then put them back together again, in the order that the universe intends. At the same time, ritual can challenge the interpretation of the intended order or even the intention of events. Given that ritual is the forum for the transmission of myth, the fact that, as a practice, it reminds us of the instability of the final interpretation means that the instability is part and parcel of the story. There is always the possibility of redemption, or of change. There is no end point: the ritual will be repeated, the tradition perpetuated. Each time it will vary a little, if only in historical time; in this inherent variation is the knowledge that it might—it can—end differently this time. The chances are slim, but you never know: ritual is the little spark of fire that both supports the myth and undermines it. There is a historical element to John's story, to be sure. This history is also his myth. But the shamanic vision is the origin story of the ritual—and so it is the shaman to whom we turn. (John's bases are covered: he is both John Constable the playwright and performer and John Crow the shaman.) He shows us how, in one go, the healing process lies not only in the repeated performance of ritual, but also in the capacity for social change whose potential is contained in its enactment.

Such is it that myth can both refer to a time without time (the opposite of history, in Eliade's [1954] famous rendering) and be grounded in actual historical time (thereby, as in this case, giving itself the scientific credentials to be a movement of the twenty-first century). By rejigging the terms of fusion and fission—by deliberately combining history and myth, or time and timelessness, on one hand, and by splitting himself apart, into narrator and shaman, on the other—John both connects and separates these two temporal frames. He unmoors our reference points: by unifying the mythic and historical lenses into one perspective, John frees us up to think about the underlying structures. What stays the same, in time and out of time? It is an ethical way into the question of universals, of truth, a contested business if ever there was one.

One element of perennial truth is social hierarchy. Prostitutes appear to be nearly universally at the bottom—or even outside—of those hierarchical structures. Social hierarchy, institutional hierarchy, graveyard hierarchy: these are the tales of history and thus of myth that both embody and expose social worlds, and the individual lives that inhabit them. Who is on the bottom, and who is on the top? Why can certain people claim elite status, while others cannot? Why are some buried in the churchyard, while others are relegated to mass graves? These questions throw into relief the sociality and its ordering—in multiple, particular forms—of the human species. We all intuitively know that where we are in social status is a matter of to whom, where, and in what historical period we were born. There are no predetermined rules of rank in our blood or in our bones.

But are there universal social ones? Certainly men tend to come out higher than women (Ortner 1974), and sex workers tend to come out lower than most, however their trade is cast. While promiscuity is not universally maligned, and patriarchy is not universally held aloft, these are nonetheless sustained cultural patterns that describe a great swath of human history, including European culture in general, and English culture in particular. Although the terms of cultural value are in no way universal, these hierarchical structures of society may be. Some societies may be more egalitarian than others, or more democratic than others: hierarchy will not be uniformly presented. But it appears to be fairly constant, even if the terms of status—and the symbolic tropes through which those terms are upheld and legislated—vary enormously.

While we have a certain amount of evidence that patriarchal hierarchy is part of our eternal landscape—then and now, here in the backyard of the Southwark parish—we also, seemingly, have an eternal hope of making things better, of releasing the pain of the outcast, the underdog, the disadvantaged, the abused, the suppressed. There are multiple ways to exorcise these social, personal, and physical tensions: there is the shamanic ritual, there is the performance, there is the revolutionary rebellion or, slightly tamer, the activist outburst or cry of the outcast. To be oppressed is not, at least, to be repressed.

Here, then, we have a myth that refers to history, accurately in some parts, and more freely in others. To get us going, we have a ritualist who is both shamanic activist and playwright healer, and a ritual performer in both guises. And to keep us there, we have a myth in three parts—or, better, in three times—all of which conspire to bring us to the potential of the present political moment against the backdrop of perennial debates that play upon the symbolic utility of sexuality and sex work, as well as point out to us the material power of monetary, bodily, and familial exchange.

First, we have the narrative of the origin of the group, referring to the vision that inspired the gatherings that take place here. This is the present (and, to some small degree, the past): we are the contemporary activists and listeners and participants of the ritual, and our group is the formation of society that we have produced. Second, we have the narrative of the history of the site, tracking—through parallel stories—the nature of being an outcast, at this place, for close to a thousand years: we can see how what happened here parallels what still does. And finally, we have the narrative of mobilization, looking toward the future. Whether it is TfL, or the memorial garden, or the church, or erotic freedom, the social consciousness that underlies the ritual gathering is one intended to bring about change, the very possibility of which invokes what lies ahead. Through hearing the story of outcasts in the past, there is a possibility of not only camaraderie in the present, but also a shared consciousness of endurance, longevity, tradition, and transmission into the future.

The past and the future thus occupy equal places in this—and arguably any—ritual: they act as bookends. And so it is that a ritual may encompass time even as it transcends it: ritual makes different frames parallel, interweaving temporalities as the occasion demands it. Text is fleeting; only practice matters. Here, we are mobilized not with doctrine but with myth: the story around which we orient and toward which we act is at once historicized and made eternal.

Coda: Intimacy and Commerce

The anthropologist Claude Lévi-Strauss (1963) shows us how myths of particular societies enable their very social structures: symbols stand in for each other such that, in concert, they can build up the architecture of a society's mind-set. But history happens when a particular configuration of meanings as interpreted by the actors in a particular social network is articulated in particular ways, and these are never fixed: a "traffic in symbols" results in a dynamic, diachronic set of constellations that we might also call a social process (Geertz 1973:45). There is meaning to structural configurations, in other words, and it is that meaning—or indeed the order, or the core nodes, or where the crease folds in the accordion should lie—of the layers of a given structural makeup that is contested, argued about, disagreed over, and acted upon. It is in these inner symbolic relations that the nature and the definition (not to mention the priorities and the regulated production) of a given social system emerge.

To review, then, what is the story of unceremonialized dead sex workers meant to effect? Explicitly, it is a question of integration: of ourselves, and of society. But why are sex workers the chosen symbol for this message, and the operative terms of this event? Silent though they may be, they speak to a fascinating historical tale, to be sure, one that touches on the remarkable history of this local neighborhood. But, more importantly, they unveil an ambivalent position that the medieval church held in relation to sexuality and commerce, and for all the social changes we have charted over time, we learn that this intractable nexus still holds today. Sexuality is at the core of human being, and those who offer it as needed have continued to operate throughout human history: they serve a powerful bodily and material—as well as a significant symbolic—purpose.

When intimacy becomes part of a financial exchange, theologians, scholars, activists, and policy makers through the ages are thrown into a conundrum: how is this essential element of human life—always difficult to manage with its untidy physicality and capacity for enormous emotion—to be contained when it becomes a commodity? Indeed, one could argue that allowing sexuality to be a commodity—or at least to be offered in exchange for money, rather than for something else (like marriage, or land, or family ties)—is an attempt to make it containable and without emotional attachment: is not the point of a financial transaction that it carries with it neither muss nor fuss? Prostitution is so highly charged a matter of public concern across the centuries precisely because it touches the very heart of social intercourse. The idea that somehow other kinds of embodied social relations are equivalent (or even subordinate) to a monetary transaction seems anathema to public consciousness; permissiveness around financial exchange for sexuality appears to undermine or throw into question those alternative forms and elements of exchange that are otherwise seen as legitimate, and legitimated, in sexual interaction.

To suggest that the role of the sex worker has symbolic weight is not to underestimate the actual roles these Geese must have played in medieval England. Indeed, fleeting glimpses of the reality of their lives is attested by what little historical evidence we have, in scraps of financial documentation, in popular literature of the time, and on Victorian lists of outstanding legal cases (Shilham n.d.) that confirm that brothels were part of the scene on the south bank for so many centuries. That the Bankside ritual uses sex workers as symbols of something else—of ambivalence in modern society; of debates about religion, multiculturalism, and the search for freedom; and above all of the importance of embodied presence in the matters and affairs of human exchange and interaction—does not mean there were not real women, with hurts, and passions, and loves all their own. The concerns of today's advocates around sex work—citizenship, labor rights, the fears of global trafficking, questions of coercion, and debates about the age of children—probably had very little to do with what would have concerned the activists, advocates, and good citizens of early Reformation England in whatever political battles they were fighting. But however different the symbolic valences may have been, medieval and early modern English reformers used some of the same tropes, including the use of money and multiplicity, to invoke the same cultural reactions—the attribution of shame and segregation—in the perennial debates about the ethics and morality of prostitution.

Item we ordeyne and make that
ther shal no gret housholder leue
nor trust to noo single woman
above the summe of vj.s. and viij
d. and if they or any of them do
the contrari therof that than thair
accion or accions contempnacion
and contempnacions therof shal
utterly stonde voide and adnullid
accordyng to the olde custume yt
of hadde and made.

Item we ordeyne and make yt
noo man nor woman dwellyng
withinne the seid lordship and fran
chise of what degree so euer he or
they be of shal not commense nor

Ordinances from Winchester Manor
The Bodleian Libraries, The University of Oxford, MS e. Mus. 229, folio 17r

2 ❀ *Medieval Bankside*

So been the wommen of the styves
Quod the Somonour "yput our of oure cure!"

So are the women of the stews
Said the summoner [an ecclesiastical officer], "likewise beyond my cure!"

Geoffrey Chaucer, *The Canterbury Tales* (late fourteenth century)

Since the early decades of the Christian era, over many centuries of first Roman and then Saxon occupation, the Borough of Southwark appears to have been populated with a steady stream of merchants, migrants, and miscreants. The Borough's social and architectural roots lie deep in English history, then, but the beginnings of the Southwark we see today are best dated to the central Middle Ages, around the turn of the first millennium, when the area begins to become a diverse location of high-ranking church officials, religious institutions, and foreign travelers on their way to London. As London grows in population and prominence, its southern neighbor becomes a kind of border region of the famous city, in equal measure a pit stop and a site for the provision of services to the great English capital. Characterized by modern historians as a thriving but down-at-heel precinct—think of a frontier trading town, or a carnival atmosphere in an overpopulated, underprivileged neighborhood at the edge of a city—Southwark was a place known for prostitutes, prisoners, and immigrants. Medieval Bankside, at its center, was the strip of land lining the outer bank of the River Thames as it wound its way around London: it was effectively designated for and in practice allotted to the marginal populations of the city.

Now the very heart of the London Borough of Southwark (a 1965 designation) and in the Diocese of Southwark (since 1905), Bankside, right up against the Thames, is a prominent location in its own right, as well as a neighborhood that makes up part of greater London's oldest history. These current designations that place Bankside in the center of London date only to the twentieth century, but archaeological remains in Southwark likely reach back almost two thousand years, to 50 CE, when Romans lived on the British Isles. Even if its swampy terrain made building difficult, Southwark's very proximity to the City of London predetermined that it would be an area of high population density: from the time of Londinium, as the Romans called it, there were large numbers of people wanting to live and work close to the capital, and the city made use of this geographical fact.

The need for livelihood in a human population is matched only by the need for solace. Remains of paupers—claimed by our ritualists to be the skeletons of prostitutes, but probably dating later—in a mass grave half a mile from the Southwark Cathedral do not date back as far as the Romans (although it is not unthinkable that the Romans had prostitutes and maybe even in Southwark, but the archaeological record can offer us no evidence). The Romans stayed for about four hundred years, when they were likely driven out by environmental conditions (Sheldon 2000). Southwark, then a marshy swamp, appears to have been uninhabited for half a millennium, until 900 CE, when the Saxons moved in. And soon after, we have material evidence that the world's oldest profession popped up its lovely and resilient head.

The earliest date for an ordinance of prostitution is contested, as is the identity of the bones excavated from Crossbones Graveyard, but there is not a lot of debate in the historical literature about the presence of brothels, or working places for prostitutes, in Bankside for many hundreds of years. The stews were fully operational between 1267 and 1546—this duration at least is documented, insofar as they were effectively legal in Southwark during that period—but they very possibly were also extant more than two hundred years in either direction. They were opened and closed through various statutory or regulatory public and popular proceedings in this seven-hundred-year history, but one thing is sure: they seemed to keep coming back, whether shut down by local residents incensed by the illicit practices of migrants or by Henry VIII in the last year of his reign. We know, through moments caught in historical fragments—mostly financial, attesting to the rents or the fines (which in medieval administration translated into an annual payment or licensing fee)—some of the ebbs and flows in the popularity and public availability of prostitution in Bankside. But it is harder to assess what daily life looked like—especially given the span of centuries—at any given moment in time. In these matters, perhaps the present is as good a model for the past as vice versa.

By exiling prostitution across the river, easily available but conveniently set apart from respectable circles, London had a place—nearby but separated by a body of water—where undesirable but needed services could be outsourced. Conditions would always be hard in such circumstances, and competition would likely be fierce given the tendency toward urban migration when labor opportunities are available; we know Southwark was a place where many migrants from the Continent arrived throughout the medieval period (Carlin 1996). It is not hard to imagine that women would choose to make a buck performing services for the city's residents. Indeed, there appears to be ample evidence that sex work could be a relatively lucrative profession, and English legislators worried as much about how to dissuade women from wanting to earn money through the sex trade as they did about the sinful effects of sexual commerce.

Despite the efforts of some of the most powerful monarchs in the world, historical evidence suggests that sex work was never entirely driven away in Southwark. No ruler, Tudor or otherwise, in English history seems able to have suppressed it completely. In England as anywhere, sex work is a lasting human profession, whereby sexual services are acknowledged to have value, sullied though it might be, and are available for hire at a price. (Various institutional relationships must be negotiated along the way, and the political stakes appear surprisingly high for a set of social dynamics that is so enduring and so obviously part of the human condition.) Our search for intimacy is so deep that there is no changing this basic human configuration. And the symbolic reverberation of all that sexuality conveys is contested and reinscribed with every encounter, such that the social group of those who offer it publicly is the inevitable repository of that which is ambivalent and complicated about relations with the other.

Scholars marvel—and rightfully so—that we have extant manuscripts documenting the treatment and the terms of the employment of sex workers in the medieval period. These materials governed the intimate lives of Southwark residents more than half a millennium ago, and they point us back to the ground of our ritual: this history is public. Why should we not compare these accounts with contemporary representations of the sex worker, in John's ritual rendering and in the world at large? It is the paradoxical setting apart of the sex worker while also being aware of her value as a laborer—in the statutes that guided the manor of Winchester or, implicitly, in contemporary religious, secular, or capitalist ideologies—with which the symbolic nexus of our ritual is concerned. From the Plantagenets to the Tudors, England acknowledged and maintained a system for the provision of sex work and for the protection of sex workers under the church. These edicts were at least in part an attempt to put into place rules for ethical tenancy relations between landlords and their tenants—given that the wisest among them saw that, try as we might, the various forms of exchange of sexual intimacy for material livelihood cannot be legislated out of the human population.

Stews in Southwark

London banned prostitution in 1266 or 1267. London banned prostitution again, following a "morality campaign" in 1382 (Post 1977:418), in 1383 or 1384 (Carlin 1996:213). Neither of these prohibitions did the trick. In a pragmatic adjustment, another official ordinance in 1393 banned prostitution from central London, but this time explicitly sent sex workers to other designated areas nearby, to Smithfield in the north and to Southwark in the south (Karras 1989:117). In this attempt, rather than working or living on the streets of London, prostitutes were ordered to "keep themselves to the places thereunto assigned, that is to say, the Stews on the other side of Thames, and Cokkeslane" (cited in Carlin 1996:210). Unsurprisingly, this effort to displace rather than to ban prostitution was no more successful than its predecessors, as evidenced by further attempts to rid the city of prostitution, issued again in 1417, again in 1483 (Karras 1989:109), and possibly again in 1485, when an edict emphatically tried, seemingly by polemic this time, "to eschewe the stynkyng and horrible Synne of Lechery" (cited in Brundage 1987:528).

None of these ordinances worked, as evidenced by their frequency. But the effective legalization—and subsequent regulation—of displaced brothels in Southwark meant that the sex trade in the southern, service-heavy Borough could thrive. With London's repeated attempts to drive the practice of prostitution out of the city, Bankside—sometimes called Stewside (or "the Stews side"; Karras 1989:117n69)—became a well-known and established red-light district across the river (along with the smaller but appropriately named Cock Lane in Smithfield, just north of the city). In contemporary parlance—and even in juridical terms in India or in Holland—a "red-light district" is meant to regulate by setting apart geographically what is marginally permitted but also revulsive or reprobate. Indeed, given that London-based clients needed to cross the Thames in order to get to Bankside, a new tactic had been tried in 1391, when it was the boatmen who were punished if they brought prospective clients across the river. They were penalized if they brought men "to the Stews between sunset and sunrise," and they were warned not to "tie up their boats within twenty fathoms of the shore during that time, 'lest evildoers be assisted in their coming and going'" (Carlin 1996:213). That didn't work either; apparently the boatmen were as resilient in their trade as the prostitutes were.

Thus it was that the Southwark stews, or bathhouses—brothel-saloons—moved into full swing by the mid-thirteenth century (at the latest), and they stayed that way until the mid-sixteenth century when, in 1546, King Henry VIII issued a royal proclamation to close them down once and for all (or so he thought). For these three hundred years (and in public lore much longer, up to and including the present), the Bankside brothels were a famous draw of the area. Fines paid and recorded in the pipe rolls (the annual budget books of the medieval manor) of 1252–1253 and 1253–1254, and again in 1262–1263, make reference to "girls" (*puelle*); right around 1300, we see two annual recorded payments to the bishop's court on the part of someone who looks to be a madam, Cristina la Frowe (her surname is likely a reference to her Flemish nationality [Carlin 1996:211n11]). In 1381, seven male householders are listed as "stewmongers"—despite Cristina la Frowe's pioneering role as a female taxpayer, it was intended that brothel owners be established men—who have paid their poll tax (the medieval equivalent of rent). This number more than doubled by 1506, when eighteen stewhouses appear on the books (Carlin 1996:213) before yet another (unsuccessful) attempt to close them down. Twelve appear to have opened right up again (Karras 1989:112).

Stewhouses were not allowed to keep their own boats, but they were permitted to advertise their wares "on the whitewashed walls of the houses, so as to be visible to river traffic" (Carlin 1996:215n29), and they were brightly named. The Red Hart, the Bell and Cock, the Unicorn, and the Antelope (Carlin 1996:213n23) must have been frequented as known entertainment joints, as one might visit one's local pub today. A visitor from London traveling to Southwark for the afternoon or evening could have stopped in at a stew as part of a jovial postprandial outing: stews couldn't serve food or drink, but they offered nourishment and satisfaction of another sort.[1]

Even in Southwark—which did not fall under the jurisdiction of the city and which, by this juncture, was a site known for the procurement of such services, and a rowdy, bawdy Borough on its own terms—there were various attempts to shut down houses of lewd behavior over the course of the centuries. Being a brothel owner was not (and never has been) an unchallenged occupation: a 1460 panel tried to end prostitution in the area; in 1506, the stews were momentarily shut; and in 1519, a number of "suspicious persons [were] arrested at the stewhouses" (Karras 1989:113). And yet, despite it all, as recorded by archivist J. B. Post, "a subsidy return of 1524 cheerfully listed a dozen householders—ten women and two men—separately, as 'the bawds of the Bank'" (1977:418). What we may glean from this contested back-and-forth between moralizing ordinances that repeatedly attempted to erase prostitution, on one hand, and practical legislation around the enduring reality of resilient brothel life, on the other, is that sex work may not have been the object of popular ire per se, but was rather accepted by both officials and the greater populations of Southwark and London.

The effort to close the houses may have been more directly a response to the fact that many sex workers (and brothel owners too, some of whom were women) were foreign. Flemish was the nationality cited here: in one instance a complaint was filed against a "Flemish monopoly" (Post 1977:418n8); in 1381, a stew with Flemish prostitutes was attacked; in 1393, London blamed Flemish women for "such [a] shameful and dolorous life" (Karras 1989:116–117). Two hundred years later, projecting back, John Stow would explain to his late sixteenth-century readers that medieval stewmongers were often from Flanders because no Englishwoman would have done that sort of thing: "English people disdayned to be baudes. Froes of Flaunders were women for that purpose" (cited in Karras 1989:116–117). The custom of foreign clients, too, caused some of the troubles, as when violence erupted between native Englishmen and their traveling counterparts at the locations of generally sinful activity (Karras 1989:111).[2] The honor of women is often thought to be encoded in nationality.

Whether sex work is the baseline marker of opprobrium, on one hand, or foreigners taking over native land, housing, work, and women is, on the other, the convergence of prostitution and migrant labor is charged, and ascertaining which social travesty has the power to incite the violence of the response—even if it is in the name of the other—is difficult. It may have been that it was easier to countenance foreign women engaging in such morally bankrupt activities—or indeed that it was a profession that had been "cornered by" or understood to be the domain of Flemish migrants, in an area of town that was already known for a relatively large immigrant population. And certainly prostitution on the Continent seems to have been a more widespread and less dubious practice than in England, where it was viewed censoriously, with Southwark being a notable exception (Carlin 1996:219; Brundage 1987:528). That one symbolic threat can so easily stand in for another is part of what is at stake in an analysis of the layered representations of a given historical or cultural logic.

Regulating Prostitution in the Fifteenth Century

Contractual agreements between the prostitute and her place of work, or her stew, were not laid down in writing, but, extraordinarily, some of the labor arrangements through which sex workers were employed are known to us. Contained in a kind of tenancy agreement between stewmongers and their landlord, the manorial estate of Winchester, which owned the properties occupied by the stews as part of the London (or near-London) residence of the bishop, we have medieval ordinances that lay out in careful detail what was and what was not permitted as far as the functioning of brothels and the treatment of prostitutes by brothel owners went. These folios appear to display an acute awareness about where the fine lines between protection and exploitation lay on the part of the medieval bishopric: they attempt to determine the relationships between the sex worker, the stew, and the bishop's estate (or the subtenant, the tenant, and the landlord), and they lay out in precise form what was expected of manorial occupants—the stewholders, the sex workers, and the clients who visited them. The text is a thorough and noble attempt to clarify who was responsible for what in the delicate matters of sexual and financial exchange.

If the original manuscript is as old as it says it is (which is sadly doubtful), these would have been edicts issued by the Bishop of Winchester during the reign of the Angevin King Henry II. Attributed to 1162, the "customary," or a document offering an account of conduct as it should be, decreed the treatment of and relations with "the women that are at common brothel" (Karras 1989:129; or, in Middle English, "the women that ben at common bordell" [Post 1977:424]).[3] As we have seen, there was no shortage of common brothels by the mid-fifteenth century; archivist Post (1977) suggests that it was in this period, when "Bankside stews evidently flourished" (Carlin 1996:213), and not earlier—despite its claim—that such a charter on the freedom of prostitutes was likely produced, and subsequently expanded upon. The customary itself makes multiple mention of "old customs made . . . time out of mind,"[4] indicating that the practices had been around since before legal memory (or, to be specific, before 1189, when Richard the Lionheart acceded to the throne), but needed some ethical updating in written form (which may be why the author felt the need to date the manuscript three hundred years earlier than he was very likely writing it).[5] We have always reclaimed our history with a little bit of poetic license.

Whenever it was written, there is not much that is prudish about these papers: the usefulness of a prostitute's sexual service is implicitly acknowledged. Ironically, it is in this use that the estate sees fit to ensure her protection, such that her sexuality enables rather than counters the moral ethos in which the church sees itself as operating. What good will she do anyone if she is not able to earn her keep by offering her services as a woman, and what would the upright social world do without the offering of a sewer, to paraphrase Aquinas? An explicit recognition that a prostitute was working a trade (and Southwark was the source of many of the city's services and trades [Johnson 1969:37]) justified the patronage the church offered. Prostitutes were not to be explicitly penalized themselves for their station, even if it was morally reprobate.

However ambivalently such women were held in moral terms, through these ordinances, the estate of Winchester made explicit efforts to safeguard the freedom of women who were offering sexual services, and to protect them from potential exploitation by brothel keepers. In short, as far as the church was concerned, prostitutes worked for themselves and not ever for the stewholders, which would have been entirely a different arrangement (analogous to pimping or, if women were brought under force and not permitted to leave, to today's trafficking [Hausner 2005]). The stews were thus workplaces, and stewholders were the landlords—and nothing more—of the sex workers who conducted their business there. If they were financial mediators between prostitutes and the manor of Winchester, it was as landlords of the prostitutes and tenants of the bishop: they were prohibited from taking any cut from the prostitutes' earnings (or taking any money at all, beyond rent for the room). Stewholders were not permitted to "keep any of their women within the houses against their will" (A3), to loan money to prostitutes (in order to ensure that debts that could lead to further control would not be accrued), or to prevent the "free going and coming" of women who worked in the Bankside brothels (Preamble).

These rules would go a long way in the contemporary regulation of sex work. Inverting the logic often cited in today's policy debates about protecting women from the dangers of prostitution, the manorial position—not against the practice, but for its regulation—implied better conditions for women's sexual labor, not worse. As if it were a civic administration writing policy designed to maintain the healthiest social ethos for all of its denizens (whether or not they were engaged in respectable occupations), the estate legislated illicit behavior in good faith by ensuring that the work prostitutes were doing was as beneficial as it could be for both Londoners desiring their services and for sex workers themselves. Sex work as a well-regulated commercial venture (understood at the time as the unfortunate but appropriate location for the release of pent-up societal ills) meant that it made sense to assure the reasonable treatment of prostitutes—they needed to be in good nick—and that they were looked after (relatively) well, precisely because they offered a needed service to a large community of city-dwellers who were bound to go in search of intimate encounters.

Freedom of Movement

Both elements—the ethical and the financial—of this complicated moral and economic set of labor arrangements are abundantly clear in the "acte and ordinaunce" written to encode the maintenance of the medieval stews (Preamble). The opening passages oscillate between ensuring that women using the brothels for their work (a woman "that lives by her body"; B2, B10, B12, B14, B23) be permitted to move where they wished, on one hand, and ensuring that they did not work on holy days, on the other. The practices of prostitution, it may be inferred, were legitimate, after a fashion, as long as they did not interfere with religious or conventional, mainstream life. On the contrary, it was assumed that they enabled it.[6]

As if anticipating the debates of the twenty-first century, prohibiting any arrangement that could be called forced prostitution was one of the primary motivations for the document. The apparent concern of the church was to guard against keeping women against their will—"trafficking" in contemporary political language—and to prevent stew-holders from making money on a woman's bodily labor, in which case they would have been pimps, not brothel owners. This explicit protection—and the attendant analytical clarity governing the terms and conditions of sex work—underscores the tone of the ordinances as a whole, which go on to govern the stipulations through which the provision of sex work and the maintenance of the stews might be most ethically upheld. In the preamble, protecting the freedom of movement of the "single women" of the brothel is highlighted as a primary concern:

> We ordain and make to the said lord's [the Bishop of Winchester's] avail divers ordinances and constitutions to be kept forever more with the said lordship and franchise, according to the old customs that have been used and accustomed there time out of mind, which now of late

> were broken, to the great displeasure of God and great hurt unto the lord, and utter undoing of all his poor tenants there dwelling, and also to the great multiplication of horrible sin upon the single women, who ought to have their free going and coming at their own liberty, as it appears by the old customs thereof made before, time out of mind. (Preamble)

This was no endorsement of the single women's sin, nor was it a treatise or petition railing against it. It was rather a subtle statement against the mistreatment of women who were involved in the practice in any event, and a clear claim that, sinful as their acts may have been, "single women" had to be "free" to come and go "at their own liberty": to be sinful did not justify penalty, prison, or abuse. Indeed, to treat such women as prisoners because they sold sexual services, or to create a situation in which they became indebted laborers or indentured servants would not only disable a seemingly functional system of old, but would add "to the great multiplication of horrible sin" already negotiated in these arrangements.

Significantly, in light of modern legislation that sometimes conflates prostitution and trafficking (see Hausner 2005; Vance 2005), a sex worker could not be kept against her will in these ordinances: "First, therefore, we ordain and make, according to the said old customs contained in the customary, that no stewholder nor his wife hinder any single woman to go and come at all times when they wish" (A1). She was protected as a rent-paying subtenant in good faith. Not only was it ordered that women's movement must be free ("no great householder shall keep any women to board"; A2),[7] but checks would take place by "the bailiff and constables . . . four times in the year, that is to say once every quarter," who would "make a due search in every great house, whether there be any single woman found and kept there against her will that would depart and leave her sin and never come there any more" (A5). During these rounds, the officers would question the stewholders: "Does he prevent the women [from] coming and going freely?" (B34); "Has he imprisoned any person in his house for debt or trespass?" (B35); and also, "Does he beat any woman belonging to his house?" (B40). These regulations were designed to protect the freedom of movement and the bodily integrity (to the extent possible) of a prostitute; the questioners were aware of where the abuses might lie.

There appear to have been no circumstances when a prostitute could stay on in a stew beyond her working hours, for better or for worse. Whether a sex worker needed to return to her lodgings elsewhere to eat and sleep, or during holy days when the brothels were shut, or if she wished to leave the trade altogether, or even if she wished to live or board in the stew, stewholders were not permitted to keep sex workers in their lodges. Prostitutes had to have their own autonomy.

Religious, Legal, and Financial Considerations

The early passages of the document are as concerned that the stews close down during "holy days" as they are to assure that sex workers have freedom and mobility, and sometimes in the same breath: "Also, we ordain and make that no great householder keep open his doors upon any holy days according to the old customs and customary, not keep any of their women within the houses against their will, upon pain of a hundred shillings" (A3). "Holy days" included Whitsuntide, or the week following Pentecost, the seventh Sunday after Easter, when commercial establishments were shut down: stewholders were required to stop running their taverns (and there may have been fewer local clients for the latterly called Geese). The ordinances cover their bases, however: stews were meant to close on holy days, but even if they didn't, prostitutes had to leave the manor entirely—they very likely lived just outside the estate—except for two hours at lunchtime (between 11:00 AM and 1:00 PM) and at night (between 5:00 PM and 8:00 AM), when other, respectable businesses in Southwark would resume as usual (B11). Summer working hours in the stews started at 6:00 PM and ended at 6:00 AM, to account for the longer days—and presumably to keep laborers at their posts as long as there was light before they called off work and headed to Bankside.[8]

Prostitutes were also required to leave the manor even at night when Parliament was in session, as the king was nearby in Westminster: "if any woman is found within the lordship after the sun is gone to rest, the king being at Westminster and holding there either Parliament or council, until the sun is up in the morning, after the custom of the manor, she shall make a fine at every time she does so of six shillings eightpence" (B16).[9] Although the bishop's manor lay across the bridge from London and constituted its own administrative territory (Johnson 1969), it may have been thought prudent to keep a lower profile when His Majesty was in the area, so as not to provoke his ire. More importantly, perhaps, the bishop would likely have been in residence himself, on hand for the royal sessions; his aides and scribes might have thought it appropriate that the neighborhood be cleaned up in preparation for his arrival (Karras 1989:117–118).

These motivations might well have been two sides of the same coin: the bishop's land had a juridical and financial authority all its own, known as a "liberty," and the customary was determined to uphold the manor's commercial independence, without the interference of either the city or the king. To ensure that the bishop's citizens were governed by Winchester and not by Westminster (let alone London), the ordinances insist "that no man nor woman dwelling within the said lordship and franchise, of whatever degree he or they be, shall commence or take any action or process against another for no matter or cause in any court of the king, but only within the said lord's court, to be determined and ended there" (A7). Impressively, it was the liberty—both territorial and financial—that the text intended to preserve, for the manor and for the morally dubious category of prostitutes.

This set of ordinances is not a canonical debate about how to bring women out of the trade. A practical air pervades the text: how best might such terms be articulated so as to ensure optimal arrangements? One of the questions meant to be asked of stewholders and their subtenants on weekly rounds was: "Does she take any money to lie with men and not perform it?" (B54). The prostitute had a job to do, and the ordinances were designed to make sure she did it well. Both stewmonger and prostitute had rules they must follow; by fulfilling their responsibilities and obligations, they were presumably protected from unethical or untenable arrangements that the other party might try. "Those who hinder the officers in making their weekly searches" would be fined "a hundred shillings" (B9); officers who hid any breach of the ordinances from the court would be imprisoned (B17); those who wrongfully offered bail (when a defendant should go to prison) would be fined (B19). These documents put ethical considerations along with brute realism about human behavior into play at every station; they are remarkable in the nuance of the regulations that attempted to maintain institutions theologically understood as sinful with the least possible social damage.

Prostitutes paid fourteen pence a week for the use of their rooms in the stews: "a woman that lives by her body [must be permitted] to come and go (as long as she pays her duty as old custom is, that is to say every week fourteen pence for her chamber) at all times shall have free licence and liberty, without any interruption from the stewholders" (B2), who would be questioned during officers' rounds about the rents they accepted (B33). The relationship between sex worker and stew was governed by the higher-order tenancy agreement between the stewholder and the manor, but the stewholder was under no circumstances permitted to use his (or her)[10] mediating financial position to abuse the sex worker (and questions were asked to make sure of it): the terms arranged were those between laborer and landlord, or prostitute and stewholder. Stews were manorial tenants and were maintained with the understanding that they were places of work, not residence.

While the main caution of the customary was to ensure that practicing prostitutes were not abused, equally important was to ensure that no one mistook them for respectable women. Indeed, it appears that the system was sustainable precisely because they were visibly classified as a category of women available for hire, who were seen as other than (and beneath) both "[r]eligious women and wives," who were "not to be received in the stewhouses" (B4). To be doubly sure of the social categories at work, prostitutes were not allowed to wear "clothes which are called aprons" (B8); these were the adornments of women in publicly acceptable professions. As long as they—and everyone else—knew their place (that is, the denigrated place of the prostitute), sex work was a trade that could, in the end, be more beneficial to the social worlds under ecclesiastical jurisdiction here (the prostitutes, their clients, their landlords, and the bishop) than damaging. If the customary was followed to the letter of the law, no one would be harmed, no one would be deceived, no one would be constrained, and the rightful charges would be made for services and accommodations, both, with no agents taking any wrongful cuts and no one getting duped about either financial or emotional matters.

The ordinances thus juggle guarding against the potentially malevolent (or greedy) actions of the stewholders with the potentially deceptive (or greedy) activities of the sex workers. They also try to strike a moral tone: just as prostitutes were to be questioned on a regular basis as to whether they took money but failed to provide the service for which they were paid ("women who take money to lie with men but do not do it"; B20), stewmongers were to be questioned as to how many laundresses were in the house (since having extra women was viewed as an inherent danger of the stews; B31) or whether "he keeps in his house any woman of religion or any man's wife" (B36). The text is not overly piteous, however, and stewholders are mandated against too much kindness as well as too much cruelty: they are prohibited from making loans too great (although such a provision is likely stipulated in order to prevent the claim that debts were owed, which could result in a woman having to stay overtime to pay them back, creating a form of indentured servitude, which is what the ordinances are most concerned to prevent) or from letting prostitutes "board," which, again, means refusing to give stewholders a way to keep sex workers trapped.

But one can imagine a case where a place to live or a loan of a few shillings might have gone a long way, and these exigencies are not available in the text. One hopes that, in the reality of medieval social encounters, adjustments to the rules were found as needed. Still, the ordinances are very clear that if a woman was with child (B23), or diseased with "any sickness of burning" (B25) (or "the perilous infirmity"; B45), she would summarily "be put out" (B25) of the manor and allowed nowhere near the stews: in neither case was she any longer a suitable employee. The stews may not have been prisons,[11] but nor were they places of refuge.[12]

Emotional Clarity

As we know, early medieval canonists were convinced that sex work was a depraved act and a deeply immoral practice; its public nature, its multiplicity of partners, and its quality as emotionally deceptive all built upon the basic sinfulness of sexuality to begin with (Brundage 1989 [1976]:82). Prostitutes carry the burden of such depravity in these canonical discussions, and presumably they did in real life, too. But the ordinances from the Winchester manor start from the premise that the penalties for such behaviors were not exclusively a prostitute's to pay; in these instructions we see the fines (and thereby some of the responsibility or putative blame) for an illicit manipulation of the system placed elsewhere, namely on an abusive stewholder or, at further remove, on a duplicitous officer of the manor. These measures constitute at least to a small degree some symbolic protection of the prostitute, which, even if it is meted out in small doses, is significant.

It is human lust that leads the manor into such murky terrain to begin with, and arguably it is men's emotional vulnerability that structurally requires the moral denigration of the women who might show them up for it. Along with the stews and the manorial officials in these ordinances, men have to be kept in line in this medieval attempt to make sure the system is not more immoral—or morally contaminating or explosive—than it already is. Attempts are made by the City of London in 1351 and again in 1361 (and customs documents that may date from a century earlier also refer to such efforts) to keep prospective clients away from Bankside by penalizing the boat captains who would ferry them across the river to "les Stuwes" or "les Estouves" (Karras 1989:111n46). But these seem half-hearted—or at least self-consciously symbolic—in the face of the 1393 ordinance that explicitly sends prostitutes out of London (again) to the Southwark stews. In condemning the practice, the city denounced all those involved—clients, stewholders, and prostitutes (all of whom are tended to in the manorial ordinances), and boat owners, too—and was determined only to displace it, or to ensure that it happened elsewhere.

Once in Southwark, we know that women were not restricted in their movements: this edict is very clear. Men, too, were assured freedom of movement, even when they failed to pay up: stewholders were not allowed to "detain someone in their houses because of debts"; no proprietor could "[keep] any man against his will within his house as prisoner for any debt that he owes to him" (B3). Interestingly, though, no clause of the ordinances monitors client behavior: by the time the rules governing prostitution are devolved to the manor, it is almost as if clients are free from the scrutiny that the rest of the system undergoes. This seeming absolution provides evidence for the argument that however sinful the single women must be, their clients get away scot-free.

If sex work was to be countenanced at all, it was certainly not men who should be critiqued for their conduct.

There were practical reasons, too, that clients' behaviors were not interrogated in the way that those of "stewholders" (B30–B46), "common women" (B47–B57), and "officers" (B58–B62) were: the customers of the stews were the commercial visitors to the manor, and their payments kept the system afloat. From the perspective of any franchise, the clientele needs to be kept happy. So the estate had to ensure that paying customers were looked after, along with their service providers. For starters, if anyone held "the goods of another in custody and [did] not want to give them back," the stewholder would have to pay a fine of twenty shillings: "if any man comes into this lordship to any stewhouse and leave any belongings with the wife . . . or any other woman therein . . . he [shall] have deliverance of his belongings again at his going" (B6). No one was allowed to take advantage of him by stealing his clothes while he was out of them.

Further, matters of the heart and body are delicate ones; for a comprehensive moral and economic system, the manor had to provide (via its tenants and the common women who rented their chambers) a service that would satisfy the men who crossed the Thames to come to the stews. The requirement that a client be able to spend the night with a prostitute in her stew chamber, for example, was an assurance for the man who had paid for such a service, but also seemingly accommodated his desire for the emotional intimacy that might come of such a liaison: "if any woman takes any money to lie with any man, unless she lies still with him until it be the morning and then arise, she shall make a fine of six shillings eightpence" (B20). As we have seen, in canon law, one of the moral crimes of which a prostitute was considered guilty was deception, and the ordinances offer a number of attempts to curtail the willful behavior of women who were presumed to have access to a large repertoire of emotional tactics. A prostitute was not allowed to solicit, to make a fuss, to have alternate employment (such as spinning; B13), or to have her "own lovers contrary to the custom" (B12): if she was working in the manor, she would be available on the terms specified.

These terms meant behaving with some degree of modesty, prostitutes though they were. A sex worker was not allowed to "scold contrary to the custom" at pain of both imprisonment and a fine, and the clause is specific as to the kinds of behaviors that were not acceptable: "if any woman that lives by her body chides any man or makes a fray, she shall be in prison three days and three nights and make a fine of six shillings eightpence" (B14). Further, if she "casts a stone or makes any face at any man going by the way, either by water or by land, she shall make a fine of three shillings fourpence" (B13). No faces, no ruckus, no scolding, and no abuses were permitted. She was not to explicitly entice, or "draw men in by the clothing or otherwise" (B7; but neither was the stewholder's wife, fairly, for whom the penalty was stiffer, to the tune of forty shillings [B8]). These were not becoming actions for women of any station, but more importantly, stews were not supposed to solicit or actively promote their services. As the customary puts it, "if any woman of the brothel hinders any man, other than sit still at the door and let him go or come, choose which they will, or if she draws any man by his gown or by his hood or by any other thing, she shall make a fine to the lord of twenty shillings" (B7).

It is hard to imagine that women held to these rules, in truth, or that they were always strictly enforced. Our image of bawdy women (the etymology of "bawdy" precisely derives from this period) with sharp tongues implies that a publicly lewd suggestion on the streets of Bankside might indeed have been welcome, or taken with a good deal of humor and a pinch of salt, or even a mutual acknowledgment of human suffering in urban peri-London: no one was blind to these social dynamics. Indeed, the root hypocrisy of the system was that even as prostitutes were engaged in order to accommodate the physical—and also emotional—needs of men, their own emotional needs were of no concern. They were allowed to have intimate relations only with paying customers for the good of others but never for themselves, on pain of prison, fines, the "cucking stool" (a structure of public humiliation; see Carlin 1996:61n206), and being required to leave the manor (which was effectively the termination of employment with the Bankside stews): "if any woman that lives by her body holds any paramour against the use and custom of the manor she shall be three weeks in the prison and make a fine of six shillings eightpence and then be set once on the cucking-stool and forswear the lordship" (B12). In this construction we might find the greatest indicator of denigration (although it could be argued that bringing a personal relationship into the workplace was appropriately frowned upon): even in a chamber she had paid for, where she had no obligation to the stewholder other than to be a good tenant, a prostitute was not allowed to have an intimate relationship on her own terms.

It is hard too to know what life felt like on the streets of Bankside in the Middle Ages, in the vicinity of the stews where sex-working women plied their trade. They were not supposed to scold; their clients had presumably left nagging wives at home and would not pay to be subjected to feminine fury all over again. But from court records it appears that sometimes they could hold their tongues no longer: sex workers are listed as and "along with accused scolds" in ecclesiastical court rolls from Winchester, Smithfield, and Westminster (Karras 1989:124n95). And yet no number of edicts or pipe rolls can tell us what really made a medieval Englishman's heart race in his choice of partner, never mind that he might have to pay for her services. For some, they may have been all the more sexy when they were sassy—sharp wit has never gone awry in the history of English flirtation. It is not difficult to imagine that the cleverest-tongued Goose was the prize of them all, if a prostitute could ever be a prize, or that a rousing verbal exchange between Goose and prospective client might have been the catalyst for a robust interactive transaction. Certainly a regulation against chiding does not seem to have stemmed the predilection to speak out when life's circumstances became too hard to bear.

The Rule of the Monarch

In the last year of Henry VIII's reign, the brothels were closed for good. After many attempts over hundreds of years, the King "hath by advice of his council thought requisite utterly to extinct such abominable license and clearly to take away all occasion of the same" (Hughes and Larkin 1969:365, proc. 265). The king's proclamation was firm in its intention that those "dissolute and miserable persons" who engaged in "abominable and detestable sin" would cease and desist such activities by the time of the next holy festival, Easter, twelve days after his proclamation was issued, and return to their native places:

> [H]is majesty straightly chargeth and commandeth that all such persons as have accustomed most abominably to abuse their bodies contrary to God's law and honesty, in any such common place called the stews now about the city of London, do, before the Feast of Easter next coming, depart from those common places and resort incontinently to their natural countries with their bags and baggages, upon pain of imprisonment and further to be punished at the King's majesty's will and pleasure.

Women that in the manor of Winchester's ordinance "live[d] by their bodies" are here thought to "have accustomed most abominably to abuse their bodies contrary to God's law": what was a practical arrangement now becomes not only sinful but no longer natural.

The houses that had lodged the prostitutes would have to be cleared out. Their owners and leaseholders would have to publicly forswear such activities in the future (and further would have to present the names of prospective tenants to the royal council for approval, who would have to do the same):

> All such householders as under the name of bawds have kept the notable and marked houses and known hostelries for the said evil-disposed persons; that is to say, such householders as do inhabit the houses white and painted with signs on the front for a token of the said houses, shall avoid with bag and baggage before the Feast of Easter next coming upon pain of like punishment. . . . [T]he same owner or mean tenant intending to make lease as afore do present the name or names of such as should hire the same to the King's majesty's council, and . . . before them the lessee hath put in bond and surety not to suffer any of the said houses to be abused as hath been in times past with the said abomination.

In other words, working prostitutes were to be sent packing, and the stews were to be summarily shut down as establishments of that sort. In the fervor leading up to the holy festival of Easter 1546, Henry VIII's last, the area around the stews had to be cleaned up once and for all. Nor would Bankside vendors be allowed to sell food, drink, or other services: "all such as dwell upon the banks called the stews near London . . . do before the said Feast of Easter cease and leave off their victualizing and forbear to retain any guest or stranger into their house either to eat and drink or lodge." One can compare this policy to a city's clearing of an impoverished area, a slum, or an insignificant village in order to make way for a new development, a dam, or an international event like the Olympics, with little regard for the circumstances of the people who live there.

Why does Henry change his tune at this late date, after thirty-seven years on the throne, during which time the stews seemingly operated without restriction or restraint?[13] By his own account, in the practices of the stews:

> There hath of late increased and grown such enormities as not only provoke instantly the anger and wrath of Almighty God, but also engender such corruption among the people as tendeth to the intolerable annoyance of the commonwealth, and where not only the youth is provoked, enticed, and allowed to execute the fleshly lusts, but also, by such assemblies of evil-disposed persons haunted and accustomed, is daily devised and conspired how to spoil and rob the true labouring and well-disposed men.

It appears that Henry—or perhaps his advisers—has become less patient with the ways of ill repute in Southwark, and is no longer willing to accept them by default. There is no countenance of the ways of the flesh in these words, nor pity for the prostitute, who appears herself to be the temptress ready to bring otherwise healthy and normal men down into the sullied worlds of destitute and depraved lust and sexuality. Nor is there any ambiguity in the monarch's view of the practice of prostitution. Blame is clearly apportioned: prostitutes are the bane of the social order, and the order is given to close the brothels, which are seen as the places that enabled such practices, in a dramatic shift in tone from the ordinances that lay out the terms of viable or legal encounter so comparatively reasonably.

But nothing really had changed in the nature of the sex work that had been conducted in Bankside for centuries at this stage, and we must look elsewhere to understand this sudden shift of mood. Perhaps the mark of a monarch who knew his reign was coming to an end, or that he was soon to meet his maker, Henry threw down the gauntlet once and for all in this proclamation. Beyond the progress of the Reformation and Henry's getting on in age, we might ask what political move toward the appropriation of the powers of Winchester was intended here.[14] That the Bishop of Winchester was technically in charge of the stews may indeed have inspired Henry to make this proclamation—until this point he had no jurisdiction over the liberty of the Winchester estate or indeed over Southwark. In his sweeping proclamation, the King took radical action, claiming royal jurisdication over the territorial and tenancy affairs of the bishop:

> The King's most excellent majesty also chargeth and commandeth that no owner or mean tenant of any such whited house or houses, where the said lewd persons have had resort and used their most detestable life, do from the said Feast of Easter presume to let any of the houses, heretofore abused with said mischiefs in the streets called the stews aforesaid, to any person or persons before the same owner or mean tenant intending to make lease as afore do present the name or names of such as should hire the same to the King's majesty's council.

In this injunction is a royal claim to dominion over the manorial court leet, and a clear statement that the owner of the stews—the ecclesiastical estate of the Bishop of Winchester—would bow to the Crown rather than operate independently. Much as we may marvel at the acceptance if not the outright endorsement of prostitution by the church prior to and in the early Reformation, and the relatively ethical treatment of prostitutes in church doctrine as a result of the acknowledgment of this social reality, the position of prostitutes was left in no doubt by this final declaration on the matter by Henry VIII. The banishment of sex workers from the bishop's estate appears to be one final means through which Henry VIII intended to consolidate territorial and legal power before his death: it was one of his last proclamations, as he would die within the year.

In a sense this late decree could be seen as an uprising of moral fervor at the end of Henry's life; not every royal proclamation was so insistent upon rooting out sin. In the beginning of his reign, in fact, as befitted a new monarch intent on gaining the respect and loyalty of his subjects, he wiped the slate clean. Four days after he acceded to the throne, on April 25, 1509, he pardoned all major criminal acts, including "high treason, petty treason, murder, and all other manner of felonies" (Hughes and Larkin 1969:81, proc. 60). This was a good beginning. Two years later, he was concerned with cleaning England of all riff-raff, in a proclamation that reinstated Edward I's 1285 Statute of Winchester, which treated matters of adjudicating felonies and the keeping of highways free of underbrush alike. Idleness was a crime in itself: "vagabonds, idle people, and suspect persons living suspiciously" could be incarcerated without nourishment for a day before being sent back to "such city, town, place, or hundred where they were born, or else to the place where they last dwelt or made their abode by the space of three years" (Hughes and Larkin 1969:85, proc. 63). Migrants, like beggars, were to be evicted. This focus on clearing the streets of immigrants remained a mainstay of Tudor proclamations through Elizabeth I's reign—and it appears to be a preoccupation not far from twenty-first-century consciousness as well.

The role of women in brothel-like situations was a public concern of Henry early in his reign, too. In his 1513 decree "Proclaiming Statutes and Ordinances of War for Calais," a list of rules for the ensuing war with France (the price of French wines and abstinence from meat are a frequent concern in the Tudor proclamations, as we shall see further during Elizabeth's reign), Henry issued an outline of prohibitions regarding "bordel keeping in the host," or any bordello under English dominion. Calais, the port from where operations to the Continent invariably began, belonged to the English until the mid-sixteenth century and to the French thereafter; it is a border town that still serves as a migrant detention center and a thorn in the side of both French and English authorities. Henry's early sixteenth-century proclamation about war with France throws into relief the fact that women migrants being kept as sexual companions—either brought into England by men coming home or taken out of England by men leaving—was a weighty moral matter. Henry decrees

> that no man bring with him any manner of woman over the sea, upon pain of forfeiture of their goods to the marshal and their bodies to be imprisoned, there to remain at the King's will. And that no man hold no woman within his lodging beyond the sea, upon pain of imprisonment and loss of a month's wages. And that no common woman presume to come within the King's host, nor nigh the same by the space of three miles, upon pain if any so be taken to be burned upon the right cheek at the first time. And if any be taken with the host, or within three miles of the same, after she or they have be[en] so burned, then she or they to

> be put into ward of the provost marshal, there to remain in prison as long as shall please the marshal and to have further punition as by him shall be thought convenient. (Hughes and Larkin 1969:113, proc. 73)

These are strict orders, and they reflect Henry's obviously deep concerns about the lengths to which men and women might go to be in each other's intimate company, and the perils that might ensue—to the perpetrators but more importantly to the state—should prostitutes distract soldiers or claim royal naval patronage or resources.

By the end of Henry's reign, his stance has hardened to apply to the Southwark stews as well. Whether a refusal to condone loose morals in the kingdom or a move to conquer Winchester's dominion under the royal hand such that no jurisdictions fell outside the purview of the King, here as elsewhere, sex work is the symbolic nexus for other political agendas, one that is capable of mobilizing populations through the base drives of sex and war. The Southwark stews marked a differentiation between the bishop's jurisdiction (and financial holdings) and the King's: Henry's Reformation would unite the two under one Crown.

Henry's proclamation shows us in no uncertain terms how sexuality and the exchange of sexual services are regarded in his court in the mid-sixteenth century, but it also breaks from the attitude of permissiveness that seems to have characterized the Southwark stews and the practices of prostitution in Bankside for several hundred years. That he makes such a decision so late in his reign indicates a change of heart in some way, or a gentrifying zeal taking hold toward the end of his life. Closing the brothels (or a wrathful attempt to) is a harbinger of theologies to come, a claim of control over the symbols and practices of sexuality that Elizabeth, his daughter, would take up with renewed passion, or at least vigor, in the years of her reign and her lengthy leadership of the Church of England.

Coda: Churches, Churchyards, and Contemporary Mobilization

None of these brothels exist anymore, nor is prostitution legal or even visible to most observers on the streets of contemporary Southwark. We have the manuscripts that describe the rule of the land—or what it was meant to be—at a particular moment in time, and we can see when stews and the practices therein were made legal and illegal, and for what ostensible reasons—as well as, in some cases, the underlying historical and cultural factors that were really at work (and that may have differed quite considerably from what the public record may state). We can document some of the behaviors or actions that underscored or accompanied these variable relationships. We can see in some measure, just by virtue of the laws that arose, or the ordinances that were written, or the petitions that were signed, what a general ethos dictated, and what the competing interests were. And we can investigate certain cases that might indicate what the financial arrangements between different parties were, and that suggest the relative values of different kinds of services rendered between or among different groups of people.

We cannot so easily see what life looked like for the women who offered their services in the arts and ways of the "fleshly lusts" and for the men who took them up on it. But a nuanced understanding of cultural location can help fill in our imaginations. Poverty is a difficult lot, in death as in life. Funeral rites are a communal way to say goodbye to a departed one, but a churchyard is for the burial of the bodies of respectable parishioners. Indeed, if women who "lived by their bodies" were not allowed to be taken for—or even to be in consort with—householder women in life, how could they be buried for eternity alongside them in death?

An early historical account of the stews, written not long after they were closed down, was produced by the Tudor chronicler, John Stow, who in his 1598 *Survey of London* offers a potted history of Bankside and the customary we have just reviewed. Stow tells us that: "I have heard ancient Men of good Credit report, that these single Women were forbidden the Rights of the Church, so long as they continued that sinful Life, and were excluded from Christian Burial, if they were not reconciled before their Death. And therefore there was a Plot of Ground, called the Singlewoman's Church yard, appointed for them, far from the Parish Church" (Strype 1720:II.iv.7). Denying Christian funeral rites—which is implied by a separate graveyard setting—may have been a policy for the early medieval church. Someone with means and the status which may or may not come hand in hand with wealth would be buried with a rite and a gravestone, while someone low on—or outside—those social hierarchies would be buried communally. It is a simple way to display where someone ranks; it does not have to be cognized as such, but it is apparent enough in the symbolic placement of the body of the dead and the absence of a tombstone.

So, when the Jubilee Line, poised to extend its remit in Southwark, hit upon an unmarked bone, it was in some sense only logical to assume that the land was part of John Stow's "Plot of Ground." It is clear that what was found by the Museum of London's Archaeology Service in the graveyard at Southwark in 1992 could only have come from a large, public burial ground that had fallen out of use: 148 skeletons were exhumed from the Jubilee Line site, mostly paupers (Brickley and Miles 1999). It would seem we have come upon our graveyard for the poor. This information is tantalizingly close to the material evidence we have been looking for: a burial location where we can honor our dead, and a place where the medieval whores of lore—and historical account—can find their final resting place with respect, at last.

It is thus understandable that our ritualists equate this excavation site with the single women's graveyard so carefully noted in John Stow's late sixteenth-century work: it all seems to tally. Close to (in contemporary terms, anyway) but not on the grounds of what became the Southwark Cathedral, here is a gravesite that has no markings—had not even been noticed in recent times—and, upon discovery, is revealed to be full of skeletons from very impoverished backgrounds. A preponderance of the adult skeletons is female. The Museum of London tells us that only 1 percent of the site has been excavated, and that the number of skeletons is greater and the burials go much deeper than have so far been dug up. And if there are more skeletons to be found, who is to say that they do not reach back to the fifteenth century, or earlier? This possibility could be construed to suggest we have found Stow's single women's churchyard with the corroboration we think we need. Even the Museum of London leaves open that hope in its online materials, stating that the "Cross Bones burial ground served the poor of the parish of St. Saviour's, Southwark, but the ground is thought to have originally been established at least as early as the 17th century, as a single women's (prostitutes') cemetery."[15] These bones testify to the material history of this site.

There are a few problems, however. First, the bones themselves date from the first half of the nineteenth century, not the medieval period. That might be countered by saying (as the Museum of London does) that were this site to be excavated further, additional—older—remains might yet be found. But that means that we have not yet found any material evidence for a burial location or the absence of funerary rites for the women of the stews. Second, and more complicated to contend with, cartographical data tells us that there was no burial ground at this site until the mid-eighteenth century: none of the published secondary literature—apart from Stow's mysterious reference, which is based on hearsay—indicates a medieval burial plot at this location. From comparing two early eighteenth-century maps, we must conclude that this graveyard was established not in medieval times but between 1720, when there is no burial ground marked on John Strype's map, and 1747, when there is one on John Rocque's.[16] Crossbones is not a medieval graveyard, but an early modern one; it is the St. Saviour's burying ground, but it is not Stow's "Plot of Ground," which remains unidentified. This is not that place.

These bones might not have been found if it had not been for building a bigger and better contemporary London in the modern world, enabling the rejuvenation (thought by some to be gentrification) of South London and Bankside. So the Jubilee Line's extension that hit the bones uncovered a story that was ready for telling. And the story we are told rallies us, gives us a location around which to gather, literally and metaphorically, ready to mobilize on behalf of sex workers around the world, in the past and in the present. It is not a fifteenth-century graveyard, but we are in mythic time and ritual space: does it matter?

And so it is that at 7:00 PM on the dot, the bards of Southwark and a few of their friends—Nigel of Bermondsey and Niall of Hammersmith—gather in whatever configuration they may at the Urban Physic Garden, an ephemeral park lasting one summer in 2011, on Union Street, where the plants are categorized by their therapeutic effects. In the treatment room, you can have some St. John's wort; in the gastroenterology department, some peppermint. In the operating theater (a wooden stage with makeshift bleachers and cast-off logs for extra seats), the bards performed on July 23, the festival of Isis. Isis and

Osiris are the subjects of one tale, as is the demon who haunted these parts: come one, come all. Any poets who wrote something today and would like to perform?

What, concretely, would John like to effect? A memorial garden. In tandem with the community garden as the index of the healthy urbanization movement of his age, why not preserve Crossbones from the ravages of late capital in defense of a little green space? How about a public memorial for a long-standing history, a public statement against unchecked corporate capitalist expansion, and a public garden to commemorate those who were willing to be public about their multiple involvements with the most private parts of people's lives? This is the real story of Crossbones. Whether medieval prostitutes were buried here is, in some sense, immaterial to the tale. We know that they lived "by their bodies" and that they worked in Bankside within an elaborate construction of bodily and material regulation designed to facilitate their trade. There is no doubt that many or most of them died poor, and were probably buried in unmarked graves. When all is said and done, whether it was *this* grave in which their bodies lie is less materially important than the history this site now tells, and the memory that our mobilization brings to life.

Memorial Gates

3 ❁ Shamanism and the Ritual Oscillation of Time

> Next, on this Bank, was sometime the Bordello, or Stews, a Place so called of certain Stew-houses privileged there, for the repair of Incontinent Men to the like Women; of the which Privilege I have read thus.
>
> John Stow, *A Survey of London* (1603 [1598])

What shamans do, the world over, is heal people. They are the conduits to other worlds where cures are available, when the ills that might plague an individual do not lie in this one. Like anyone else on the borders of society, a shaman occupies an ambivalent role: he is powerful and dangerous, necessary but marginal. He may know the ways of nature—and probably does, better than most, because he is closer to it—but as a result he may be seen as farther away, in symbolic terms, from being human. Sherry Ortner's (1974) famous parallel between women and nature is about polarity: distance from culture, or any given culture's understanding of civilized humanity, places someone lower on the totem pole. This duality is often but not necessarily gendered.

In keeping with these structures, shamans are usually men: it is often seen as too powerful a role to relegate to a woman. But it does mean putting a man on the margins, which may complicate the continuity of the institution: a shaman must be strong enough to inhabit his double role. That strength will likely be conveyed with a certain charisma, or aura, or perceived or acclaimed power—power that will translate into the capacity to perform rituals. As suspect a figure as he may be, a shaman is entrusted with the ability to be efficacious. He may need to change form, for example, so as to take on an animal persona if the needed cure lies in the realm of the animals or in the domain of a particular animal (whether it be a particular species or an individual creature). Shape-shifting is no small task, and the ability to do it and to do it well is worthy of the respect that is accorded the shaman.

This particular shaman, John Crow to you, is interested in social healing. He exposes an old, deep wound in the community around him. No one has ever really bothered about this six-hundred-year-old story before. Nor was anyone duped: it made sense that harlots were on the bottom of the social order—and the combined motivations of promoting ethical conduct; the possibility of redemption; mercy; pity; and financial reward meant that the church treated them as well as anyone ever has, if not better. But social mobilization needs to rely on contemporary symbols and activating agents, and in the early twenty-first century (if not perennially), sex work is something that catches people's interest. Winchester Geese are a good way to tell that story, or to ask us to consider an issue au courant. If anyone, anywhere—past, present, or future—may be healed as a result of John Crow's shamanic journey to visit with the whores of old or his contemporary performances describing or reenacting those mystical visions, more power to him. More power to the patient, that is, and also to the shaman.

If shamans can shift shapes to do their healing work, they can also shift time. For a qualified shaman, there is no problem posed by living in multiple dimensions simultaneously: the nature of existence is change, so it is possible and even desirable to be able to function in many temporal frames at once. Shamans make it their business to mediate time, and temporal manipulation is the method by which they set things right. They can reach into other dimensions and sort out troubles that began generations ago, healing a person's ills or a community's fractures, unconstrained by the worldly space-time that limits the rest of us. They do so in our present, adjusting historical wrongs of the past so that we may redirect our movement into the future with less trace of the wound.

John Crow too shifts our sensation of temporality, at least rhetorically: he asks us to consider the goings-on at this very place—the place from which he speaks and we listen—hundreds of years earlier. The intention of this ritual is to demonstrate how some of the same human patterns, emotions, and experiences that we live in the early twenty-first century were happening in the sixteenth century, too, in the same spot and for some of the same old reasons: exclusion, or loneliness, or the general human business of looking for love. By holding the place fixed, he asks us all to travel in time, and look for the universals, not the specifics—neither the particular culture (although he draws from many of them in his incantations and is himself a product of one or more), nor the particular moment in historical time. It is the human condition we seek. Luckily, we have plenty of material with which to find it, right in Southwark's own backyard.

John Crow

Shamans may or may not feature prominently in the indigenous English religious landscape, but in a globalized era, ritualists come in all guises, in every part of the world. Born John Hamilton Constable in 1952 in Oswestry, England, our native shaman is an Englishman. He is also a man of his time, namely part of an early generation of Western Europeans who came of age in an era of radicalism. A scholarship-trained graduate in English literature from Cambridge, John came of age in the '60s, at the moment when Europe and the United States were exploding with activism, exploration, and mind expansion, and London was at the heart of it. He was—and remains—part of a local (and, to some degree, transnational) artistic scene that dabbled widely in psychedelics, Eastern mysticism, and deep psychological exploration.

As made iconic by Jack Kerouac with the publication of *On the Road* in 1957, the Beat generation started traveling to North Africa, South America, and the so-called Far East in the 1960s and '70s, following the 1960s civil rights movement in the United States, the summer of love in 1967, the social uprisings in France and Italy in 1968, and the Beatles-inspired free love and antiwar movements on both sides of the Atlantic in 1969. Coinciding with the surge of 1970s feminism, this was a time of radical departure from the wholesome postwar Euro-American conservatism of the 1950s during which John was reared. He identifies one reason for being "out there" (and indeed he was not alone—it was a sizeable enough cohort that we identify it as a historically significant social movement on its own terms) as a reaction to "the figures of my youth [who] used to sell cars and personal hygiene." This characterization is not a compliment.

A scholarship to public school (meaning, in the English context, private school, now known as independent school, as in not state-funded) was the only way John could have been prepared to study at Cambridge in those days, before equal opportunity was a priority in the British education system. Even from humble beginnings, he must have dazzled Cambridge admissions tutors with his brazen, youthful eloquence. In the roaring '60s and radical '70s, he might not have been easy to manage, however: he thought he was being chased by poltergeists as a child (and perhaps he had a higher propensity for the supernatural even then). Unsurprisingly, obedience or deferral to authority was an issue throughout his education: he clearly had talents but very little interest in cultivating them in the ways disciplinarians told him to. His natural intelligence may have been exceeded only by his inclination to buck the system and to act out against authoritarian structures in sometimes unruly ways. Still, the institution had faith in him, even as he resisted, and made him sit the Cambridge entrance exam, for which John wrote a defiant essay about how the Beat writer Allen Ginsberg was the greatest living poet. He got in.

Getting in was one thing, but getting through Cambridge was touch and go. Matriculated at Queens College, he did make it to Finals (the final examinations all Oxbridge undergraduates must take to receive their degrees), but he attained insanely erratic results. He flunked an essay arguing that David Bowie was the greatest living songwriter-poet ("if I had been writing about [Bob] Dylan, I would have gotten away with it," he muses forty years after the fact), but he got a double-starred First for his submission on William Blake, whom he described as being able to capture and epitomize the "visionary language" of the Bible. In the end he got a Third Class degree, described by a friend of John's as "the next best thing to getting a First: it was a badge of honor, really, because it meant you'd done no work but could still write your name." He refused to return to Cambridge from Italy to pull the mark up to a IIii (which was the college's request; "for shame!"), moved back to London in 1973 "to be an actor, or writer, or rock star," and finally hit the road properly in 1977 to see the world for himself.

Europeans and Americans who did hit the road to discover so-called Oriental cultures encountered Asian paradigms in their own context, and many found their lives permanently influenced by their wanderings. In John's case, Japan was the first stop (Zen remains a touchstone), followed by Indonesia and India; John recounts spending a couple of days with naked ascetics in the Himalayas smoking hash and doing yoga. He was not alone in his interest in exploring new worlds; whether psychedelics themselves or foreign travel (often supplemented by a generous dose of whatever mind-altering substance was locally available) had a greater impact on this generation—transnationally—is up for debate.

Even in the West, these years signified an era of mind expansion. As a young man coming of age, John was interested in psychedelia at the moment it was at its peak on both sides of the Atlantic, with the public experiments of R. D. Laing in Scotland and Timothy Leary at Harvard. You didn't have to travel to India: toying with altered consciousness was part of public culture (or, rather, counterculture) in the United States and in Great Britain. Those like John who felt that they had never fit in found to their delight that there was a larger society of people like them, willing to explore the nature of mind and the universe through alternative states as well as psychological inquiry. These explorations of the mind—understood through both the individual psyche and the common or collective unconscious, in a Jungian paradigm, a Blavatskian one, a Gurdjieffian one, or any comparable or parallel expression of mysticism in an ancient or a modern form—were the raison d'être of his cohort, and art was very often its medium. John's art is one of language, and his obsession is the beauty and capacity of the English tongue.

For twenty-five years John has lived on a small church square in the Borough of Southwark, ten minutes on foot from Shakespeare's Globe in one direction and from Crossbones Graveyard in the other. He has made his livelihood and his way in the world as a local poet, performer, artist, and activist since he was a teenager, and sees no reason to stop now; it is his life quest. His flat has Tibetan carpets, incense, many icons of Kuan Yin (the Chinese and Japanese goddess of compassion, whom John identifies as "his goddess"), and collaged mementoes from the heart of the pumping London art world of which John has been a member for forty years.

John identifies as neither a Christian nor a non-Christian; he is a product of (and views himself as contributing to) neither a religious culture or upbringing, nor a secular one. These are not the terms through which he operates or expresses his shamanic work or vision. Nor does he eschew these paradigms, however: "It would be wrong to say that Christianity has been a constant in my life . . . but the Bible was read a lot" in the home where he grew up, on the Welsh border. A Christian background did not foreclose radical experiments with the human mind and mythic consciousness, but for these to be given proper—or somehow universal—expression, John felt he must search elsewhere, both to locate what must necessarily be a universalist worldview and, now, in the context of the ritual, to ensure their representation in as accurate and inclusive a way as possible.

So references to Hinduism and Buddhism—and even more so, references to indigenous or ancient religions—sprinkle John's theology, but he has not entirely replaced Christianity as a worldview. He has rather accommodated religious difference by bringing varied canons into conversation with each other, in a radical, personal poetic act of determinedly nonhierarchical ecumenicism. One could say that he follows the consumerist model of an eclectic pick-and-choose late capitalism, or a hippie everything-goes, catch-as-catch-can, multilayered, peace pipe—some might say piecemeal—inclusivism, but John views it rather as holistic. These are all viable models for religions of the New Age: take the best of each and live by the amalgam. It is the era of the melting pot, after all.

John Crow the shaman refuses to be categorized as belonging to any one religion or movement, or to none. He emerged from John Constable's consciousness to tell a story and to do its bidding, namely the healing work of a particular society and its contemporary denizens. The point of the ritual is not, as John (Constable and Crow) insists frequently, that it is religious or part of a religion. "We're not a religious cult, although it might look that way. We're not a united, single belief system," John explains. What he has effected is a ritual, without the grounding of a singular religion, designed to show ourselves and our histories to ourselves and our futures. Religion and its categories are beside the point.

Shamans as Healers

For a group of people who are known as healers, shamans are feared or disparaged by surprisingly many. They are no straightforward lot. To take the most oppositional case, sometimes shamans are seen to perform ill, as with the Putumayo in Colombia in Michael Taussig's (1987) complex rendering. As in many places (including in our Southwark context, although arguably with a lighter spirit), shamanic work is to commune with the dead, which is not usually a safe or wholesome task. Further, for the Putumayo and for others too, "some dead seem more dangerous than others"; in the Colombian case, "the evil wind... may kill" (Taussig 1987:371), one crime, at least, of which sex workers are not usually accused.

Still, these two graveyards both reflect a social hierarchy, which is not unusual; parallels between John's performances and the shamanic rituals in Colombia as described by Taussig are apparent: "Here the whites are the superior caste: they bury their dead in the part of the cemetery nearer the church and memorialize them in brick and mortar, while the Indians make do with that section of the cemetery farthest from the church, marking their graves with small wooden crosses that time soon turns to dust" (1987:370). Perhaps the women and children buried in Bankside had wooden crosses laid at their graves, too, or stones, pebbles, or flowers. One can only imagine. But even if the categories of medieval English society were other than white and Indian—they might rather have been cast as parishoners and pariahs, their women as wives and prostitutes—we can take these signifiers as indicative of structural relations in a hierarchical society.

The comparative spatial and material dimensions of community graveyards can tell us a great deal about hierarchical relations in the past, but even more germane to the tale being told here is how invoking the dead can mobilize consciousness and change in the present. Far from pointing out any differences in culture or geography, there appears to be much in common in the intended means of efficacy of these two shamanic rituals: the mode of organizing for social change among the Putumayo in Colombia presents in a similar form to that found among the former hippies of South London. That is, ritually memorializing the outcast dead by drawing from the apparent spatial dynamics of graveyards also acts as a call for new social relations among both the Colombian Putumayo in the 1980s and Southwark Londoners in the early 2000s. When Taussig—working in another part of the world that operates within an entirely different set of cultural symbols—wishes "to consider the slumbering power of the imagery of the dead in their redemptive relation to the living in shamanic ritual" (1987:370), he could just as well be describing Southwark.

Not all features of shamanic ritual will traverse cultural location. Shamanism is viewed as a potentially dangerous form of "sorcery" in the Putumayo context—especially if one is part of the social order that is being questioned—but shamans are generally viewed as competent healers, able to move through time, form, and state of consciousness in order to get the job done, restoring order and balance where it is needed. Eliade locates the seemingly universal source of shamanic power as an ability to cure oneself, an act that reveals the shaman as able to effect a necessary shift. It is this demonstrated ability to heal that confers his status: "the shaman is not only a sick man; he is, above all, a sick man who has been cured, who has succeeded in curing himself" (Eliade 1970 [1951]:27). Across the world and throughout history, shamans appear to be a kind of social worker who can draw on both natural-born and cultivated powers (they will need training and will likely be part of a lineage) to enable, heal, or redirect.

Paradoxically, then, shamans are healers although they themselves may be thought to be sick. Eliade explains: "For if they have cured themselves and are able to cure others, it is, among other things, because they know the mechanism, or rather the *theory* of illness" (1970 [1951]:31). In these cases, the implication is that they are healthy despite the outer signs: they understand the causes of illness, and sometimes display them, but in so doing they are able to heal unusual symptoms.

This inherent ambivalence is the source of a shaman's strength in society, and arguably his power. Alfred Métraux, writing on the *piai* (shamans) of the Amazon, explains: "The intensity of religious experience, which is the very condition for shamanic practices, gives the *piai* a position that is both privileged and marginal within their group" (in Narby and Huxley 2001:98). Indeed, many scholars have noted just how far out on the margins shamans from all over the world seem to be. They are considered "mentally deranged" (George Devereux in Narby and Huxley 2001:119), "on the verge of insanity" (Czaplicka 1914:172), "impostors," and "ministers of the devil" (Denis Diderot and André Thévet, respectively, in Narby and Huxley 2001:32, 13). Like ascetics, they can be considered—and can actually be—mentally ill, and yet they are turned to for any number of social and physical problems. From a universal point of view, Eliade describes shamans as "those who experience the sacred with greater intensity than the rest of the community—those who, as it were, incarnate the sacred, because they live it abundantly" (1970 [1951]:32). We may want to quibble with Eliade's definition of the sacred, but that a shaman is in some measure too exuberant for—or does not easily fit into—everyday life or quotidian time, refusing to cede to convention, should be apparent.

Or, as Graham Townsley puts it in the case of the Yaminahua in Peru, "shamans understand things in a way that other people just do not. They understand them better and more profoundly" (1993:449). While a mind-altering substance for many may be a means to the end, Townsley "was told on a number of occasions that the *koshuiti* [capacity to heal through blowing] of a really good shaman would be effective even without the drug." He argues that shamanic knowledge is not about a preexisting repertory of meaning but rather "an ensemble of techniques for knowing" (1993:453). Shamans heal through practice, in other words, such that what they do—sing, speak, perform rituals—is the source of their knowledge. The ritual event does not have to be semantically cognized, either by shamans or by their patients, to be effective: indeed, it is precisely the action that counts.

It could be argued that John Crow's (and his cohort's) propensity for psychedelia and the mind-altering drugs that were popular in the Beat era is cognate with—or gives itself over to—a kind of shamanic persona, or at least a mind-expanded one that relies on some of the same means, or the same ambivalent relationship to conventional reality, as shamans do. Of course, not all acid droppers or peyote eaters are shamans (although it is likely that a great many shamans are ayahuasca takers or chang drinkers). What the use of mind-altering substances implies is that the kinds of knowledge accessed and delivered by shamans are not available in (or easily translated into) everyday frames of consciousness.

A practitioner who sings and speaks in ways that are designed to direct or redirect the attention of spirits—"the living and the dead," in John's words—will by definition be someone who does not speak or act in conventional modes. He needs to be able to catch and "twist"[1] someone's—a spirit's—attention, which is no mean feat, and all the more so if the spirit he needs to attract is resistant or initially uncooperative: not all spirits are easy to communicate with, especially if they were ill-treated in life. It follows that those who are asked to heal are often the most marginal of the group, able to use their powers on the edge of society in order to help it find its balance. Through being the recognized outsider, a shamanic healer (or the spirit he communes with and may effectively channel) can facilitate belonging among diffuse members of a group, who now have a visible symbol (either the shaman's behavior or, in our case, the spirits who represent the other, even if they also represent the self) by which to locate the opposing poles of social normativity and extra-temporal dimensionality. If a shaman is really effective, he may even enable a sense of belonging across those two spheres of social experience—the conventional and the outrageous—but that is a challenge even for the best of them.

Time and Narrative

Often it is through song that a shaman's power is wielded, meaning that both sound and language do the work of traversing time; spoken narrative or oration may also serve this role. As we have seen, it is not unusual for the shaman to do the work of speaking to the dead; this performative ability indicates that he is capable of traversing time—which is both his chosen vocation and the vocation for which he is chosen. (The cause and the effect are tautological here; the shaman demonstrates that he is capable by invoking the dead even as he does the work that is needed.) Time travel is thus both a demonstration (a performance) and a means to an end. The shaman's narrative (itself a diachronic act), although offered in the present, communicates across time and effects a ritual impact by reminding us that we are not limited to what we see or experience in what we think of as our time: as ritual participants, we too are capable of transcending time, or at least connecting to those in other times. Springing from the present, ritual time expands outward—forward into the future, while hearkening back to the past. Herein lies the possibility for change.

In Ricoeur's famous rendering of narrative as the mechanism through which time (and thus self) is constructed, he argues that "mimesis . . . draws its intelligibility from its faculty of mediation, which is to conduct us from one side of the text to the other" (1984 [1983]:53). Narrative constructs linearity in time or, in another rendering, time impels the production of narrative, or of moving through the text. Similarly, the shaman's performance or mediation draws his listeners from one temporal realm to another, asking us to oscillate between the present and other times in our recollections or anticipations—the future and the past are mental states (as well as temporal realities) that mediate and are themselves mediated through our experiences. A text might also be transcended, of course: mimetic narrative appears to play the same role as liminality does in the study of ritual or, better, mimesis *is*, for Ricoeur, ritual, that activity which can transform one point in (social) time to another, having reproduced—and recalibrated—as necessary. It is the capacity of ritual to encompass all these acts at once, via practical action rather than via textual discourse, in one multivocal gesture of accomplishment.

Ironically, it is John's narrative linking human beings in the present with human beings in the past that precisely takes us (and them) out of time: the historical link serves as the ground of a ritual that facilitates the connection between times. Our ritual appears to mediate history, in fact, and even time itself, such that the structures of human societies are laid out as bare as the bones of the dead. There is nothing to hide—and indeed the church never tried to conceal the ambivalent position in which it held the prostitutes who provided the outlet for social stability. At first glance, ritual's capacity to mediate though time—or across time—gives it its power. But even more significantly, this ritual explicitly mediates between social groups, striking a chord or a nerve as it exposes the ambivalent relations between elite members of the laity and those whose bodily actions seemingly sustain the social order. The present and the past are as uncomfortably linked as the upright insider and the trod-upon outsider.

Might ritual mediation thus be understood as a kind of healing, or at least a reconciliation of these polarized realities of past and present, high and low? Certainly the ritual narrative impels that meaning. But we have here a paradox in that, through narration, both an act in time and a story about the past that it brings to life in the present, John removes history as the most salient factor of the human condition—as, indeed, he attempts to remove hierarchy. Ironically, all societies in past and present produce—and even depend on—hierarchy. One can remove history but not remove elitism. Even though the terms change—who is up, who is down; whether those who are downtrodden are given protection, or respect, or not; whether it is possible to be redeemed, or incorporated back into the mainstream with no trace of stigma, or not—hierarchy as a feature of human societies cannot be easily transcended. And yet, by incorporating the past (and the future) into the present, we are analogously—illogically but powerfully—able to incorporate our outcasts into the whole of society. We must negotiate all the elements of this matrix, and by doing so, we may be able to adjust the terms of difference, just a little.

Healing and the Social Psyche

These oscillations—between times and between people—in many ways reflect classical modes of understanding social relations. By any reckoning, the psyche is a dialogical mechanism: if the relationship between self and other is an unfolding interaction that occurs through time, social change—or, in this instance, social healing—may be precisely understood as a historical process. Take, for example, the work of Claude Lévi-Strauss (1963), where the shaman is explicitly the psychoanalyst, or the healer of psychic or emotional wounds, in "primitive" Bororo societies. Here, for John Crow, the same holds true in twenty-first-century South London.

John knows that there is a psychoanalytic interpretation of what he experienced as a mystical vision: "a Freudian would say the Goose is my unconscious." He has projected her outward, a symbolic representation of the workings of his mind; in his narrative, the Goose arrives to tell her story, but it is upon John's consciousness that the tale is imprinted, and from there re-told in ritual. If he tells the story of the Goose so that we may hear his narrative, we congregate so that he may do the work we cannot do ourselves: look squarely in the face of those dynamics that are all too easy to forget, repress, or sublimate. Inequity will always mean poverty; human passions will always mean money for a woman who has nothing left to lose but her reputation. We do not have to look far to confront hypocrisy, even within ourselves. By giving this truth a space, a time, and a story through which to unfold, John reminds us of life's harshness, even in—and sometimes especially in—death. His shamanic performance renders to us the human condition in digestible form: it is too painful otherwise, too close to the bone.

Lévi-Strauss pairs the shaman and the psychoanalyst through the shared metaphor—an aural one, in both cases—of oscillation. In describing the song for difficult childbirth in a Cuna Indian society in mid-1940s Panama, he tells us that he will recount the shamanic cure in a kind of mythical rendering that might approximate the local experience of healing: "The next ten pages offer, in breathless rhythm, a more and more rapid oscillation between mythical and physiological themes, as if to abolish in the mind of the sick woman the distinction which separates them, and to make it impossible to differentiate their respective attributes" (1963:193). Lévi-Strauss argues that shamanic "manipulation" (1963:192) is at the heart of the cure; thus he makes equivalent the role of the shaman in the so-called primitive, collective world and that of the psychoanalyst in the modern, individualistic one.

The techniques of a shaman are surprisingly close to that of a psychiatrist, and Lévi-Strauss is clear about the comparison:

> The cure would consist, therefore, in making explicit a situation originally existing on the emotional level and in rendering acceptable to the mind pains which the body refuses to tolerate. . . . The shaman plays the same dual role as the psychoanalyst. A prerequisite role—that of listener for the psychoanalyst and of orator for the shaman—establishes a direct relationship with the patient's conscious and an indirect relationship with his unconscious. (1963:197–199)

In this construction is also a reassertion of the equivalence between the "mythical" and the "physiological": by placing the Amazonian shaman, or *nele*, in structural parallel with the Western psychoanalyst,

Lévi-Strauss reminds us that suffering can be experienced bodily or mentally, at the individual or collective levels, in somatic experience or in time. All these forms and frames must be considered in tandem and as contributing to each other in experience, and in analysis.

If humans—and even apes—have a natural inclination to imitate each other, what are we imitating? A heartbeat, perhaps, but also an oscillation between two points or poles, in blood or in breath, that keep a sense of self alive. We copy activities in time—a facial expression, a gesture—as diachronic movement, but we also copy a sense of rhythm, and thus enable synchrony with others (Dunbar 2012). Oscillation—babies miming their parents, or lovers mirroring each other; narrative play between then and now, past and present—may be a natural way of doing and feeling things. Barbara Myerhoff, experimenting with shamanic journeys during her fieldwork, calmly describes how her "body assumed the rhythm of the passing trucks" (1974:41). The sine curves of time, pulse, and rhythm are the templates through which we commune with each other.

If the psychoanalyst heals the patient, the shaman heals society. Healing may—nay, must—happen at both individual and collective levels; this double effect or double target is part of the shaman's investigative work. By healing the individual, the collective is soothed; by healing the collective wounds of memory, individuals in the present may suffer less. At Crossbones, frayed white ribbons bearing the names of individual sex workers are strewn over the gates so that we do not forget: at the ritual we may think, appropriately, at the level of institutions and their outcasts, but we must also remember that they were individual bodies—people, women—who bore the brunt of those social burdens. Either way—whether the patient is an individual person's body or a collective's social body—the mechanism of cure is the release of emotion, such that the patient (individual or collective) can move through the presentation of the same circumstances, or social symptoms, on future occasions without reverting to a patterned response that is frozen in time from previous or earlier trauma.

If a social world can be thought to be ill and in need of healing, the work of a shaman might be needed to cure it. Here we have the heart of our ritual. In contemporary Southwark, the figure of the sex worker is "a fusion of symptom and symbol," as Obeyesekere (1981:34) puts it:

the social body needs its psychoanalyst, too, if it is to assess its own role in the fractures that have been exposed, and be able to redirect its responses. Paraphrasing Murray Edelman, Catherine Bell sees "ritualization . . . [as] a process to which a conflicted relationship is subjected in order to facilitate both the escalation and resolution of a struggle that otherwise would destroy the relationship" (1992:88–89). In this particular instance, John Crow's ritual is simply to reveal a "conflicted relationship," and to show its intractability through time, thus offering, perhaps sustainably, a step toward resolution. The shaman's work is to be the mediator of time, but he is also the agent of change.

Whether illness or wellness can be transmuted from self to collective is an open and indeterminable question, but if anyone can do it, shamans can. The woes John Crow aims to heal are social ones: individual distresses, in his narrative, reflect structural exclusions, and the individual is soothed here, as by so many shamans throughout history and across the world, by virtue of righting—or at least recognizing, through telling—wrongs that may not have had any direct bearing on the patient who displays the symptoms. Here in Bankside we are reminded that social—and indeed sexual—exchanges will always be bodily ones, and that to be present, now, at this place in time, is a mode of human interaction that must not be forgotten, even as the global glorification of capital goes on around us.

Through shamanic mediation, then, we are consciously directed to where the wrongs took place in the past: there was no glamour to bodily exchange, and we know that the women who did it were maligned then as now, if in different discourses. But we hear this tale as we stand together on a street, gently resisting the ways the world has alienated us further. In recognizing historical injustices, we tacitly trace them into the present, to a world where bodies seem to have no clout at all. And yet, of course, they do. We are here. We are released, if only momentarily, from the structures that constrict us, and thus come to know—bodily, experientially—a new kind of relation with our social world.

The Response

And thus do those who have themselves practiced sex work come to John's ritual for their own healing. On April 23, 2015, when John asked the collected assembly whether anyone had any thoughts he or she wished to speak about to the group, a young woman who had not previously attended stepped forward. She wanted to explain the pain of the profession, but with no bitterness or regret about her own practice of it. Instead, she argued, it was the public perception of what it was to be a prostitute that caused difficulty in sex workers' lives: "It's not our work that is damaging. It's the stigma that is damaging," she asserted. In this eloquent construction, the denigration of sex work is itself the source of the public health and social harm that prostitution may bring about; the ritual that she was now part of could be instrumental in ameliorating some of that damage. Her testimonial was one way of participating in the ritual effort to reclaim the image of sex work, and in so doing contribute to the work of healing.

Other women and men who currently or previously practiced sex work participated in other ways. After the completion of the ritual one evening, before she went to meet her friends from the gathering, one woman spent a long time praying at the gates and lighting small votive candles, in a personal world of what appeared to be a somewhat pained moment of private reflection. She was not engaging in conversation, but her actions and attitude gave an impression that the work she did brought with it a fair amount of suffering. This occasion, where sex workers were honored, rather than harassed or maligned, offered a rare opportunity to consider the exigencies of prostitution without shame, and thus to grieve what may have felt like the impossibility of belonging or integration—the loss of what might have been—outside of this ritual location. Such a ritual of mourning can be a catharsis, and can, hopefully, refresh a broken spirit with a renewed sense of support.

Many have practiced or experienced sex work at some point in their lives, even if it is not an enduring profession for them. At a picnic following the July 23, 2014, ritual (the day after John's birthday and so an occasion for a party after the regular gathering), one woman explained that she enjoyed participating in these events because she knew what it was like: "I did the trade for a while, you know." She had done it for the money, because at the time she had been addicted to hard drugs; she was glad the episode was over—it had been a bad one—but it had left her with a lifelong empathy for the down-and-outers who found themselves in desperate straits, financially and emotionally. She could relate to the story being told, and wanted to be part of a gathering that would tell it.

Not all the participants of this group have experience with sex work, however, and not all expressions of loss are about social marginality. Every month, John offers the opportunity to speak about individuals who have died; sometimes names are simply stated, one after another; sometimes full testimonials are offered, as in the case of a man who spoke about losing his adult son, and the way he experienced first parenting and then unexpected grief. In this way, the ritual becomes a true memorial and serves the purpose of healing as at a funeral, when the living reconstitute themselves in the absence of a recently lost, close member of their tribe.

The ritual is also an opportunity for wholesome, hands-on community efforts: stalwart participants bring us all carefully cut ribbons to tie onto the gates every month. John's partner, Katy, has crocheted a number of web-like medallions to decorate the railings, and handmade embroidered or quilted flags and emblems consistently appear as new offerings to the shrine. Some write their own poetry, inspired by the tales heard here, and affix these shreds of paper to the gates; others bake cookies and pass them around. On one occasion, a devoted group of attendees lovingly printed the names of people whose records they had found in local history sources, along with the year in which each had died, on a series of long white ribbons. In this way, John explained, we could commemorate not just the idea of those long dead in this area but actual individuals whose archival traces still existed but who needed some material memory-making. The careful crafting of history takes place here not just through narrative form but through embodied work in the present.

Our emphasis on materiality and natural processes does not end at the gates or with the completion of the ritual. This is a neighborhood event, after all, and similarly inclined, historically spirited naturalists and traditionalists who value organic life are happy to join in when they can. Every autumn, nearby Borough Market is host to a festival called October Plenty, which celebrates the harvest with great fanfare and processions of apples, berries, root vegetables, and their Corn Queene;

musicians and theatrical performers stage renditions of Tudor dramas and folkloric concerts. The neighborhood's very own Green Man—a living impersonation of all things natural (and a figure of pagan nature worship who shows up in British forests and gardens everywhere)—is a Crossbones regular. And where does the October Plenty festival end, after a day of apples and cider? All together, in communal spirit, in honor of and love for nature, everyone goes to Crossbones. If we esteem nature enough—and history enough, in this corner of South London so saturated with stories told and untold—we can move forward into the future not tethered to our desks or the digital construction of our world, but with a rejuvenated, enlivened respect for the health of our bodies and our earth.

Coda: Mimesis and Oscillation

The malady may be experienced in the present, but if the anthropological literature on possession may be taken as an indication of "primitive" beliefs of healing, as Evans-Pritchard (1953) would have it, the cause of an individual's symptoms might be understood as an unheard spirit; in Nordic mythology, a curse. Histories may need to be outed, the strange twists of longitudinal fate exposed. Ancestors may need their wrongs righted, or to settle the scores for a long-ago grievance. Patients are usually individuals, but they are sometimes whole groups, or whole societies, who present physical, mental, or emotional symptoms needing redress. Sometimes, if the symptoms of the present are caused by the troubles of the past, the remedies must take place in another time altogether. Both parties—those wronged in history and those who suffer in the current moment—are grateful for the appearance of a practiced and qualified mediator who can heal things efficiently.

Shamans, in having a larger capacity for time travel and otherworldly experience, are those who can meet, engage with, and imitate those who might require a little intergenerational or intertemporal mediation. The sometimes quirky (if not downright insane) actions we might see in this world become perfectly acceptable if they are understood as the means for communication with another. Shamans must muddy the waters of linear time: they are operating diachronically at one level (in historical time, or in this-worldly temporality), even as they are functioning synchronically (that is to say, in mythical time) at another. Also, any given moment in shamanic ritual time can be taken either as a snapshot or cross-sectional event or, equally, as a response to a particular set of historical and cultural factors and influences. Shamans are already oscillating between (as well as within) multiple kinds of time; it is their vocation. Their oscillations may imitate those in other worlds: they reveal them for us to see, but we do not need in turn to mimic the shaman. We know his actions take him to the brink of madness. He reaches out so that we do not have to follow.

On the other hand, to be nearby is to mimetically fall in step, especially in this flock. Underdogs, unite! Let us oscillate together. We gather on the understanding that times will be crossed, and the trajectory between past and present will be exposed. The point of John's shamanic vision is to propel us through time—diachronically—in order to identify common experience, and also to dissolve time, such that we see that hierarchy is constant, and that matters pertaining to bodies, exchange, finance, and livelihood do not disappear from human society. Curiously, we arrive at the same place through either diachronic or synchronic means: we are here in a time where sex work remains marginal, but also where currently acceptable modes of exchange no longer involve bodies—and indeed may no longer involve money—at all. Finance is virtual. The body is outmoded. Materiality comes best in the form of the Shard, an oil-funded skyscraper that towers over all of us.

The shaman's mechanism is the manipulation of time, in precise defiance of material fixity—but in determined assertion of the meaning in bodily presence. Even though he is the first to transcend temporal limits, he counters the virtual move. We are not alone—look at all the others around you who share at least some ideological space—even in our experiences of solitude. Similarly, that some are placed low on the totem pole is a universal social fact: hierarchy is part and parcel of human collectivity. Alone though we may be—and unique in history as our time may feel—we are neither solitary nor isolated in our subordination. John Crow might be a gentler, London-based Fanon (1968 [1961]) of our time: wretched of the earth, across history, unite! Resist, accept, acknowledge, know.

This shaman's work, then, is not to tend to the individual so as to reach the collective, as so many shamans do in their curative rites, but to reach back to the past so as to help fix the present. (And perhaps, in healing our contemporary collective, as individuals we may become more connected to our bodily beings and to each other.) Bringing two temporal frames into conversation with each other gives a new perspective on each, and on the human condition.

Telling the story in the present of the past allows us to consider the future. We carry the wounds of history, but we are not confined by them. How we mobilize our troops and how we narrate our tales may or may not be historically accurate, but we can evoke the sense that matters now, and that mattered then. In some ways it is irrelevant whose bones are buried here: it is an unmarked graveyard, which tells us that the bones belonged to those who did not have gravestones. We know prostitutes were poor. We know societies have always had to negotiate poverty and livelihood, and the lives and deaths of human beings who themselves had to negotiate bodies, lust, and desire. The tale here is one of human suffering, and the goal here is one of human dignity. We do what we can. We tell their story. And we attempt to understand how the symbols and truths of femininity, sexuality, and embodied being touch all of us as the deep cultural markers of humanity.

In his oscillation between defiant one and man of the community—the accordion actions of social change and social healing—John encompasses both poles of social participation: to be central and lauded for it, and to be peripheral and feel marginalized—if possibly also mobilized—by it. His shamanic ritual is designed to show how we oscillate between these two ostensibly incompatible poles, and to do it with enough eloquence and grace that each side of the continuum notes the hierarchy that he is explicitly exposing. As Bell reminds us, "Ritual mastery is the ability—not equally shared, desired, or recognized—to . . . take and remake schemes from the shared culture that can strategically nuance, privilege, or transform" (1992:116). John Crow is social and antisocial all at once: socially defiant and locally respected, he uses this ambivalence in the spirit and pursuit of revelation.

In its oscillatory capacity, ritual has a time-ceasing or time-transcending quality: this is what van Gennep means when he writes of liminality, what Durkheim means when he writes of collective effervescence, what Leach means when he writes of upside-down social relations. Things stop. Or, better, they get jiggled around through some palpably temporal rupture in an otherwise linear narrative in history—such that a shaman is able to reach back and diagnose the source of contemporary social illness in a story of the past. And so he does.

Queen Elizabeth I ("The Ditchley portrait"), by Marcus Gheeraerts the Younger.
© National Portrait Gallery, London

4 ✿ *The Virgin Queen and the English Nation*

FALSTAFF	Where's Bardolph?
PAGE	He's gone into Smithfield to buy your worship a horse.
FALSTAFF	I bought him in Paul's, and he'll buy me a horse in Smithfield: an I could get me but a wife in the stews, I were manned, horsed, and wived.

William Shakespeare, *Henry IV, Part 2* (1597–1598)

KING HENRY V And you, good yeoman,
Whose limbs were made in England, show us here
The mettle of your pasture; let us swear
That you are worth your breeding; which I doubt not;
For there is none of you so mean and base,
That hath not noble lustre in your eyes.
I see you stand like greyhounds in the slips,
Straining upon the start. The game's afoot:
Follow your spirit, and upon this charge
Cry "God for Harry, England, and Saint George!"

William Shakespeare, *Henry V* (1599)

Redcross Way, the location of our modern ritual, is home to the spirits of a flock of dead prostitutes who are buried in land that lies somewhere between a modern London transport system and an Anglican cathedral. Communing with these spirits and with the London of old—nay, with the Southwark of old—we have a contemporary shaman, who reminds us that we stand before a "singlewomen's graveyard," although in truth it is a much later site than the one he refers to in the account of the Tudor chronicler and lay cartographer John Stow. And attending these memorials of "singlewomen" or Geese (or prostitutes or paupers), we have a committed group of countercultural seekers who make their way every month to the lacy gates that demarcate the reputed burial site, the symbolic heart of medieval Southwark and its complex nexus of poverty, politics, and power.

An important question in the anthropology of any society is how we have arrived at the place to which we have come: what are the cultural flows that have brought us to the contemporary moment? As it happens, the British share this fascination with the historical roots of their nation and their character: they know, as ethnographers do, that action, thought, literature, and history—at the highest social echelons and at the lowest—combine to create something we call culture. The analytic at work here suggests that the particular group—or subculture—on which this book is based wishes to resist the unhindered spread of capital and its attendant threat to embodied social relations on a site known for its historical honesty about carnal desire and sexual practice. But how, we must then ask, did England move from an economy based on human, sensory interactions to one where people and bodies have become almost secondary to market forces? How did England as a nation both create and become defined by this shift in the nature of encounter and exchange?

What follows is an anthropological musing about how a new kind of English (and global) economy emerges over the course of the Reformation—coinciding with the closure of the stews. Brothel economies are at base embodied ones; in calling for a reappropriation of their value, our ritualists defy the comparatively disembodied modes of exchange that have come to define the nation and the world in the modern era. The period of early modernity is one of enormous change, and its traces define much of who we are now: not only do the economies of exchange that begin to emerge in the sixteenth century set us on course for what we know of the modern world up to and including the present, but the way we see ourselves as individuals, as free agents, as choice makers, and as religious or secular beings all arguably date to what happens under the reign of the tumultuous Tudors.

Even as economic modalities become less about bodily exchange, it appears that they remain gendered; the less embodied an economy is, the more the politics of gender seem to rise to the fore. Indeed, the symbolics of gender—and the legitimacy of sexual exchange—change dramatically in England over the course of the sixteenth century, which starts with a king who cuts off his wives' heads when they fail to produce male heirs, and ends with a queen, his daughter, who rules singly and powerfully, and who engenders the beginnings of what will eventually become an empire that rules the globe, to the tune of her national glory. At the other end of the social spectrum, at the beginning of the sixteenth century, prostitution is a normal and public institution; by the end, it is an underground and depraved practice. Paradoxically, under the reign of the misogynistic king, prostitution is legal and monitored, while under the rule of the glorified queen, sexuality—even within marriage, let alone outside of it—is kept under strict control. Female power at the apex of the social order does not translate into sexually liberated moral ideologies. (This is a universal truth: nowhere is it the case that the mere presence of female deities—and Elizabeth was frequently represented as a goddess [Doran 2003]—means that a society displays gender equality.)

The Protestant Reformation in England has been cited as a period when male control of the family is tightened in comparison to gender relations in pre-Reformation Europe (Crawford 1993; see Roper 1989 for the parallel German case). And yet female power is arguably at its zenith in the person of Queen Elizabeth I; her reign is a period when the English nation and the newly consolidated church thrive, as do the arts and a nascent but burgeoning trade empire. She rules partly in the guise of a man, for everyone doubted whether a woman could be a real monarch. By refusing to become a wife, however, in one fell swoop—although it pans out over several decades—she roundly defies popular conceptions of womanhood. As an unmarried monarch—a "singlewoman" in a different social echelon and register—Elizabeth is in an unprecedented position to place a unique set of social and exchange relations into motion between England and her potential trading partners, first on the Continent and then in the world.

The precise beginning of the consciousness of English nationhood or nationality has been a bone of some contention among scholars of Western European history. Nations, it turns out, are neither natural entities nor easily dated as concepts or as rallying cries. While scholars may wrangle over when English nationalism precisely began, it would be foolish for us to imagine that a sense of Englishness would remain unchanged, or that we would be limited to a single formation of something called nationalism over the centuries. What England means—and what nation, gender, and sexuality mean in relation to each other, to whom, and with what implications—will, of course, shift through the ages. We must allow for different symbolic configurations of the English nation over time: such is the meaning of history.

The History of the English Nation

If relations between nations and the national ideologies or consciousnesses they form take different shapes over time, what, we may wonder, returning to our historical narrative, was taking place in the sixteenth century, just after Bankside's brothels were shut, and the Church of England had advanced in its negotiations with other Protestant movements in Europe? Queen Elizabeth I—not the first English queen, but the first of any considerable power and, notably, as a single woman—came to power, in the wake of a decade of national power grabbing inflected against the volatile religious politics of the country and the Continent. So our story of womanhood continues, but from the top down here, rather than from the bottom up, and we return to the perennial questions of gender and sexuality to ask: how did the deployment—or, in this inverse case, the withholding—of female sexuality underscore the construction of the nation under Elizabeth I, the Virgin Queen, a female monarch who, over the course of her forty-five-year reign, proved to be one of the most powerful in Europe?

Until Elizabeth's reign, relations between European nations had been articulated in terms of marital relations between monarchs: the network of constituent nations in the region had been upheld by kinship dynamics whereby the descendant of one royal family would marry and solidify connections with the descendant of another. That marriage can establish or strengthen political relations between different groups is obvious—and it is a practice that is still upheld to this day, the world over. This is classic anthropological theory: kinship establishes relations, and the intentional creation of these networks helps us understand how and why groups or clans or cousins marry in the ways that they do—in the villages of Nepal (Allen 1987); in the Amazon

(Lévi-Strauss 1969 [1949]); or, in Radcliffe-Brown's (1952) review essay, among the southern Slavs, multiple North American Indian tribes (notably the Omaha and the Choctaw), the Masai in East Africa, the Twi of West Africa, groups in Oceania (particularly in Melanesia and New Guinea), and the Nagas of Assam—or, indeed, in the monarchies of medieval Europe. Gayle Rubin (1975) shows specifically how it is the exchange of women that establishes these links. Might kinship theory help us understand how states or nations came to define themselves and each other in early modern Europe?

Marriage becomes particularly important when large territories and fortunes are at stake, and Europe's monarchs were well aware of the political advantage a well-placed marriage could promise. Take, for example, Elizabeth's half sister, Queen Mary I, who, in marrying Prince Philip of Spain (who became King of England when he married Mary in 1554, and then King of Spain when he acceded to the throne in 1556), became equal party to the royal franchise known as "Philip and Mary, by the Grace of God, King and Queen of England, Spain, France, Jerusalem, both the Sicilies and Ireland, Defenders of the Faith, Archdukes of Austria, Dukes of Burgundy, Milan and Brabant, Counts of Habsburg, Flanders and Tirol," as their title told it. Marriage extended the jurisdiction of power and cemented the relations between European states and territories in absolute terms and in the eyes of royal subjects: enormous power was to be gained by marrying the right prince and establishing a fortuitous alliance.

By contrast, Elizabeth's refusal to marry meant that—indeed, required that—a different kind of relation was put into place between England and her Continental neighbors. To begin with, if marriage could bring about power, the promise or potential of marriage could serve as diplomatic leverage, which Elizabeth used on multiple occasions, particularly in the length of time she took to refuse Philip II of Spain (her half sister's widower) or Alençon of France. But further, however, her refusal to marry anyone meant that she ultimately retained the power that marriage might rather ironically disperse: if one gains power through one's royal husband, one's royal husband gains power through one. And while power, like love, may not be a zero-sum game, one's royal husband may also be seen to dilute one's own capacity to rule: certainly Elizabeth appeared to take this stance. Refusing to marry to gain power also meant refusing to marry to cede it—as well as holding out the promise that she might yet do so, and therefore be open to new trading partners, as it were.

In Elizabeth's resistance to marriage and to not only the conventional role of women but also the conventional mode of establishing regional relations, England was no longer married to the Continent but rather consolidated its own power in the institutions of both church and state. To prove the point, Elizabeth was famously known in her own lifetime as saying that she was married to her people and thus to her country: it was said that she held up her coronation ring during her first Parliament as evidence of the marriage that mattered to her. By the end of her life, she was explicit on the subject, when she spoke of "all my husbands, my good people" in 1599 (cited in Haigh 1998 [1988]:24). She was also famously unconcerned with succession (and again emphasized her role as the mother of England). She chose rather to harbor the power of the political body that was England in the undiluted icon of herself—the personification of the monarchy, the church, and the nation all in one. (Consider by contrast just how dispersed power was only a century earlier in medieval Southwark, for example, where the Bishop of Winchester had his own manorial courts and bailiffs, impervious to the king.)

Historians of the Reformation in England disagree about the pace and the direction of the spread of Protestantism during a contentious period (see Haigh 1993, 1995 [1982], for a review of the positions). What is clear is that England as a Protestant nation emerges victorious once and for all under the reign of Elizabeth, even if it was her father, Henry, who established the seeds of the contemporary church in and of England in the first place (tellingly, Elizabeth actively cultivates comparisons between her rule and his; see Haigh 1998 [1988]:24–25). This focused intention to contain and combine the joint power of the nation and the church into a strong, unified England is apparent in all of Elizabeth's policy decisions.

Elizabethan England is the beginning of the nation as we know it today; as such, it is also the beginning of transnationalism as the predominant contemporary form of global commodity capitalism. Transnationalism, after all, requires a nation to transcend in the first place. Even as England's church and nation are strengthened on their own terms, relations with the Continent remain significant, in terms of the expanding Protestant world in France, the Netherlands, and Geneva, and also in terms of the perennial concerns about the price of fine wines and victuals. Elizabeth's antipathy to marriage (even while she toys with the idea and teases possible suitors for much of her reign), and the national and religious consolidation that such a stance enables, bring about a different kind of trade relation. In the end, it is commodities, not women or royal partners, that become the objects of exchange between England and her trading partners on the Continent and, in due course, across the world.

Elizabethan Womanhood

Under Elizabeth, prostitution and marriage were two poles in perennial opposition to each other, and they stood in even more dramatic opposition to herself, a powerful, unmarried regent known for her virginity. In walking this tightrope of gender (along with the "political tightrope" she walked "with great skill" in matters of accession as well as those of church and state, all highly contested during the Reformation [Haigh 1998 (1988):8]), Elizabeth ultimately inverted both modes of female sexuality: she would be neither the mother nor the whore. She was the Virgin Elizabeth, analogous to but different from the Virgin Mary, and she would be available to no one—no buyer and no husband—except, of course, to her subjects, her church, and her nation, for whom she was willing to occupy all the female roles, and all the male ones, too.

To avoid—or, better, to supersede—the confined set of options and the multiple expectations that faced women in sixteenth-century England, not to mention the misogynistic perspective that women should not rule, which she faced for the duration of her long reign, Elizabeth frequently confounded the question of her gender, and not just by remaining single. On multiple occasions, in a host of famous quotes, she referred to herself as a man both to account for and to bolster her strength and her power: in 1581, she proclaimed, "I have the heart of a man, not of a woman, and I am not afraid of anything," and in 1588, in her celebrated speech rallying the troops against the Spanish Armada, she declared, "I have the body of a weak and feeble woman, but I have the heart and stomach of a king, and a king of England too—and think foul scorn that Parma or Spain or any prince of Europe should dare to invade the borders of my realms" (see Haigh 1998 [1988]:24). It is said that, during one of her frequent discussions around the negotiation of marriage, an ambassador quipped, "Your Majesty thinks that if you were married you would be but queen of England, and now you are both king and queen!" (Haigh 1998 [1988]:18). She deliberately cast her gender as complete within itself.

This masculinization, or sometimes a notable absence of gender, or sexlessness (which should remind us of another famous anthropological principle that very high-ranking women are often treated as "honorary men"), also explains how it is that having a powerful queen does not translate into feminine power in popular, everyday settings. Haigh reminds us that one of the ways Elizabeth ensured her popularity despite her female gender was to play along; in public, she "often derided her own sex" (1998 [1988]:23). Rather, she rose above it: the Queen's negative comments about womanhood, along with her deployment of her virginal status and resistance to conventional ideologies of marriage, engender other ways of constructing herself as a monarch and England as a nation. Her fierce, unsexed independence sets into motion historical patterns (arguably still gendered if not directly confronted as such) that produce the English nation as we know it, namely an autonomous state that becomes a powerful trading nation. It is no longer women who are being traded, either in the stews of Bankside (at the lowest levels of society), or as royal wives across the borders to the Continent (at the highest), but commodity exports—goods in a soon-to-be-global market.

Prostitution

Henry's proclamation to close the stews, now finally seemingly enforced, may not in practice have been any more successful than the medieval attempts to banish prostitution in Southwark, but there is no further evidence of regulated prostitution after the middle of the sixteenth century. Needless to say, prostitution does not evaporate: the disappearance of legal or semi-legal prostitutes from the historical record—not the literary one, of course, as English was coming into its own as one of the most elegant tongues in the world, and the legacy of the acceptability of sex work in Southwark was already enduring—does not mean there were no longer practicing prostitutes in Southwark.[1] As our Tudor narrator John Stow tells it, Edward VI (Elizabeth's half brother, who ruled from 1547 until his early death in 1553) receives Hugh Latimer, the Bishop of Worcester (not to be confused with Winchester), to hear that the moral troubles in Bankside persist after his father's decisive attempt to end the sinful acts that had taken place there over such a long period:

> [T]ho' the Sin was no longer allowed in this Place, yet the same Sin still remained. For this Complaint was made before King Edward the Sixth, by a Reverend Father, Latimer, in his blunt, but honest way of preaching: "One thing here I must desire you to reform, my Lords, you have put down the Stue's; but I pray you what is the Matter amended? What availeth that? ye have but changed the Place, and not taken the Whoredom away. I hear say, there is such Whoredom in England as never was seen the like. I hear say, there is now more Whoredom in England than ever there was on that Bank. These be the News I have to tell you: I fear." (Strype 1720:II.iv.7)

But sex workers would now have to practice under entirely different institutional circumstances,[2] never mind symbolic ones. They might have earned their keep in more dangerous conditions, given that their livelihoods were no longer ideologically or administratively protected by the church. A long association of criminality in Southwark would also have attached itself to newly arrived underworlds, as well as established ones, and prostitution's social demotion would have meant that it was no longer widely thought of as an unfortunate reality but instead as a delinquent offense.

In short, a different sexual morality took hold—one that would rather push the practice underground than acknowledge it upfront and find ways to cater to and accommodate the bodily and financial needs of the populations around London. An entirely changed ethos surrounding the exchange of sexual intimacy and such services for money arose as the Reformation grew in strength over the course of the sixteenth century, consonant with the consolidation of both the church and the nation in England. These processes all began under Henry's reign, but took full force under Elizabeth's. Under Elizabeth, prurience would have to be transformed into purity: prostitution is not a light matter in the religious Elizabethan homilies (official sermons) "against whoredom" (see Crawford 1993).[3] They do not, perhaps, contain critiques of sex work so different from those contained in the multiple petitions that tried to close down the stews, but there is no longer room for legal sex work, and the brothels do not open again.

Virginity

Prostitution is a far cry from the cultural values around sexuality that began to be put into place under the reign of Elizabeth, who used her unmarried status to glorify her office (and her nascent national church) with a tacit comparison to the Virgin Mary. It is not too far to see how Elizabeth's antagonism toward marriage (MacCulloch 1990) not only buffered the state, but also produced a strict theological ethos of chastity. As is widely known, under Elizabeth, virginity—or at least chastity—as a moral value increased: she was the Virgin Queen after all, becoming iconic of the state and the purity of Protestantism over the course of her reign. Chastity *is* purity, and indicative of the purity of faith in a faith of purity. Womanhood was not denigrated, exactly, but female sexuality—as a source or as a tool of power, or as something that can or might be used as a livelihood even within marriage, itself anathema to Elizabeth—sat as the polar opposite to the ethos of the nation.

That women have power was apparent in her reign (although at times she underplayed her gender, as we have seen). And that attraction between the sexes is a mainstay of human existence was not denied in Elizabethan culture, if Shakespearean writing can be taken as any indication of the way life was experienced and performed during Elizabeth's reign. But that sexuality was something best kept at bay (as insisted upon in early canonical writings of the church) was exemplified by the Queen, and is amply evident in nascent Protestant doctrine. This confirmation of a basic theological tenet only served to consolidate Elizabeth's power—she lived the symbolically unsexed life, ostensibly, thus avoiding the conundrums much Christian theology had to face about sexuality even in marriage and for procreation (if not conundrums over succession). Her near-divine status in this regard meant that she legitimately ruled over both nation and church, each as an independent entity, and she could, from her stance of purity, determine the economic and symbolic relationships between the two.

As in any era, the representation of women's sexual desires and attendant behaviors is a particularly malleable symbolic nexus. Consider the symbolic valence of virginity, as taken up by Marina Warner, who points out that Elizabeth may not have been a virgin, necessarily: "Elizabeth I was hardly entitled the Virgin Queen because she refused lovers—a succession of favourites characterizes her reign" (1990 [1976]:48). We do not know the precise relations between Elizabeth and her lovers: being unmarried is the virginity that is referenced here or, as Warner interprets, "her virginity principally indicated she could not be subjugated or possessed" (1990 [1976]:48); the implication is that the Queen—as well as both the state and the church—might be sullied if she were subjected to any kind of diluting influence.[4] She would pass down a whole, pure England, not one irremediably mixed up with other nations. The Queen herself would be the best symbolic representation of the nation that was England: undiluted and uncontaminated, but rather complete as a singular entity, its boundaries and borders intact.

Marriage

Chastity is a symbol, as we have seen (even at the popular level, Macfarlane [1987] finds that actual virginity was not necessarily held up as an unassailable virtue): the Queen had many serious flirtations over the course of her reign. She engaged with many men and had many marriage proposals from the nobility of England, Austria, Sweden, and Saxony (Martin Luther's neck of the woods), as well as France and Spain, some of whom she strung along—Haigh calls her a "royal tease rather than a royal tart" (1998 [1988]:17)—but her refusal to marry was in due course shown to be adamant. This resistance was the cause of real concern to her advisers early in her reign—she was supposed to marry: then, and now to an only slightly lesser degree, "that is what women did" (Haigh 1998 [1988]:14). And whatever social pressures to marry popular women might have experienced were not lifted in the case of the Queen, but heightened, for the sake of succession. In 1559, 1563, 1566, and 1576—until Elizabeth was forty-three—Parliament begged the Queen to marry and was prepared to put all kinds of limits on the powers of her husband as monarch (as indeed Philip II was constrained by an Act of Parliament upon his marriage to Mary).

As with religion, Elizabeth kept her own views on the matter of intimate relationships rather close to her heart. What is clear from the outset is that she must have had a rather distasteful view of marriage: one does not have to be psychoanalytically inclined to see that her father's marriages—not just to her mother, Anne Boleyn, whom he subsequently had beheaded, but to his succession of wives—might have left her with a deep distrust of the institution (see Strachey 1928). By 1563, the year she turned thirty, she appears to have been fairly explicit on the subject, explaining in an uncharacteristically straightforward moment, "If I am to disclose to you what I should prefer if I follow the inclination of my nature, it is this: beggar-woman and single, far rather than queen and married"; a year later, in private anyway, she stated that she was "resolved never to marry" (Haigh 1998 [1988]:17–18). (Parliament kept up the pressure for another twelve years nonetheless.)

Haigh also clearly delineates how "marriage to a subject [an Englishman] was too demeaning" when Elizabeth was paving an already difficult path in a domain that questioned the rights of women to rule, while "marriage to a foreign prince [was] too dangerous . . . , bringing fixed foreign entanglements." She knew the hard way that "keeping her own counsel and exercising power alone" (Haigh 1998 [1988]:18) was the safest and yet the most open-ended route to productive domestic and international relations. Not coincidentally, Elizabeth's rule was a time of exceptional economic growth.

Singlewomen

Elizabeth cast herself either as a man or as a woman above the rank and performative (and procreative) duty of ordinary women. For a start, marriage was that which the Queen forewent, and clearly distrusted, for good reason. But in sacrificing a Tudor lineage, Elizabeth created the English state as an avowedly Protestant one, in opposition to—or at least irrespective of—the European monarchies with whom the English kings and Mary I had been allied in marriage for centuries.

This mode of behavior was all very well for a queen, but what about Elizabeth's subjects? What of gender relations in popular terms? If the status of the prostitute was confirmed as depraved in its immoral and robust sexuality, with virginity held up as the opposite symbolic pole, the status of marriage was complicated in Elizabethan England. "Singlewomen," a term that conflates unmarried women with widowed women and with prostitutes (in the narratives of both our ritualists and the Elizabethan historian John Stow [Karras 1999:131]), all of whom there were plenty, comprised a significant demographic, or up to "20 percent of the adult population" or more over the long period of medieval and early modern Europe (see Bennett and Froide 1999:2). The trades of brewing ale and weaving cloth were taken up by singlewomen in medieval England (Bennett 1996), and artistic singlewomen "could take apprentices in their own names" (McIntosh 2005:138), but these opportunities started to wane under the reign of Elizabeth: a peasant or a woman in the urban working class does not afford the same privilege or offer the same advantage as being a single queen. By the end of the sixteenth century, singlewomen were still engaged as domestic servants but were beginning to work in subsidiary (and now coded as more feminine) trades, like lace making: "[w]hatever the work of not-married women in 1600, it was viewed . . . as low-skilled and low-status work, and it yielded . . . poor remuneration" (Bennett 1996:59). The status of women in relation to their husbands—and to their work, with or without husbands—was changing.

Ironically, then, as we have seen, Elizabeth's power as a female ruler does not appear to have translated into a more generalized ethos of women's access or strength: on the contrary, women's behavior seems to have become more restricted. (Elizabeth, as we know, sometimes ruled as a man but "gender resistance," if that is what it was, took place only at the very highest level; it was not a popular movement.) The symbol of female sexuality—seen as voracious and loose in medieval times, something best used to the good of society when it was too capacious or if there was too much of it in a population—becomes tight and rigid, needing controls, in early modern Elizabethan England. Malleable as it is, here as everywhere, women's sexuality appears to represent the integrity of the entire nation, as reflected in the person of the English queen. Making that symbol literal—putting into practice a refusal to marry—and effecting an explicit resistance to that blurred set of interactions or lack of differentiation that marriage or the sharing of women inevitably produces means that the Queen single-handedly enforced the boundaries of Protestant England.

These ambivalences are part and parcel of everyday life, and there is some dispute in the secondary historical literature as to whether the ideological differences about the sexual lives of men and women were prosecuted differently (compare Macfarlane 1986:243 with Crawford 1993:43; see also Collinson 1994). There is much evidence that men and women worked alongside each other, sometimes as husbands and wives together (Bennett 1996; McIntosh 2005), although there is general agreement that women were meant to uphold stricter standards as part of the public face of chastity, and were probably excused less easily, single or not. Whatever contradictions may have held in real-life Tudor England, we may say with certainty that sexual purity was symbolic of containment, at the level of the individual, the family, and the nation, and was idealized as such.

Elizabethan Protestantism

Henry VIII founded what would become the Church of England by encompassing church affairs under those of the state, but arguably English Protestantism was consolidated into a robust religion on its own terms, one that would begin to develop an enduring global appeal, under the rule of Elizabeth. When Elizabeth ascended to the throne upon the death of her half sister, Mary I, in 1558, English Protestantism found its new patron; her reign marked a new era in the Church of England, with the Virgin Queen at its head. The Church of England had broken from Catholic doctrine and authority in order to enable Henry's divorce and the subsequent union of Elizabeth's parents—quite apart from her doctrinal loyalties or religious practices, Elizabeth would be devoted to Protestantism as the literal origin of her own begetting. Protestantism became a faith that identified as one of purity and, in a transitive relationship, as we have seen, her chastity was indicative of the purity of that faith: she was the Virgin Queen. To a degree, her subjects might engage in religious practice however they saw fit, but from the time of Elizabeth, England would be known as a Protestant nation: Elizabeth would defend the church and the state, in equal measure, with her very person.

One might argue that her father, with a disreputable series of successive marriages that ended in divorces and beheadings, was not particularly concerned with sexual morality, but Henry VIII felt he was supremely concerned with such: his attempt to gain the Pope's approval for a divorce from Catherine of Aragon was genuine, motivated by his ardent quest for an heir. Beheading those who committed treason was the widespread practice throughout the sixteenth century (and could be argued to have been more humane than burning traitors at the stake, or boiling them in oil, also tried and true methods of eliminating opposition both within and without the family). Henry was naturally concerned that his nation had a robust lineage of monarchs to lead it. In the truth of history, Elizabeth's rule meant that this desire was realized, although not as he imagined it: as MacCulloch succinctly reminds us, "Henry could not foresee that the birth of [Queen Anne's] daughter, Elizabeth, in 1533 had furnished a worthy successor to the throne" (2009:626). With the added perspective of hindsight, it is even more astonishing that Henry turned out to provide an heir in precisely the way he had wished to: with a child he had by Anne Boleyn, for whom he had supplicated the Pope for his divorce.

By virtue of her reign, Elizabeth proved that a woman could rule ably—*pace* Henry—and also lead the faith. Her father's desire for a stable, long-ruling, capable heir that would bring England fame and prosperity would be fulfilled in full, and England would do well by its church. Although their approaches to sexual morality could not have been more different—whatever sexual mores might be attributed to Henry, Elizabeth was not remotely interested in questions of marriage or lineage—royal father and daughter shared a vision for England, and for the role of the church in creating and sustaining it. She and her supporters (possibly to an even greater degree) would cast Protestantism in England as Elizabeth's own in style: pure, noble, and unerring. The independence of the Queen would stand for—and would indicate publicly to the region and the world—the independence of the state, thereby claiming not only a legitimacy but an autonomy for the nation she ruled that neither her sister, Mary I of England, nor her cousin Mary, Queen of Scots, had been able to achieve prior to her reign. That both the Queen and the nation were seen as having their borders intact only furthered the metaphor.

That she would defend the church with her very being was obvious to everyone, as MacCulloch (1990) notes. But Elizabeth's claim to the Protestant nation was an embattled one, and considerably set back from the relatively brief period of Mary I's rule after Edward VI's also brief but consolidating one. During Mary's five-year reign (1553–1558), many Protestants had left England, and renewed alliances were forged with both Rome and Spain: the church allied again with the Pope, and Mary herself married Prince (soon-to-be King) Philip of Spain. These Continental links did not take too long for Elizabeth to undo, however: after her sister's death, she recalled her faithful from their exiles in France and Switzerland, in 1572, England broke with the Pope.

The English Reformation under Elizabeth

Although the ending of England's ecclesiastical ties with Rome was done relatively quickly by the new Queen, it would not be fair to say that Catholicism was easily vanquished in Elizabethan England, nor indeed that such was the goal of all future English Protestant movements and sects. The Reformation was a period when warring factions were battling for territorial and political allegiances in the name of religion: the affiliations and powers of the church, the structures of its institutions, the liturgies and prayers that would or should be common and practiced by all were again up for debate, and sometimes violently so. Puritans wanted less Catholicism in their church structures; Calvinists wanted a spartan soteriological view. These were not cerebral political matters: the Reformation was a volatile period when many people on both sides of the Christian divide—lay and clergy, both Protestant and Catholic—were killed in brutal and sometimes vicious circumstances for practicing or preaching religious faith of the wrong kind.

Such violence tells us that much was at stake, on all sides, although more of the violence was perpetrated by the Puritans—Protestant reformers who felt that the Queen did not go far enough—than by Elizabeth herself. Even as he correctly identifies the outcome of the Reformation for the state religion, Tyacke's (2001:37) comment that "Catholicism may have withered away" diminishes the Protestant nationalist efforts that Elizabeth took up amid much religious and political change. One can fairly easily make the claim that protecting England in the name of the faith was Elizabeth's primary motivation, regardless of her theological beliefs or particular religious orientation, although these would have underpinned the character of her actions. Plots on the state or against her life were tried for treason; one trial resulted in the execution of Mary, Queen of Scots (who claimed that she too had been plotted against, as an aspirant to the English throne).

Here, too, in matters of church as well as those of state, Elizabeth's status as a woman was a complicated one. The matter was partially resolved by establishing her title as Supreme Governor (rather than Supreme Head) of the Church of England: this adjustment meant she could monitor the church in her role as head of state with a slightly modified title. In England, the monarch has been responsible (since the Reformation) for establishing the terms of the relationship between state and church. As Supreme Governor of the Church of England, then, Elizabeth immediately positioned herself in extreme contradistinction to her sister, Mary, a Catholic who married a Spaniard and thus allied not only with Rome but with the whole Continent, over which, as a married couple, Mary and Philip had joint jurisdiction. (Elizabeth's interest in aligning with the Continent was, by contrast, very limited, even when aides tried to convince her to support diplomatic missions, let alone marriages, to other Protestant nations, namely the Netherlands and Calvinist Switzerland.)

Her position—and extraordinary strength—as a single woman ruler was noted even by the popes whose claim to religiosity she rejected for the English church: in 1588, at the height of Elizabeth's power, Pope Sixtus V could not help but be impressed: "Just see how well she governs! She is only a woman, only the mistress of half an island, and yet she makes herself feared by Spain, by France, by the Empire, by all!" (cited in Haigh 1998 [1988]:179). Even the most displeasing of institutions for Elizabeth, marriage, came under the jurisdiction of the state rather than that of the clergy under her rule (Crawford 1993:55). Her own inclination to avoid the alliances of marriage in relation to Europe was mirrored in the theological stance that was opposed to the marriage of the clergy.

The Practices of Early Protestantism

What kind of Christianity did Queen Elizabeth choose to consolidate, of the 1,500 years from which she could choose? Henry had been ardent in his passion to set up a new church, and to make it a law of the land. But the question of succession had been a fraught one, for the monarchy and for the church, and finally it was Elizabeth's near half century on the throne that established the foundational tenets of the Church of England. Reformation historians confirm that the "Protestant breakthrough came only in the reign of Elizabeth"; whether dramatically or incrementally (which is debated), there were concrete ways this still new form of religion took hold in England:

> [T]he early phases of the Reformation were indecisive, and . . . major Protestant advance took place only in the Elizabethan period. It was only in the latter part of the sixteenth century, when a Protestant regime remodelled commissions of the peace and diocesan administrations to give power to supporters of reform, when the redistribution of clerical patronage weakened conservative interests and when the universities produced a supply of committed preachers of the new religion, that Protestantism had a real and widespread impact. (Haigh 1995 [1982]:24)

Indeed, because she had to settle the question of religion in England quickly, the two formal Acts of Supremacy and Uniformity (together called the Elizabethan religious settlement) were passed in 1559. They declared England's allegiance to Protestantism, but tried hard not to alienate Catholics too dramatically, by offering a set of theological compromises: they named her Supreme Governor; allowed the clerical use of vestments; and reinserted in the communion ritual in the Book of Prayer references to "the body" and "the blood" of Christ, so as to leave open-ended the highly contentious question of whether the literal or symbolic presence of Jesus was felt by congregants (MacCulloch 1990:26–27). These specifications did not satisfy all parties, but they at least made the point that England would be a Protestant nation that would not penalize gestures to a former Catholic practice.

The attempt to consolidate and rationalize the religion of England began almost immediately, as would have had to be the case what with the jockeying between the Catholic and the Protestant churches in the late and post-Henry eras: much was at stake in England and across the Continent. Along with the religious settlement, Elizabeth issued four proclamations on the importance of national religion in her first year on the throne: she "Revived the Statute for Holy Communion" (proc. 454) in March 1559; banned public performances on religion (proc. 458) in May; issued a full set of "Injunctions for Religion" (proc. 460) in July; and on the same day approved her half brother Edward VI's book of "Homilies to be Read in Churches" (proc. 461; all Hughes and Larkin 1969) in a proclamation that also mandated everyone's attendance in church on a weekly basis. Still, Elizabeth appears to have believed that identifying as a Protestant was what mattered, rather than the details of how people worshiped a Christian God.[5] Very likely for the purposes of expediency—and the longevity of her rule—Elizabeth tried to cut it both ways: "in religion, she refused to choose between unequivocal Protestantism and hard-line Catholicism: she tried to sustain a Church which offered inducements to conformity for all but the recalcitrant on both sides" (Haigh 1998 [1988]:177). Her subjects, though, and especially her bishops cared very much about the details of religious practice (see, for example, Tyacke [2001:54] on arguments over whether images in glass or altars in stone might be protected and where the table for communion should be placed).

Interestingly, Elizabeth's own religious beliefs are not much known to history, and we can surmise that her insistence on the privacy of such became part of the Church of England's theology. It would seem that a legitimate Protestantism under Elizabeth was deliberately constituted as a broad and even eclectic field. She was herself very religious in that she frequently ascribed to God her power and position as Queen; nonetheless, very little is known about how she viewed theological matters. She tended rather to identify with the domain of Christendom and leave it at that.

There is evidence that those close to her consulted astrologers, notably the famous John Dee, although she herself appeared less taken with the movements of the stars (Thomas 1971:299). Still, it is clear that large numbers of the public adhered to a worldview that likely included calculations of the cosmos, and that saw natural forces as demonstrations or manifestations of the work of God; Elizabeth herself healed scrofula through touch, like her medieval predecessors (Crawford 1993:46). Such popular interest in prediction and the possible permutations of auspiciousness and inauspiciousness were not encouraged by (what we might call retrospectively) Elizabethan Anglicanism, however, and this was one kind of religious practice that fell out of the remit of English Protestantism. Although the court might have used astrology to set the date of her coronation in 1558, for example (Thomas 1971:290), others who consulted astrologers could be accused of witchcraft (Crawford 1993:45); by 1581 it was a criminal act for any member of the public to use astrology to calculate the tenure of her reign (Thomas 1971:344). This prohibition was more likely to dissuade any attempt to cast aspersions on the endurance of her power, however: the Queen knew better than to micromanage people's religious practices, as long as they identified as Protestant.

That the Church of England is a broad church—and this breadth, or even ecumenicism, remains a key element of its contemporary theology—dates back to Elizabeth's willingness to accommodate such variations in structure and practice under its welcoming umbrella. Such was politically necessary during the Reformation, especially with the painful seesaw of religious allegiance in the years leading up to her reign. The Church of England has been able to remain an integrated body precisely because it has so consistently adapted to the breadth of its Protestant congregations; those who had to be checked, and who caused the real political problems in the later sixteenth century, were those who wanted a narrower church, or the Puritans.[6] Heresy has a variegated past in the Christian church in Europe; Moore (1990 [1987]) argues that the construction of heresy as something that had to be put out (rather than tolerated) dates to the late eleventh and early twelfth centuries: Elizabeth's Parliament repealed laws against heresy in the first year of her reign (MacCulloch 1990). Execution for treason against the state religion did not cease completely, but the loss of heresy as a guiding principle was a subtle tweaking of the Elizabethan church, one with profound cultural effects.

A theology of self-sacrifice roots a tradition where it is more honorable to die for one's principles than to assimilate, as was true for both Catholics and Puritans during the Reformation, and as is true today in the context of any civil, religious, or political movement that produces martyrs for its cause. Elizabeth's Protestant church chose rather to accommodate a difference of opinion such that one body—the state—could encompass a diversity of well-cultivated beliefs and practices without losing its overarching identity. As far as this legacy goes, consider the debate that was encouraged in the development of the King James Bible between 1604 and 1611, the first post-Elizabethan decade: six companies of translators conferred for close to a decade on an authoritative text (and it still was not published as "authorized," unlike its late sixteenth-century predecessor [Moore and Reid 2011]). The Reformation was undeniably a bloody period, but now, five hundred years later, its legacy is such that a minority stance has become a source of strength for contemporary Anglicanism, which allows for a loudly voiced diversity of opinion.

The national church, of course, would continue to have a say in how people lived and how they were governed in Elizabethan England, but the state now emerged as an equally dominant force, sometimes using the theology of a particular church to help forge that shared national identity. Although a pride for and loyalty to England must have been fostered since the Saxons began to consolidate separate kingdoms just before the turn of the first millennium, it was not until Elizabeth inherited the throne that England and her church began to stand in for each other in a sustained, systematic way. Protestant Christianity was held up as the defining symbol of the nation, and together they claimed the right to rule over the land. Nationalism here must be understood as forging a sense of belonging (in contemporary parlance), first and foremost, but it also carried the twin characteristics of being distinct from other territories, in the first instance, and being greater than—or able to encompass or engage with, on one's own terms—other states, in the second.

Elizabethan Nationalism: St. George and the Redcross Knight

Elizabeth's was a strong, strident, and chaste model of feminine power, one that befitted the Queen of Reformation England. Over the course of her long rule, England had a figurehead around whom to rally: her particular form of English Protestantism became the call of a gallant nation ready to distinguish itself from the rest of Europe rather than align with it on Puritan grounds. Forming—or reforming, as is etymologically indicated in our references to the Protestant Reformation—the church was the symbolic way Elizabeth could present and strengthen the new political position of an England with many ties to the Continent, but with no binding ones.

Elizabeth was a legend in her own time, quite literally. In Spenser's (1976 [1590–1596]) hagiographic telling of *The Faerie Queene*, hearkening back both to Arthurian legend and to the worship of their queen by ancient Rome, Elizabeth is held aloft as like no other ruler (see Spenser and Percival 1893 [1590]). The Faerie Queene in the story rules over a realm that is virtuous and faithful, like Rome must have been; Arthur, here still a prince and not yet a king, both loves the Queen and perfects the qualities of the Knights of the Round Table. Arthur and Rome are a potent combination: no one has been seen as more noble or gallant than King Arthur, and no empire has ever been more valorized by the West than the Roman one—with the possible later exception of the British, born in practice (and in name, by astrologer John Dee) under Elizabeth.[7]

The mythical figures in *The Faerie Queene* are two sides of the same person: St. George and the Redcross Knight. Saints are the mystical beings who often sacrifice their lives in defense of their faith; knights, on the other side of the coin, are as brave as they come when defending their land or, in this case, the moral culture of the royal realm of England. As the presiding Queen in the tale of combined twin figures—the formerly Catholic saint and the English knight—Elizabeth, in the figure of Gloriana, is shown as able to transcend the ideologies of the warring churches, and to indicate the truth of Christianity with the virtues of "holiness," "temperance," "charity," "friendship," and "courtesy," as each book in turn relates (Spenser 1976 [1590–1596]). These qualities refer to the purity of the original practice of the faith, allegorically aligned with the Arthurian kingdom and Camelot—which, as it happens, was identified as none other than Winchester by Sir Thomas Malory in his fifteenth-century rendering of the tale. Here, then, England—Protestant England—is the overarching institution that encompasses these many times and many churches in the attainment of glory. And it comes to its most exalted fulfillment in the realm of Winchester.

St. George was taken up as the icon of the English kings in 1348 by Edward III, in another, earlier era of forging national identity; Edward also founded the Order of the Garter, whose motto—*honi soit qui mal y pense*, "shamed be he who thinks ill"—was used consistently by the Bishops of Winchester throughout the medieval period (Morgan 2006). Henry VIII went further, assigning George the role of patron saint of England. In the Elizabethan era, invoking Arthur alongside St. George was meant to indicate the purity of ancient English worship: no one would have disputed that pre-Saxon Arthurians were the true Britons—and the true Christians. Protestantism here was thus shown to be not an innovation but a return to the origin (as it was meant to imply for the Tudors themselves). St. George became the embodiment of the symbolic complex that is England, the nation—and the language that is its legacy to the world.

The Redcross Knight is the icon of Protestantism; his scarlet cross is the real and pure English nation, there on the heart of St. George. Ultimately it is the Protestant faith that is the base of the patron saint, made mythic in the figure of the knight who is slain only to be revealed as St. George. Protestantism is England, much as England is the church: it is a transitive relationship based on analogous (and even blurred) identities, not oppositional ones. First, the knight bears a representation of St. George upon his breast (just as thereafter St. George is shown wearing a red cross on his tunic), but it is later revealed that he is himself St. George. In the end, they are indistinguishable: true faith is shown to be the heart of an eternal England. Like Dorothy in the Wizard of Oz, Gloriana the Queen discovers what was there all along.

The real George was a third- or fourth-century AD figure in history, and a naughty fellow (no one who cannot riposte is worthy of being the patron saint of Shakespeare, and one has to know how to live it if one is to tell it as it is); he was either a rogue from Cappadocia or a heretical bishop. When no one could establish Shakespeare's birthday, St. George's Day was thought to be the most appropriate date for the great poet of England. And St. George is no less loved in contemporary times; the red cross flies on British flags across the country on national holidays, and from people's houses and car windows during international football tournaments, so as to rally on the English team. Also the symbol of the care and generosity of the nation, the organization called the British Red Cross still offers medical services to people who have suffered violence in conflict, regardless of their political orientation. Every April 23, St. George's Day, Google UK designs a new doodle of a knight slaying a dragon. England is a nation enchanted by its own myth.

Similarly, King Arthur's legacy is sustained until the present day: Queen Elizabeth II bestowed the Arthurian title of Royal Knight Companion of the Most Noble Order of the Garter on her grandson Prince William on April 23, 2008. (Apparently young noblemen still aspire to be as brave as the Knights of the Round Table.) On June 23, 2011, a group specially named Red Cross Bards for Crossbones met two hours before the ritual for an evening of poetry and music, at the end of which everyone strolled up the back alleys to participate in the ritual as usual on Redcross Way.[8] (For the first time, it started early.)

Was producing a new English nation in the image of Gloriana a novel way to stay on the throne, to consolidate power in Elizabeth's person rather than in her marital or religious alliances? The complex mythical layers in *The Faerie Queene* indicate the impossibility of separating any one aspect of the truth of English faith and national heritage: they are interwoven as shared features of the same body. As was true for any monarch before her, Elizabeth *was* the state, but, unlike her predecessors, in fashioning herself a "virgin mother" of the nation (Haigh 1998 [1988]:24), she produced an England that did not rely on the loyalties of any Continental neighbors: England alone was the focus of her rule. In one sense, this position must have been strategic, as there were many who wanted to see her deposed: women were not supposed to rule, and plots to get a Catholic back on the throne were plentiful.

But in another sense, her unilateral identity with the nation that was England must have been a product of her unique upbringing and deep immersion in the worlds of political (not to mention gendered) intrigue from a very young age. The obvious lesson she had learned was that she could trust no one but herself, and she preferred to use that protective psychology to create a church—and, in turn, a nation and a state—that would thrive under her reign than to look elsewhere for alliances. MacCulloch jokes that a news headline of the time could have read "1559 Settlement Passed by Parliament: Continent Cut Off"

(1990:6). The very idea that England had seceded from the politics of the Continent indicates how clearly English religion under Elizabeth had taken on a new and distinct national form.

Elizabethan Expansionism

Geographically speaking, early modern Europe faced a paradoxical moment. In one sense, the world was getting bigger: Spanish explorers had discovered what was for them a new world in 1492, laying the ground for centuries of Spanish colonialism in the Americas, great wealth in the Spanish Empire as a result, and the expansion of the purview of the Pope beyond the region of Europe. On the other hand, a nation like England was beginning to develop a corporate identity as a country that might govern its own territory, developing international alliances but with ultimate responsibility for itself. Contradictory as it may sound, it is perhaps not so surprising that as empires expanded, so too would a sense of integrated statehood. Or, to put it another way, as England consolidated herself into a single national unit, not a kin-based entangled one, she could look further afield for the transnational opportunities that would come in the form of commodities that could be carried in the cargo holds of ships, rather than in the form of alliances that came out of royal marriages.

Is not transnationalism about the transcending of nations, or conceiving of or understanding states as blurrier entities than we had thought, rather than more fixed ones? Transnationalism is a vision of the world that understands nations as interconnected in ways that scholarly or policy focuses on individual states would not take into account: marriage among monarchs in Europe before Elizabeth's reign, for example, was a way of creating transnational ties. But by establishing the nation as a state with boundaries, primarily concerned with its own interests, its own territory, its own policies, its own government, and its own religion, a clearer actor emerges in any diplomatic or international encounter. The scale and the scope of the kinds of trade that emerged under Elizabeth's reign show how these two processes—the consolidation of national identity and the forging of transnationalism—may be understood as two sides of the same coin.

It is not surprising, then, to learn that the early configurations of international trade law begins in this period: Ivan Strenski (2004) writes that the theology that was being written at this time, first in Spain by the famous Francisco de Vitoria, and picked right up—and then contested—by the Italian Protestant jurist Alberico Gentili, who lived in England from 1580 as the Regius Professor of Law at Oxford (and who would inspire the more famous Dutch theorist Hugo Grotius). This body of work, which sets the theological and, more importantly for Gentili, the political ground for the position that "every nation is free to travel to every other nation, and to trade with it . . . forms the fundamental legal ground for the condition of trade that we call globalization" (Strenski 2004:644–645; see also Schröder 2010). The seeds of economic globalization are thus shown to derive from theological law as interpreted by an Italian refugee in England.

The explicit notion of international trade does not feature prominently in these early treatises—it did not exist as a concept in the sense we know it today—but is rather implied in the juridical and theological discussions of encounter, and in the questions of claimant rights between nations (Kingsbury and Straumann 2010). For the Protestant jurists, of more concern than the concept of free trade (which would emerge in the centuries to come) was the right of free passage (like medieval harlots, nations need to be able to navigate freely through the alleys of the world): "the right of free passage forms the fundamental basis for the legitimation of the perceived universal and natural right to trade across the boundaries of states. . . . It is, in short, more than any other idea the legitimating principle upon which globalization rests" (Strenski 2004:645). The free passage that European theology began to insist upon in this period enabled Elizabethan economic policy to start traveling the seas with intent,[9] in both a western direction (with an unsuccessful expedition on the part of Sir Walter Raleigh toward what was to become the United States) and an eastern direction, toward the Ottoman Empire and India, in much more successful efforts. In 1581, Elizabeth established the Turkey Company (later the Levant Company) with a patent to obtain currants; in 1600 she founded the East India Trading Company in search of a direct route to the Asian spice trade, leading to three hundred years of global imperial power, threatened by none.

It is important, too, to recall that Europe was breaking apart, in some senses, between the papal legacy and the Protestant reformers in Germany, Switzerland, and the Netherlands—as well as significant minority populations in France and across the Continent.[10] England had split from the Continent under Henry, and Europe proceeded to dissolve as a unit under the Pope. Refusing a marital alliance meant agility in these complex matters of church and state: no kinship ties needed to be considered in England's military, ecclesiastical, or diplomatic affairs. (Indeed, much has been made of Elizabeth's style of protracted marital negotiations, which, in multiple cases, appeared to effect a sense of enduring possibility with various European allies.)

Elizabeth was the mediator here: she inherited a nation that, arguably earlier than any other, had started to form a distinct identity. When she refused to marry, something else needed to be exchanged with other European lands in order to cement the bonds, and commodities or goods come to occupy that particular mode of establishing (object) relations. Foreign trade negotiations became, then, a new means of establishing ties between European nations, in a way that was bound up with neither marriage nor religion (when England refused to trade with Spain after 1588, it was not because the Spaniards were Catholic but because they had been aggressors), and then, of course, farther flung: the Ottomans and the Indians did not have to be members of Christendom to be consumers and producers of goods.

Elizabethan Trade

Let us turn to the royal proclamations of the Tudors to see if we may trace a difference in the attitudes toward the independence of—as compared to the alliance of—England, as articulated in commodity and trade policies from the time that Elizabeth I ascends to the throne.[11] There are glimmers of trade agreements under Henry VII (r. 1485–1509), Elizabeth's grandfather, who "Renew[s] Trade with Austria and Burgundy" in 1489 (18), although he is careful, in 1493, to "Prohibit Unlicensed Trade" with the latter (31). (Here we see the first insistence on "Outlaw[ing] Foreign Coins" [20.7], which would have diluted the English economy.) Trade as an abstract, transitive interaction between European nations is literally not mentioned again until Elizabeth's reign. Henry VIII does not make a single proclamation on the subject. Edward VI and Mary I each "Regulat[e the] Wool Trade" once, Edward generically (331), and Mary "with the Low Countries" (397).

This picture of commodity exchange changes dramatically under Elizabeth, who, within ten years of becoming Queen, "renew[s] trade with the low countries" (530, in 1564), and thereafter "continu[es] trade with the low countries" (537, 546), in three separate proclamations. She "renews trade with the low countries" twice more during her reign (595, in 1573, and 639, in 1579)—these were long-standing policies—and once with Portugal (620, in 1576). And, naturally, trade is prohibited with Spain (737, in 1591), following the Spanish Armada.

Wages, too, which might be understood as a formal mechanism of exchange for labor (unmentioned in any of the proclamations of her forebears, except when Henry refers to the wages of shipsmen) deserve fifty notices, referring to twenty separate locations. She grants monopolies (for starch [794] and saltpeter [718, 776]), regulates insurance rates (605) and exchange rates (618), issues licenses for shipping and for the import of wine (a concern for every Tudor monarch—but Elizabeth is the only one to grant licenses by proclamation), and ensures that markets are stocked (490, 541, 686, 789). And for the first time in English history, she issues a proclamation to "enlarge [the] export market of cloth" (690, in 1587), rather than "punishing," "prohibiting," "limiting," "control[ling]," or "preventing" the "unlicenced" export of grain, victuals, gold and silver, butter, and cheese. (By contrast, Edward VI "permit[ted the] export of grain" once [280].) Elizabeth "licenses" export, too, of grain (532, in 1565) and of ordnance, the metal for artillery (747, in 1592).[12] She prohibits the export of arms to Russia (481), though: some things never change.

There is no doubt that cloth and then wool were important commodity exports in the thirteenth century, well before Elizabeth's rule (Barron 2004:89); within England, trade was a significant part of medieval market life (Macfarlane 1987:150). Barron describes how "[b]y the first two decades of the thirteenth century England's average annual export was between 25,000 and 30,000 sacks of wool" (2004:89) but also how, puzzlingly, London ship merchants kept a "comparatively low profile" (2004:92) in comparison to the Spanish, Italian, Flemish, and Dutch, among others. "England," she argues, "appears to have been the passive goose laying golden eggs for the benefit of others" (2004:92). Imports, by contrast, appear to have been the real focus here: French wine, Flemish cloth, and Italian luxuries of all sorts—silk, velvet, gold cloth, spices, sugar, fruit, glass, and paper—were important to the English market.

Certainly, over the course of the next 250 years, exports grew, particularly in the form of the cloth market, which returned to English hands from Flemish in the mid-fourteenth century (Barron 2004:100 and fig. 5.4). But imports remained an equal if not greater focus during this period, both to support the cloth trade with imported dyes and tools, and to keep London's culinary tastes satisfied with salt and wine. It is clear that "the economy of England was undeveloped" (Barron 2004:116–117): basic cooking utensils and even beer (not to mention books, reading glasses, girdles, and knives) had to be imported because they were not produced in England or were more cheaply available from abroad. Barron concludes her comprehensive discussion on medieval trade with the assurance that "the situation was changing and the English merchants were cultivating those skills which would, in the next century, take them on trading ventures, in English ships, to all parts of the known world"; indeed, she tells us, "[t]he dramatic rise in English overseas trade was to come in the sixteenth century" (2004:117). Under Henry, most of the trade focused on materials needed to keep up with the wars that he waged, and much remained focused on import, including armor, gunpowder, saltpeter, naval supplies, and handguns. Those exports he did oversee were largely to supply his navies and armies serving abroad with arms, food (grain, meat, cheese, fish), and clothing: the famous term "whitecoats" refers to the undyed cloth with which English soldiers' uniforms were made (Gunn 2015). Dye was not locally produced.

And so it was under Elizabeth that the foreign commodity market intentionally expanded and not for the sake of war; these were economic policies designed to build England's fortunes through export. England's independence and her chosen mode of commodity trade were not separate features of the political and economic landscape; they constituted each other. As Steven Gunn puts it, "Elizabeth's government gave her blessing to . . . entrepreneurs" (2015:n.p.). McIntosh writes that "economic credit grew in importance and became increasingly separate from social credit over the course of the sixteenth century" (2005:12). It is widely recognized that the sixteenth century was a period of dramatic economic growth (although it was not without periods of depression from high food prices by the end of the century and the Queen's reign). Elton eloquently proclaims that the "Elizabethan age witnessed England's entry into transoceanic trade" (1991 [1955]:250). All these assessments indicate that under Elizabeth's rule, the early modern era delivered an early manifestation of what we recognize as a commodity capitalist system.

Trade is not dependent upon the refusal to marry: Spain had been at the forefront of maritime expansionism and conquest—and without its monarchs being single women. But England, as a lone island, had been in no position to rival the Spanish (and had no need to, given the marital relations first between Henry VIII and Catherine of Aragon, and then between Mary I and Philip). By the time Elizabeth refused Philip, however—and even more so after the Spanish Armada, by which time Elizabeth was fifty-five years old, in her prime but well past the stage of a young bride or the potential mother of a king—England began to expand in earnest. She did not need a marital partner on the Continent to do so: her ships were more powerful than even those of the Spanish, and from this single and consolidated position, Elizabeth and her nation could grow. And so she did. Elizabeth determined not just what could be traded, but where she would trade, and with whom: these were the terms through which transnational relations were established, cultivated, enabled, and disabled.

The English Nation and the Origins of Transnationalism

This is not the end—or even the beginning—of the story of the English nation. Historian and anthropologist Adrian Hastings (1997) locates the roots of English national consciousness a good thousand years earlier, in the time of Bede and the turn of the first millennium, when the notion of a common Saxon, Norman heritage first starts whipping a sense of English nationalism into play. What Hastings and his intellectual forebears (he is not the first to assert that the English nation comes into being during the Anglo-Saxon period) identify as the seeds of nationalism—knowing who one is and where one belongs, territorially and ethnically—speaks to something quite different from the dynamics described by theorists who date nationalism much later, to the eighteenth century, when what it means to be a person in a state begins to be defined as individuality during the industrial revolution and the early Enlightenment.

Part of the trouble with identifying the beginnings of nationhood is that the nation, and the swell or support around it, like the measures to uphold and protect it, take notably different forms at different moments in time, and offer considerably different dynamics. Shifts in definition should not surprise us, but they rightly confound easy efforts to identify the beginning of nationalism. It follows that the contours of a nation and the emotive nationalism that attends such an entity will not always take the same form, or have the same impacts on the citizenry, or on those opposed to that population. In tandem with the different sets of symbolic constructions that attend nationhood at different moments, that sense of national coherence and identity will have different qualities and align with different bodies of thought over time.

What Hastings and others find in the eighth and ninth centuries is the beginning of English consciousness. What Gellner (1983) and Hobsbawm (1990) identify in the Enlightenment, a millennium later, is rather a structural body that can be governed as such: citizens within a state. And in the period of analysis here, something else again is taking place in the Reformation, as identity politics (as they would be called today) realign Europe along the lines of religion. But England also is asserting herself, if in solidarity with other parts of Protestant Europe, as a new nation, and these efforts create a new kind of relation with other nations on the Continent.

If English nationhood comes into the analytical frame just before the turn of the first millennium, and the formalization of the English nation-state comes to fruition just before the turn of the second, what role does the Protestant Reformation play?[13] First, clearly, the establishment by England of its own church and the complex negotiations between the two wings of the nation—the church and the state—emerge as the power play of Henry. Religion becomes the tool of the nation in the early Reformation (see Asad 1993), as well as its identity marker. Second, and equally importantly, by her refusal to marry as a way of consolidating relations with other Western European nations, Elizabeth makes concrete—objectifies, if you will—an exchange relation with those states. Running alongside the development of the Church of England as it consolidates its formal state structures, scriptures, and hierarchical bureaucratic institutions is thus the advent of transnationalism in Western Europe. Earlier monarchs had solidified relations with the other states of Europe through marriage; Elizabeth's antagonism to the institution means that a different relation is put into place between nations during the later Reformation. Tariffs, market rates, and the formalization of commodity trade relations in Western Europe are the legacy of Elizabeth I's nation of England.

This state of historical affairs means that transnationalism in the sense of commodity trade and regulation in the sixteenth century precedes the formal bureaucratic procedures and mechanisms of nation-states in the eighteenth. But why should this not be the case? Transnational relations—in all their dynamic complexity—deserve a genealogy alongside that of the development of the nation-state, in Hastings's or in Gellner's terms, and of capitalism in its various formations. And it should follow that nations, nationhood, and nationalism have developed in a manner that is fitting to the way transnationalism, too, has changed over the centuries. Neither the nation nor the transitive or hierarchical relations between a multiplicity of them are static formations.

Key is the understanding that all these sets of phenomena are dynamic. The first glimmerings of a sense of self-consciousness as an English people emerge as an element of the early medieval constructions of self and other (in addition to Hastings 1997, see Moore 1990 [1987]); many centuries later, industrialization—following the Enlightenment—allows such consciousness to take new, and newly material, forms, including trade. The intermediary stage is the materialization process, which Elizabeth formalizes in trade agreements and export arrangements, now necessary—now possible—as she removes herself from the marital equation.

Coda: Sexuality as Capital

If the Virgin Mary could birth a new religion, the Virgin Queen could birth her nation anew, defending her faith all the while. Married to her subjects, Queen Elizabeth begot an England that was to become a powerful trading empire—on its own terms—in place of the transcontinental marriage of its mother. Elizabeth's relation to the church was instrumental in her construction of the nation, and historians actively debate whether her position was primarily theologically motivated. Most likely, Elizabeth's own beliefs were less important in her governance of the church than were her political motivations for England. Her successful consolidation of the church did honor to her father, but the successful delineation of England's own religion did honor to her mother, whose marriage to Henry VIII could only be permitted if he broke from Rome. The precise form that the English church would take was less important than that it would thrive as England's religion. Of course, religion and politics are never so easily separated—the point is that one sphere can stand it for the other—and in her prescient way, Elizabeth appears to have known this truth: the Church of England and the nation of England were—or became—one under the rule of Elizabeth I.

As in so many contexts across the world and across history, women's sexuality is emblematic of the values of a particular culture or country, and the idealized purity of their containment. The fear of diluting female (or national) purity (or, conversely, in many terrifying examples, the conscious use of rape and miscegenation as an act of war between groups) has mobilized many nationalist movements. By contrast, in the Elizabethan context we see the deliberate manipulation of an antimiscegenist ideology to precisely and proactively construct an English nation on its own pure, unadulterated terms. It is no coincidence that this policy decision on Elizabeth's part coincided or was correlated with rapid economic growth: by containing England, transnationalism could grow. Royal women as marital partners or the primary objects of exchange and relation between European nation-states would need to be replaced by something else—and they were, by consumer goods.

This genealogy of international trade and commodity transnationalism underscores our ritual in its alternative or countercultural, pseudo-secular stance. Female chastity in particular may be symbolic of purity and of power, but Elizabeth (and indeed womanhood in many cases) was herself symbolic of the nation. Our ritualists, contrarily, claim the power in sexual labor from the underdog's perspective—from beneath. Global commodity capitalism may have emerged from chaste relations with other nations, but a defiant English activism may remind us that a whore's sexual activity could count toward the gross national product, if only we were inclined to consider it legitimate labor. While this story is explicitly about gender politics, then, it is also about a refracting mirror of symbolic references where, through many twists and turns, from the streets of bawdy medieval Southwark to the activist artists in the capital city that is global London today, the politics of gender generate the politics of transnationalism, for the Queen in the sixteenth century and for the Londoners of the twenty-first. And the rest, shall we say, is history.

The Shard from Redcross Way

5 ❁ *Southwark, Then and Now*

> [O]ur beloved, the citizens of our city of London, by their petition exhibited before us and our council, in our present parliament at Westminster assembled, have given us to understand that felons, thieves, and divers other malefactors and disturbers of the peace, who in the aforesaid city and elsewhere, have committed manslaughters, robberies, and divers other felonies, secretly withdrawing from the same city, after having committed such felonies, flee to the town of Southwark, where they cannot be attached by the ministers of the said city, and there are openly received; and so for default of due punishment are emboldened to commit more such felonies; and they have besought us, that, for the conservation of our peace within the said city, bridling the wickedness of these same malefactors, we would grant unto them the said town.
>
> Charter of Edward III (March 6, 1327)

All politics, it is said, are local: the manipulation of time, too, must be enacted somewhere. In the story at hand, our ritual takes place in Southwark, a borough that is 300,000 strong in a twenty-first-century London that is vibrantly expanding. Formally incorporated into the City of London in its present form as late as 1965 (Johnson 1969:385), Southwark is one of the densest boroughs in the contemporary capital: the 2011 census lists almost 10,000 residents per square kilometer, double the average for London (and twenty times the average for England, which has always had a large rural population).[1] Some of this population density may be attributable to the dense office culture that has sprung up around the Shard skyscraper. But farther away from the river, the rates of migration from around the world—usually from lower economic levels, as has been the case in Southwark for centuries—remain high, and pockets like the area around the famous Elephant and Castle roundabout remain underserved and poor.

Bankside, which, as its name suggests, is as far north in the Borough as one can go, abuts the river. As we have seen, in medieval terms, it was a logical place for a brothel: a boat could ferry a customer from London right to the door of his mistress, and back again, if need be. In the twenty-first century, this neighborhood is in no way a red-light area, and it is clearly not suffering from a lack of social services. Even before Southwark became formally incorporated into the city, the area became known as the South Bank, host to everyday open-air markets, booksellers, and countless international and artistic festivals every year on an elegantly lined promenade; the designation is a 1951 name that dates to the development of the area for the Festival of Britain in that year. In the last half century, Bankside and the area around it have benefited—economically, at least—from millions of pounds of investment from city developers. The proximity of this area to the geographical and banking centers of the city means that it is—as it arguably always has been—the cultural heart of London, with the Royal Festival Hall, the British Film Institute, the National Theatre, and the more recently constructed Tate Modern lining the riverbank in quick succession. After all those centuries, Bankside is now central London right and proper; south of the Thames is today the center of the world.

Set just slightly back from the river is perhaps the most famous cultural institution of all: the Globe Theatre, where Shakespeare's plays were first performed at the end of the sixteenth century. The Globe is the icon of both elements of Southwark's history: its less-than-reputable, raucous, exuberant expression of human nature, on one hand, and its centrality as a cultural institution, on the other. This combination is what being "south of the river" means, then and now, and what our ritualists promote as the real character of Southwark: the diverse vibrancy of cultural expression in ways that are not necessarily mainstream, or high class, or remunerated at legal rates, or publicly acknowledged as valuable (until they are gentrified, reclaimed by the mainstream, and made fashionable precisely by virtue of having been underground or cultish) even though, the argument goes, they are the soul of the system, which could not function in any apparently clean or straitlaced way without its held-close-to-the-heart-but-at-just-enough-remove underbelly. There is only an upper class or a dominant culture if there is a lower class or a counterculture to maintain it.

All of contemporary Southwark—even the establishment institutions—proudly claims this countercultural history. Our ritualists are a living, breathing example of that counterculture today: in their social mobilization and their passionate and performative activism, Southwark's history lives on. Through the medieval period and the Reformation, Southwark held on as a dynamic location of activity and art, alongside institutions of the Christian church that were themselves undergoing major transformations over the course of a thousand years. These social institutions—churches and theaters, places of both artistic performance and worship—have been part of the Southwark landscape since the turn of the first millennium. They take on different guises today, as institutions do in every era, but they continue to be at the heart of life in the Borough.

Our ritualists perform right at this intersection of art and ritual, and here the two are intentionally conflated. Through the enactment of not only the ritual but also the mystery plays that emerged into John Constable's artistic consciousness (consonant with the ritual that emerged into John Crow's shamanic one), we see how social actors conduct themselves in relation to social bodies—institutions—that vary over time, depending on what is expedient, productive, and creative. John's ritual performance and his theatrical one breathe; they swing, dialectically, between criticizing the church and embracing or acting in solidarity with it. Both performances argue against what they call a hypocritical history on the part of the church, but this position is useful—even integral—to those they critique. Such an oscillation between being on the outside (questioning an institution's double-edged history) and being on the inside (positioning oneself as within the fold of a larger protective or encompassing umbrella) mirrors both Southwark's relation to the city and the diocese's relation to the Church of England.

The performance of ritual takes place outside the Cathedral, on Redcross Way, and claims a radical status. The performance of theater that relates a story of shamanic visions and sexual awakenings takes place inside the contemporary Southwark Cathedral, with the blessings of the church, since its teachings are at least partly encapsulated in *The Southwark Mysteries*, John's twentieth-century mystery play (Constable 1999). Claiming Southwark's histories of legal and illegal prostitution in one context while telling Southwark's story as a conscious reappropriation of its lower status in another constitutes a double activist performance. These variable positions—being on the outside when critique is necessary, and being on the inside when solidarity is rather the order of the day, precisely in order to effect an alliance in opposition to a larger body that needs challenging—translate into a mobilizing strategy of agility and versatility, able to navigate between the immanent realities of everyday life and the transcendent realities of universal truths of hierarchy, contingent though they may be.

Medieval and Early Modern Southwark

As we know, until the mid-sixteenth century, Southwark prostitutes worked under the jurisdiction of the Diocese of Winchester, and they were nominally under the protection of the bishop. They worked in Southwark precisely because it was not the city, but they certainly provided a service for the city. Prostitution has always been a theologically messy business, and thus it was in some sense only proper that the moral oversight lay in the jurisdiction of the church. As far as Southwark stews went, it was the bishop, not the king, who stood to reap the rents from the endeavor; that the diocese could claim these monies was perhaps thought to be a compensation for taking on such a theologically puzzling situation, which, to be fair, if the manor's ordinances laying out the appropriate behaviors of stewholders and sex workers are any guide, it tried to do with care.

Winchester Palace—a beautiful structure, part of which still stands today, including the famous Rose Window (likely built in the fourteenth century, when the rose was already a noble emblem; it was later to become a symbol of the Tudor monarchs in particular)—was the Bankside manorial residence of the Bishop of Winchester, designed to accommodate his visits to London. Sources such as English Heritage attribute the earliest construction and first occupancy to the architectural enthusiast Henry of Blois, in 1136 or thereabouts, but both the granting of the land and the erection of the palace likely date earlier still, to William Gifford, who was Bishop in the first decades of the twelfth century (Winchester House and Park 1950). Both Gifford and then Blois are reputed to have made significant architectural adjustments to Winchester Cathedral, their ecclesiastical seat, as well as to their manorial palace.

Many an illustrious figure in English history (William of Wykeham, the likely architect of the Rose Window, in the fourteenth century; Thomas Wolsey and, later, Stephen Gardiner, in the sixteenth), often simultaneously holding the office of Lord Chancellor of England, occupied these premises and ran the manor, complete with its somewhat sordid goings-on up the way. It does appear that certain blocks of land were not technically under the ownership of the church (Winchester House and Park 1950), precisely (and presciently) so as to avoid the claims that could (then and now) be made against it. Even so, the Bishop of Winchester was the lord of the manor and the legal overseer of the area—known, appropriately, as we have seen, as the liberty. He would have rightfully claimed any rents or penalties charged to stewholders whose leases he still owned, and would also have been generally aware of the activities in the neighborhood, reputable or not.

Just southeast along the river, from the thirteenth century, the Archbishop of Canterbury also had a London residence, Lambeth Palace. With the archbishop in the neighborhood, the area could become a posh suburb, in its way, or at least the most elite figures of the land did not mind living cheek by jowl with the least desirable figures, as long as the brothel owners were paying their rents—and as long as the prostitutes cleared out as they were meant to when the landholders came into town. Denigrated as they may have been, Southwark's prostitutes were not treated as lepers were in this regard:[2] they did not have to be permanently hidden away from mainstream members of society (see Moore 1990 [1987]). It is likely that Southwark's location (and role) as peripheral to the city already accommodated the desire to keep sex workers away from conventional society. Prostitutes were required to leave when Parliament was in session; on other occasions, elite members of the church who traveled to Southwark for business in the city would just have to look the other way.

In either event, clearly it was not thought that houses of prostitution and church lands had to be kept separate, which is the very premise of our story. On the contrary, in some senses, the strange demographic combination of Southwark residents may have protected stews all the more forcefully. Johnson (1969:chs. 2–3) suggests that a predominance of high-ranking ecclesiastical officials meant a collective, long-held, and logical resistance to a higher administrative or authoritative body, such as the king or the city, overseeing the area. As it was, Southwark, or south of the river in general, remained a kind of no man's land—or rather, a high-man/low-man (or low-woman, as the case may be) place—with the land owned by elites but occupied by outsiders, a place perhaps uniquely suited to negotiating the hierarchical social orders of English lay and religious life. At the higher echelons and the lower, then, Southwark has long been known for iconoclasm, a refusal to cede to the status quo, and a little bit of liberal defiance in defense of lived morality, land, and the underdog.

By the first part of the sixteenth century, in his famous dissolution of the monasteries, Henry VIII wanted to amalgamate the funds from church activities so they would be available to the state. Stews—not monasteries exactly, but a source of revenue for the church nonetheless—would have been one more way in which eccelesiastical officials were gaining wealth. Whether theologically, politically, or financially motivated—and these strains are not always so easily discerned—Henry decided that he could no longer tolerate the moral implications of such houses of sin; the stews were made illegal, or driven underground, and would no longer be legal tenants of the manor of Winchester. Whether his councilors advised this course of action, or whether Henry wished to deprive the then-Bishop of Winchester, Stephen Gardiner, of that source of income, or whether, at the end of his life, he was overcome with a moral rigor that could not sustain the thought of semi-legal prostitution or an area dense with impoverished souls, we may never know. It may also be that the general attempt to clean up moral and social life as part of the growing surge of Protestant fervor sweeping Europe influenced Henry for his England. In any event, as we know, in 1546, the stews were closed.

After the death of Henry VIII, the Borough continued to take brazen delight in its public presentation under Elizabeth I. Brothels were no longer legal, but they had been around and under ecclesiastical jurisdiction for many hundreds of years, so they might still have been notionally tolerated by social authorities. Although prostitution in Southwark must have been pushed underground from the mid-sixteenth century, it is hard to imagine that there was not a residue of the kinds of arrangements that had sustained and supported the Southwark stews for centuries. As must have been the case all over Europe, and is still the case all over the world today, prostitution when outlawed would have started to take the form of more secretive soliciting, possibly as part of a more sordid or dangerous network of underground activities,[3] or of back-alley affairs, where a woman could earn a little bit of covert sustenance on the side, rather than be under the relatively public protection of the brothel and the diocese.

To what extent was life on the margins tolerated in Elizabethan England? Certainly royal proclamations continue to order "Vagabonds and Rogues" out of town (and Southwark is always explicitly and resignedly included in these ordinances), but the sheer number of repeated orders (not to mention social knowledge) implies that they were never particularly effective in a place known for dense poverty with a history of loose morals. The stews may have been closed down, but taverns and bear-baiting continued to offer boisterous and wanton entertainment, and, most significantly for our history (and for that of the world), theaters soon opened in the place of stews in the Southwark of the sixteenth century.

Even though the Southwark stews were a thing of the past, their reputation and the public's knowledge about them lasted well into Elizabeth's reign (and indeed endures today). Many Southwark and London court cases impugned a woman for acting as a "common whore" in the sixteenth and seventeenth centuries—such an epithet appears to be a universal insult—but evidence for the ongoing existence of brothels or explicit prostitution in the Borough is slim: it is much harder to attest to an underground institution than to one that appears legally in the books. It is very likely in this period—ironically after the Southwark stews were shut—that we hear of the Winchester Goose for the first time, emerging as an angry epithet hurled at the Bishop of Winchester in Shakespeare's *Henry VI, Part 1* (1.3.52–53),[4] thought to be written in 1591. At the conclusion of an acrimonious argument with the bishop, who furiously demands, "Gloucester, thou will answer to the pope!" the Duke of Gloucester can bear it no more, and retorts, "Winchester Goose, I cry, a rope! a rope!" The dishonorable reputation of Winchester's manor—the place where wanton women went to earn a shilling—is exposed in a literary play about the political machinations of the estate well after the practice had ended.

This oscillation between condemning the practice of prostitution and acknowledging it in English state, church, and literary history is paradoxical, to be sure. But it also reflects a deep practicality in the governance of theological and political institutions, and the use of each as a check on—or an outlet for—the weakness of the other: the church's accusation of the city's materialism reflects Southwark's disdain for the rigid and capital-driven ethos of the city, while the city dismisses the acts to which people are driven for solace. The church and the state must make do with the systems they have; the balance that has held for many centuries by the time Elizabeth I takes the throne is ripe for consolidation. In some sense, Southwark is to the city what the English church is to the English state: that against which identity battles can be publicly (and privately) played out for the sake of integrity and growth, the alternative or oppositional term or underlying structure that allows the center to flourish.

How all these agendas come under one rubric continues to surprise and sometimes delight Southwark residents, as it did their historical ancestors. The Borough has an ambivalent relationship with London, playing its strange proximity and intimate dynamic with the city in different ways, depending on whose story it is telling. While Southwark is now part of London's geographical identity, as it is part of Winchester's history, it offers itself first and foremost as a place of alterity and independence, and it revels in this unfixable personality. It was the London residence of important bishops, but it was also notably separate from London, and fiercely determined to be free from the perspective of the church, the ferrymen, and Westminster. Even the efforts to incorporate Southwark into the City of London proper—astonishingly, not successful until fifty years ago, after centuries of trying (see Johnson 1969)—appear always to have been conducted with a desire for economic control of the Borough's goings-on, on one hand, and a miserable resignation on the part of upright financial and governmental institutions that something must be done to control the looseness of the way life was lived south of the river, on the other.

The extent to which Southwark is encompassed within the City of London, its juridical authority, and its capital cachet, depends, as with every other social, practical, discursive, and legal phenomenon, on the historical moment and the particular considerations or interests at stake. Being an insider or an outsider—or the capacity to assert and articulate either the identity of a member of the mainstream crowd or that of a critical activist—similarly depends on this very self-conscious perspective. As a borough, Southwark is comfortable in its ability—indeed, relishes its capacity—to move between these disjunct positions: each has its benefits.

Southwark Cathedral

Over the river though it may have been, full of low-lifes and outlaws and whores, Southwark was also a pious place. Older than Winchester Palace is a site that claims an unbroken, active religious history for close to a millennium, since the end of the eleventh century. Southwark Cathedral, or its location, at least, if not its designation, is the heart of religious life in the Borough. This geographical—call it geomantic, if you like—concentration has been remarkably consistent, even in the face of the tumultuous religious shifts during the English and European Reformations. Southwark was still outside the City of London in the sixteenth century, but it was inside the newly reformed Church of England, under the juridical authority of the Diocese of Winchester, and had to negotiate the extreme material and social politics of the era.

The Cathedral itself has a long architectural history that dates back almost as far as the site: designated a cathedral church only in the early twentieth century (the Diocese of Southwark was established in 1905), the site was likely an Augustinian priory in the early twelfth century, and there may already have been a religious structure there for many hundreds of years. The priory appears to have been an established religious institution in use since its origin in 1106, despite numerous natural and social disruptions in its function. A fire destroyed it in 1212, but it was rebuilt later in the thirteenth century, and its structural base remains largely intact, a testament to the longevity of Christian worship at the site and the dense social and religious history of contemporary South London.

Medieval clergy lived nearby, and the Bishop of Winchester held it in good standing, using it for functions and appointing clergy as its staff.

Many community events were supported by the diocese, first through the graces of the priory and then in the parish churches that sprang up around the area to accommodate a growing population. The Bishop of Winchester was involved in local Southwark politics too, through the local parishes, and this involvement meant that Stephen Gardiner was able to help prevent the destruction of the churches in Bankside when Henry was on his Reformation rampage. By transferring the lease of the priory, by then named in honor of St. Mary Overie,[5] to the existing, small parish of St. Mary Magdalene (which dated from the thirteenth century), Southwark residents were able to take possession of the former monastery, folding it into a larger, combined parish, St. Margaret's, in 1539. The new, amalgamated church was renamed the parish of St. Saviour in 1540. Henry's actions may have closed down the priory, but he did not destroy the building (and he reputedly gave a severance pay of £100 to the acting prior).

Civic activism took hold, and clearly worked well: parish life began in this period to serve as an important social nexus, a role it still has to some degree. In 1559, the new parish established a school, the first in Southwark, St. Saviour's. And in due course, in the early eighteenth century, we know that the parish established a communal burial ground, also called St. Saviour's, which lasted for about a hundred years, and which has been resurrected as the Crossbones Graveyard today. St. Saviour's Church, as it was then named, was renovated first in the 1830s and then again in the 1890s, in preparation for its upcoming status as the new diocese's cathedral structure.

During and after the Reformation, when the Church of England was struggling to determine its doctrines, liturgies, and rites, as well as the configuration of its governance structures, the Diocese of Southwark (even though it remained under the jurisdiction of the Diocese of Winchester until 1877) was developing its own identity within the larger Anglican movement. As the Elizabethan Crown solidly encompassed the church, the bishoprics too accommodated the changing administrative structures that characterized the practices and institutions of religion in England in site-specific ways. Southwark, accustomed to being peripheral—in part by virtue of being autonomous in a very central location for many hundreds of years—fashioned itself as powerful in its marginality. Then as now, its diocese saw no reason to deviate from this seemingly positive and empowering position, and appeared to take pride in occupying an unusual stance within the church, reflecting—and with no contradiction from within—its geographical uniqueness, long asserted in Southwark's alterity, smoothly integrated with its Anglican religious loyalties.

So by the time of the Reformation, and certainly by the time of the present, Southwark has had centuries of practice in holding its own.[6] The contemporary Cathedral is a powerful locus for the demonstration of the alterity that the council is aware can be reappropriated to stand it in ironically good stead: being over the river is a unique location that might as well be used to its greatest advantage. Its website welcome proudly proclaims:

> Southwark Cathedral is the oldest cathedral church building in London, and archaeological evidence shows there was Roman pagan worship here well before that. Significantly, Southwark stands at the oldest crossing point of the tidal Thames at what was the only entrance to the City of London across the river for many centuries. It is not only a place of worship but also of hospitality to every kind of person: princes and paupers, prelates and prostitutes, poets, playwrights, prisoners and patients have all found refuge here. The tradition continues in modern ways. . . . [T]he congregations reflect the age, ethnic, gender, sexual orientation and status diversities of a comprehensive world-class capital city; thus the variety of past centuries is multiplied and magnified many times over.[7]

In the twenty-first century, Southwark Cathedral is a place where women or homosexuals might be priests; indeed, it was the first diocese to appoint an openly gay priest, to much controversy, but again Southwark held fast.

Similarly, in a community spirit—as well as in a radical one—plays verging on the irreverent might be performed on the Cathedral floor. The Cathedral (which bills itself as an "inclusive" place of "radical love") was happy to stage John Constable's explicit and challenging play, *The Southwark Mysteries* (1999), which directly questions the historical role of the bishop in supporting prostitution. In this context, the Cathedral and the activist shared the status of other. We recognize the other in the other: Southwark is outside the City of London and the jurisdiction of Westminster, just as the Goose is outside the rest of the flock, and the Crow is outside the bounds of conventional society, teetering on the limits of acceptable behavior (never mind representation) with what he aims to describe and depict. Here we have a case where unusual alliances create different kinds of social (and performative) movements: strange bedfellows, or unholy allies, each with their own cast within contemporary cultural circles and each drawing on their own networks, forge together, even though they might have different ends or varied purposes in mind.

Theater and Performance in Bankside

Southwark's identity is one that is—and has always been—proud of its alterity: if you have the highest number of sexually experienced and available women around, the most fun to be had in bear-baiting, and the greatest playwright that has ever lived, you may as well enjoy your status, other as it may be. These phenomena play off each other, of course: an atmosphere of unruliness enables further lawlessness or even reckless criminality (Johnson 1969:70) and, in due course, a reputation for such, which only cultivates it further. Southwark (and the city, too) knew that it was a place where anything goes. By the end of the sixteenth century, after numerous attempts to clean up the streets and tame the criminal rowdiness for which Southwark was famous, the Borough was a natural (in the cultural sense) site for the emergence of theatrical performance, where all that unrestrained conduct could give itself over to the dense festival atmosphere of early modern spectacle (Duncan-Jones 2010 [2001]:4).

Our ritual takes place around the corner from one of the most famous locations for performance in the history not only of England but of the world. By the late sixteenth century, Bankside had become a place of theaters, or playhouses (rather than one of brothels); theater in Bankside and beyond has been as central—and as controversial—to the vibrant cultural life of the Borough as prostitution was before it. Southwark's sauciness was hardly rooted out, but it emerged in a (more) acceptable format, where audiences could enjoy publicly racy language instead of publicly racy behavior. Queen Elizabeth was convinced to close the theaters only on occasions of plague, ostensibly for the sake of maintaining public health;[8] the crowded theaters in

Bankside were risky in times of easily contractable infection (although Johnson suggests that the real reason her advisers advocated such closures was to control the "excited crowd" that an audience of theatergoers could become [Johnson 1969:224–225]). Any place people gathered in dense, usually poor settings was a place that was targeted for plague prevention, but more generally for disorderly behavior.

The Bankside of the very late sixteenth and early seventeenth centuries, where William Shakespeare's plays were produced for the first time, would support the controversial demographic theory that a poor, urban environment, where there is not a lot to go around, means that people may become more creative than ever, and that we may be inspired to find new ways of surviving—and of expressing the exigencies of that survival. Conversely, it could be argued that the economic prosperity that London and its environs—England at large—experienced under the rule of Queen Elizabeth I would support a thriving creativity: there was room to maneuver. Either way, this was a time of great literature coming out of England, and particularly the Midlands, where Shakespeare was born (Duncan-Jones 2010 [2001]:3–8). Shakespeare's birth and death days, not really known, are conventionally celebrated on April 23, St. George's Day, based on the recorded dates of his christening (April 26, 1564) and his burial (April 25, 1616). Shakespeare's biographers have long been willing to conflate the patron saint of England with the patron saint of literature.

Just north of Redcross Way, Shakespeare's own Globe Theatre, opened in 1599, was one of four in the neighborhood (along with the Swan, the Rose, and the Hope). The Globe was loved in Shakespeare's time for some reasons we can well imagine—the English language was brought to new heights onstage, and Shakespeare's plays are one of the literary wonders of the world—and for some we cannot: the experience of play watching must have been very different from the way we view theater today. "In Shakespeare's Globe, there was no proscenium arch, no artificial lighting. Plays were performed by daylight in the afternoon. The crowded auditorium [was] not dark. Watching Shakespeare in his own time would have been a communal experience. . . . The Elizabethan theatregoer always [saw] the faces of his or her fellow audience members" (Bate 1997:272). Even more than today, a Shakespearean performance was a public event.

Shakespeare's *Henry VI, Part 1* was performed in Southwark before the Globe went up; it was staged at the Rose in 1592. It was "a triumphant success, drawing some ten thousand spectators" (Bate 1997:17), and it very likely established his career. Central to the play is a rousing, ongoing verbal duel between the Duke of Gloucester and the Bishop of Winchester, who is repeatedly mocked for having been party to the sins of the flesh in the manor in which the play was performed. It goes like this:

BISHOP OF WINCHESTER Gloucester, whate'er we like, thou art protector
And lookest to command the prince and realm.
Thy wife is proud; she holdeth thee in awe,
More than God or religious churchmen may.

DUKE OF GLOUCESTER Name not religion, for thou lovest the flesh,
And ne'er throughout the year to church thou go'st
Except it be to pray against thy foes. (1.1.37–43)

The Bishop of Winchester is accused of not being sufficiently religious, and of caring too much about his political and financial position. Their rivalry continues and becomes more vitriolic, such that two scenes later, in their attempt to evict each other, we come upon our reference to the whores and, a little further into the argument, to the Goose:

DUKE OF GLOUCESTER Peel'd priest, dost thou command me to be shut out?

BISHOP OF WINCHESTER I do, thou most usurping proditor,
And not protector, of the king or realm.

DUKE OF GLOUCESTER Stand back, thou manifest conspirator,
Thou that contrivest to murder our dead lord;
Thou that givest whores indulgences to sin:
I'll canvass thee in thy broad cardinal's hat,
If thou proceed in this thy insolence. (1.3.30–37)

With this set of insults being hurled back and forth, when the duke calls the bishop, a few lines later (53), a "Winchester goose," it looks to be the bishop himself, not the prostitute, who is the Goose. Either way, the ecclesiastical authority of the Borough is the object of the playwright's satire, and Winchester is the butt of the joke, the Goose who makes a buck from the passions of men. Both the bishop and the whore are in on it, in one sense, although one does so bodily and the other from the vantage point of power.[9]

The stews may have been shut and the Geese may have flown by the time Shakespeare rises to fame, but his capacity to tell of the plight of the human soul soars during this period. *Henry VI* introduces us to the Winchester Geese—or Goose, rather, although it is likely hurled at the bishop, not at his flock; *Henry IV* and *Richard II* introduce us to the stews.[10] *Henry V*, the play that glorifies the king's battles against the Continent—but with tacit allusions to Elizabeth—was written around 1599, and was almost certainly performed at the Globe: the great playwright's exploration of the formation of England as a nation (however ambivalently he viewed patriotism; see Bate 1997:205) was presented at one of its most irreverent locations. Life was still on the streets, and in the playhouses and taverns, if not in the brothels.

Although the Globe was destroyed by Puritans in the mid-seventeenth century—playhouses sponsored too much bawdy behavior and unbecoming spectacle to be allowed to continue in a repressive era—the theatrical legacy remained strong in England, and particularly in Southwark. Despite renewed challenges in the also prudish Victorian nineteenth century, Southwark prevailed as one of the hearts of the theatrical world. In 1818, the Old Vic opened its doors as the Royal Coburg Theatre; over the course of the nineteenth century, the theater was opened, closed, renamed, and refashioned in practically as many ways as the public and the patrons would allow. It was designed for the "nobility and gentry" but, as if parroting a local epithet, in 1831, the performer Edmund Kean critiques his audience as "a set of ignorant, unmitigated brutes."[11] Such commentary refers to Southwark audiences in a way that is reminiscent of the way nobles or elites might have referred to the bear-baiting rings of the Elizabethan Borough—it was still Southwark, after all.

By the end of the nineteenth century, Victorian social mores—perhaps the logical extensions of the Reformation era's symbolic structures of gender—were determined to somehow keep the theater open without the associations of lowliness. It was no longer called a theater, but rather a music hall and a few years later a coffee tavern, and its managers asserted its decency. The theater reclaimed its status as such in 1912, when it obtained a license for performance; in 1914, the Old Vic began restaging the plays of Shakespeare. In the neighborhood if not at the theater where Shakespearean productions were originally written and performed, the Old Vic became renowned over the course of the twentieth century as one of the London locations for the world's greatest theater, with Laurence Olivier, Alec Guinness, and Judi Dench performing the Bard's greatest roles. All were knighted for their performances, that is, for their capacities to evoke a world outside a spectator's own that is still, somehow, entirely recognizable. In the twenty-first century, run by artistic director Kevin Spacey, the Old Vic sponsored programs for disadvantaged youth from London's poorest neighborhoods, with the intention of evoking for them the transcendent quality of theater, that capacity to transport someone beyond him- or herself.

Connotations of theater as a lowly art form were certainly Victorian, as is reflected in the history of the Old Vic, but they also predated their queenly namesake by several centuries. Theater in sixteenth- and seventeenth-century Southwark was not an elite institution where Hollywood directors would have made world headlines: it was a place of low-lifes who told their stories on stage, well suited to the sullied environs of Bankside. That half a millennium later, theater has become a way of uplifting young members of disadvantaged London communities shows that any institution can occupy various ranks on the totem pole, depending on the historical moment. The Globe was refurbished in the 1990s as part of the Borough's continuing efforts to rejuvenate—or gentrify, depending on your perspective—the neighborhood: as we have seen, Borough Market, the Tate Modern, and the South Bank were all regilded, and Bankside's most famous legacy, the Globe, was reopened for performance purposes in 1997, in time for the four-hundredth anniversary of its founding in 1999. Cultural institutions reflect their surroundings and the politics of those places; they feature and they also perpetuate symbolic worlds that create people's sense of who and where they are, where they come from, and what they aspire to. Like religion, theater is a place where people go to get outside themselves or, equally, to turn inward, experiencing firsthand the complexities of human emotion and experience, as narrated or mediated on stage, and as interpreted within.

Performance is a way to understand all these modes of being: social practice in a dense urban setting, theatrical extravaganzas or spectacles, and ritual events. All are designed to evoke emotion in the individual spectator or practitioner, for the sake of learning how to negotiate the complex exigencies of social existence. Performance is that practice which at its most effective brings the spectators along with the performers into other worlds, recognizable but distinct from the one they inhabited before the performance started. As Shakespeare put it, "all the world's a stage," and all the world are "players." He knew how to say, poetically, that a play (or indeed, perhaps, a ritual) is separated out from everyday activity—it is a set-apart and on-display way of representing human action and interaction.

Contemporary Artistic Performance: *The Southwark Mysteries*

The late twentieth-century London theater incorporated this proud legacy, but it also moved in other directions. For his whole adult life, John Constable has been performing art that challenges the spheres of human consciousness and the assumed social stabilities that mask its depth. From avant-garde theater in North London in the 1960s under the famous and cultic name of The Warp to an ecumenical tale of the affair between Mary Magdalene and Jesus performed in Southwark Cathedral first in 2000 and then again in 2010, John's artistic intention as both performer and playwright has been to expand the minds of his audience about other realms of possibility. These alternative views are not catastrophic or destabilizing; if seen in the right spirit, they are simply innovative, and they can unlock new doors or suggest new modes of living to people or communities who need a fresh perspective on old and stale problems. Performing a play that invokes both Christian and anti-Christian themes inside the Southwark Cathedral to an audience of hundreds was one high point of his career; the monthly reiteration of the tale to a smaller, more contained group of twenty-five or thirty on the back streets of Southwark is a performance of another kind, a ritual that creates a homegrown church in a different configuration.

John Constable's respective performances—as playwright and as ritualist—mirror each other. Each variably takes on a Protestant and a secular—or, perhaps more accurately, an ecumenical—tone, invoking an open-hearted spirit, naming the saints of inspiration (although they may not be limited to those of the Western world), inviting reflection and memory, and feeling the living legacy of the dead. Neither performance claims itself as religious, however: one expressly calls itself a ritual without being a religion, and the other is quite clearly a play. Both serve a social role, and they operate in tandem for that goal: social change is the transcendent forum here.

The story of the Winchester Geese can be told within a Christian cast, one that hopes for redemption in the spirit of pity, or within a universal one, whereby the female spirits at Crossbones are allied with Egyptian goddesses in the story of Isis, Brazilian religions of the Amazon, pagan spiritual goddesses, and the Sino-Japanese Kuan Yin to engender awareness, awakening, fertility, and strength. By holding the story as a constant, the medium may shift, from ritual performance to theatrical performance, and from an activist's or artist's supposedly secular tale to a Christian narrative one, all of which tell the story of the Winchester Geese and the paradoxical relationship of prostitutes to the social order in medieval Bankside. In either guise—whether it is classified as a ritual or as a play—it is hoped that the performance elicits among its participants and its audience a deeper awareness of the inequities of history.

The Southwark Mysteries is the play (rather than the ritual) that narrates the experience of the vision and the subsequent revelation of the story of the Goose to John Crow. It is John Constable's story about himself, at the scale of the spectacle rather than the one of intimacy at Redcross Way. It is a sassy script, never shying away from a lewd double entendre or the opportunity to remind the players and the audience that humans struggle with desires of the flesh, and with its consequences. In this emphasis—and in the setting of a church—it comes across as a Christian play, and its performance in Southwark Cathedral is not inconsistent with the ritual's sometimes defiant and critical message.

In a scene entitled "The Fall," the Goose tells Cromwell:

GOOSE

> Over me and my John Crow
> You have no authority.
> I call upon my Bishop
> As defender of my liberty. (Constable 1999:150)

Cromwell then engages in active dispute with the Bishop of Winchester:

CROMWELL	Ha! Where is the Bishop that would own this whore?

The bishop is up to the challenge, and when he shows up, the two begin a verbal theological skirmish:

CROMWELL	Ha! Methinks it is a strange Divinity That with the stews has such affinity.
BISHOP OF WINCHESTER	My God seeks to parlay With this world's imperfection. And there it is, this Goose enjoys Her Bishop's protection. Here is no Law but the Law of Winchester.
CROMWELL	Since you honour not God's Law Here is my Law of Westminster. (Constable 1999: 150)

Cromwell then uncovers the bishop to become, temporarily, Will Shagspur, the Elizabethan playwright (Constable 1999:150–151); the Shakespearean inspiration is made explicit in this latter-day Bankside performance. The Bishop of Winchester and William Shakespeare are, just for a moment, interchangeable in their historical-geographical consonance and their shared ability to understand the subtleties of the human condition, such that the story of the Goose may be told, and thereafter sustained.

Just as Southwark now inhabits a position within London yet remains conscious and proud of its history of alterity, Constable's play was performed inside Southwark Cathedral even as it critiqued the Anglican church for what it claimed was hypocrisy. Through the iconic figure of the Goose, *The Southwark Mysteries* plays out how the church upholds hierarchy: ideological mores may be grounded in core Christian tenets—pity, mercy, and the perennial possibility of universal redemption—but they create an exclusionary world as well. Such a worldview not only observes social difference, and pities those who are at the bottom (which, the play suggests, cannot be sustained as a moral stance if it comes with judgment or denigration), but is complicit with the production of inequality.

We are not equal in death, the Goose reminds us, as we were not equal in life. In John Crow's mystical vision, he was inspired by the

Goose to break all bonds with a differentiated social reality that was seemingly natural. The Winchester Geese stand in for those social differences, and he uses their tale to rally a call to collective justice. *The Southwark Mysteries*, along with the monthly ritual, is an artistic performance, but it is also a social one, told in the hope that its revelation might reverse historical wrongs. The playwright risks his loyalties to the Anglican church when he airs its dirty laundry in public (and represents simulated intercourse between Jesus and Mary Magdalene on the Cathedral floor to drive the point home, for example), but he will not keep silent about the injustices that social rankings inevitably produce. And he is seemingly rewarded for his bravery and even for his choice to expose a theological and historical paradox: such socially motivated performance would not be accepted by everyone, but it is lauded by this church. Southwark, with its history of alterity, chooses to join forces with him to reveal and to undo exclusivism.

That actors and prostitutes in Southwark occupy equivalent symbolic status is part of the message of *The Southwark Mysteries*: Southwark is accustomed to the many ways of outcasts and is willing to welcome them nonetheless.[12] In Constable's drama, the players sing:

> Now All The World Knows
> And The World May Abhor
> But The World cannot unmake Poetry:
> God's Actor is bedfellow
> Here with God's Whore
> In the Sacred Heart of God's Liberty.
> (Constable 1999:151)

The play ends with a resounding cry from the entire company: "*To Southwark!*"

To be public, as performer or prostitute, is to work with emotion in the social realm, displaying what is more prudently thought of as contained within the modest bounds of family, household, or individual person. In its alterity, Southwark is a place of public opprobrium, but over time, and with the strength gained from gradual geographic consolidation (first in itself as a borough and then within the City of London), it has learned to embrace this iconoclastic status with relish. In being known as the place of difference, the underdog Borough can continue to thrive, whatever untoward group or performance may present itself. From prostitutes to actors to irreverent ritualists, Southwark embraces the performance of alterity as a value in itself: to demonstrate otherness is a reminder to London, to the north bank, to England, and to the world that beauty, art, compassion, and human emotion come in all forms and can be conveyed in more ways than the mainstream ever could dream of.

Social Performance

What kinds of performances are permitted where, and for what historical reasons? What is interesting in our case is how, until the sixteenth century, Bankside prostitutes were not discouraged from performing their roles as public women, but required to: one of the caveats of being a sex worker in a stew was the visible proclamation of one's station. If a woman's sexuality was public, all the world had to know. With the advent of Protestantism, Bankside performances became theatrical ones, with the erection of public theaters (to make up for the closure of public brothels). If you could not live the risqué life, you could watch it on stage: entertainment became abstracted, perhaps, not unlike the commodity market.

Whatever we make of sex work and its status or moral acceptability in the Christian church, it is somewhat surprising to see and to hear an explicit discussion of sexuality and prostitution in a cathedral, even in a cast that counts armies of red cross–bearing nurses and hard hat–wearing Jubilee Line extension construction workers (not to mention enormous choirs of local schoolchildren) among its number. There is a paradox on display here: on one hand, we know we are seeing something illicit in the context of a Christian society; on the other, we know that the representation has been endorsed by the church since we are seeing it in an Anglican cathedral. Challenging representations of the history and mythology of Christianity are not foreign to the church: think of the theatrical musicals *Jesus Christ Superstar* and *Joseph and the Technicolor Dreamcoat*, both of which aired on Broadway and in the West End in the 1970s and '80s. None of these plays question the fundamental premises of Christianity, and they can be supported by the church accordingly. In the case of *The Southwark Mysteries*, the Cathedral made the decision that such a performance could be staged in a house of Christian worship, and determined that the representation of sexual love between Jesus and a Winchester Goose was not anathema to the Christian message, just as, many centuries ago, the bishop's manor made the determination that supporting a brothel economy was not inconsistent with Christian ethics. On the three evenings that the play was performed in April 2010, the Cathedral even put its regular sign outside its doors, so as to quieten passersby: "SHHHH: There is worship going on within."

Indeed, Christianity is famous for being able to handle—and weigh—multiple opinions, and for thriving because passionate views may be held in so many varying casts by so many divergent parties, in the modern as well as the historical world (see Cannell 2006; Woodhead 2002). Rigorous debate is part of Anglican history; the tradition has encouraged disciplined learning and practiced oratorical skill among its scholars and clergy, who have always been supported by the English church. And whether it is arguing for a religious or a secular cause, or from a religious or secular ground, English theater and literature are known the world over for the beauty, rhythm, nuance, and tone of their language, and for their subtle yet meaningful commentaries on the human heart. To argue a case or a passionate cause in eloquent English (and to do so in received pronunciation or, now, in any dialect or accent, as we genuinely become more accepting of class) is to slay—or at least to inspire—the attuned listener. If the tale told is one of sexual love, well, so much the better: such is the story of the human race.

Is the performance of such a play inside an institution such as the Cathedral a resolution between a marginal activist group and the larger social structure it critiques? Potentially. Certainly, there is a temporal distance from the medieval church that is explicitly criticized in the play. Both play and ritual interrogate the paradox symbolically, and thus leave open the possibility—indeed the hope—that institutions may change. Much as it may be the perpetrator of exclusion, the church may be the answer to social suffering. But there is no doubt that the play intends also to be a thorn in the side of the church (and, paradoxically, Southwark Cathedral likes it that way). It is not impossible to occupy both positions at the same time: a theology of inclusion may precisely obscure a history of hierarchy. Exposing such a contradiction—both sides of the institution of the Christian church—is the intent of the ritualists, and the point of the play.

As a play, *The Southwark Mysteries* has been performed much less frequently (twice, to be precise) than the ritual that also tells the tale (more than a hundred renditions, or monthly for more than a decade). (*The Southwark Mysteries* has also registered as a community organization, "offering creative ways for people to interact with their inner-city environment," as its publicity literature states.) The drama's rareness in this instance contrasts with the regularity of the ritual. Who should be able to tell the story? To hear it? Moving into the sphere of religion, should it be secret or esoteric knowledge, or should it be something open and available to the masses? Must the mythic tale be mediated, and if so, by whom? There are disagreements on these points from within the ritual group, in particular whether the play should be performed inside the Cathedral at all. One member of the regular gathering—someone who had spent decades traveling the world selling fake advertisements for what he claimed would be an international telex directory and who, upon his return to his native England, found his love of all things strange in this South London group—thought it was much too mainstream to tell the Southwark story from inside the church. His advice was that the play should be performed not every decade in the Cathedral but every year outside of it.

When the play is performed in the church, there is resolution—in the sense that the Goose is redeemed by virtue of having loved Jesus. His love for her in the form of Mary Magdalene reminds us that the sex worker too is pardonable. There is no eternal sin; we are all capable of redemption. Titillating though the drama may be, it is not hard to understand how the Cathedral would agree to the staging of a play that shows how Satan is vanquished by Jesus—as explicit as it is, this is a religious tale and one that is locally suitable. It is clever and irreverent: someone in the play has to remind YAHWEH, who is happy to play the lead, as he puts it, that these are the *Southwark* mysteries (Constable 1999:143). But would the play have been performed in the Cathedral if Mary Magdalene/Goose had not been redeemed, that is, if she had remained a Winchester Goose, rather than a "penitent whore" (Warner 1990 [1976]:224–235)? The medieval church spent a good deal of time considering how best to redeem whores (including by marrying upright men), and even our ordinances make mention of the women who live by their body but who wish to leave the trade. But not all of them do. In the Cathedral, the Goose is redeemed; in the ritual she is not, necessarily. The tale is the same, but not quite.

Contemporary Ritual Performance: Art, Religion, Culture

The question of performance brings us back to the analysis of ritual. Are the features of artistic performance the same as those of ritual performance? Like shamanism, theater and ritual appear to be parallel kinds of performance cross-culturally. Toffin (2010) argues for their equivalence in Newar dance-drama. Ward (1979) points out the comparable social role of actors in Chinese ritual drama and Elizabethan theater (low in both cases). Geertz (1973) shows us how the performance of a cockfight is ritual action that serves to bind a community, and consciously—even, sometimes, self-consciously—"display" a culture to itself.

Certainly for our ritualist-playwright, John Crow/Constable, "ritual is closer to art than to religion." Ritual performance and artistic performance are linked in the ways they demand an analysis of representation and display, and the relations between content and form—plot and narrative—they imply. Theater reflects human life and priorities, and if people perform stylized actions (whether or not they are called ritualized actions) with a particular set of goals or orientations (call it worldview and ethos, after Geertz), the demonstration of these moods will be religious, much as it will—or can—be political. Whether it is for amusement or for magic, the practices of performance will effect a mood swing, a social change, the next dramatic plateau from which to begin new action. The point of a ritual, much as the effect of a good play, is to bring about a semantic—or, better, an emotional—shift in the nuance and significance of meaning for those who participate. An effective ritual will adjust the resonance of harmonies in an individual's or a collective's social order, tuning the strings of the social orchestra ever so subtly so as to restore or redirect whatever imbalances were pulling them in the wrong direction or swelling them in such a way that their sounds were distorted.

Ritual is necessarily performative, or public, in the sense that, for it to come into being, it has to be displayed. This is not necessarily a question of making an action public (although if a deity may be thought to be an audience, it may be): rituals are often performed in private.[13] The performance of ritual is based upon the method—and perhaps the very base modality—of display, what Clifford Geertz means when he writes that "culture is public because meaning is" (1973:12). By putting a sequence—of narrative, of action, of theater—on show, we (the audience and also the performers; the distinction is not of the utmost importance here) see who we are and how we choose to represent ourselves.

What links ritual and theater is thus this double layer of consciousness, inherent in what everyone knows is performance. We (the players and the audience, the ritual actors and the ritual observers) identify with the scene, and yet we know that we are separate. Performance (theater and ritual) is effective precisely because we know there is—must be—at once a sameness, a shared or common ground, in the collective experience, even as there are those differences that mark how each of us responds to the event as an individual. A single audience member, as one viewer, knows that he or she is touched or affected or implicated for all the reasons that his or her world of experience reflects. Consciously or unconsciously, most viewers know that they are not being directly referred to in public performance, which by definition must touch others whose lived experience overlaps with but will also necessarily diverge from their own. And yet we may feel more connected with our fellow audience members or participants in the shared recognition that what is being represented is commonly known, or understood, as well as collectively experienced. It is not critical for these processes to be conscious: the action—performance, in this instance, either ritual or artistic—works even unconsciously.

Similarly, or in parallel, ritual or performative time acts both as a distinct and unrepeatable feature of a particular performance, and as a template, that which may come around again and again, the next time the ritual or the play is on show. Performance—of either the theatrical or the ritual variety—delivers its effect through the double-edged quality of being ephemeral: it is experienced at a particular moment in time, and yet it is replicable, or its structures are. Presence is power in this way, but latent capacity is in some sense no less palpable: the story only need be brought to the surface to be told. There will be some elements that are inherently recognizable, but always others that are fresh. It is this dialogue that makes performance meaningful, and transformative, and worth repeating in the first place.

If Geertz is right, ritual—the performance of a practice—is the same, symbolically, as the performance of a text, and can be read as such. The work of analyzing culture is not about cataloging the detail of what natives think; it is about understanding the mechanisms of social process, through individual and collective variants, rooted in history above all. It is embodied, not discursive, but it counts. That performance can take the form of either something called theater or something called ritual means that the two will sometimes overlap and sometimes not. Some theater is magical, and some ritual is dull.

The question of social performance rounds out the issue here, insofar as it will always be political. On one hand, activism relies on a certain presentation of history. But one need not be an activist to rely on the conventions of social performance to aid others in understanding what kind of person, or what class of society, or what political or religious affiliations or allegiances one holds or promotes. In any setting, performing in accordance with social convention is often the criterion for inclusion, while a performance that defies cultural convention is very likely to result in dismissal or exclusion from those social orders—unless, of course, the performance of defiance is the cultural order of the day.

Coda: Ritual Theory

It is in ritual's guise as performance that anthropologists know it best. From Turner to Humphrey and Laidlaw, interpreted through Bell, in the methods and accounts of ethnography in Africa from Leinhardt and Evans-Pritchard to the textualists in India, Heesterman and Staal, we can see that in the stories we tell ourselves, human social identities are revealed—and produced. Ever since the early twentieth century, when Arnold van Gennep (1960 [1909]) pushed our collective scholarly minds past a Frazerian compendium of rituals, we have wondered what rituals can do, and how it is that they are able to bring about their material aims. That ritual is constituted through multiple layers of representation—as hinted at in Durkheim's (1995 [1912]) wonderful masterpiece on religious life—gives us the key to the analysis, as well as the tools for the specific analytics at work in any given society.

In ritual, the practices conducted by human communities are contained; they are performed to remind us—as individuals and as collectives—who we are and the rules by which we are meant to live. Philosophers have written extensively on the powers of discourse to construct human reality and social worlds (see especially Butler 1993); ritual theory rather shows us that practice speaks louder than words. To make too fine a point of whether discursive category or behavioral practice is the more instrumental between the two in the production of collective life would be to misunderstand how intermingled they are and must be: the speech act was the original performance (Saussure 2013 [1916]; on Vedic ritual, see also Staal 1989).

Catherine Bell's (1992) exposition of ritual correctly focuses on the relation between subject and object, but she tends to place this dialogue as parallel with that between observer and observed. Drawing from the anthropology of ritual, she reads Turner's, Singer's, and Geertz's interpretations of performance as instructing the relationship between anthropological analyst and informant ritualist. This relationship personifies the dichotomy between thought and action: the anthropologist's thought cognizes the religious practitioner's action.

A similar or analogous dichotomy is at work in the religious studies language that differentiates the insider's view from the outsider's view as two primary ways of interpreting religion. Either one is of the religion (and assumed to be experiencing it) or one is studying it (and assumed not to be of it): in this dichotomy is the presumption that one may occupy only one of those positions. Participant-observation is more nuanced than the insider-outsider construction allows: the anthropologist is not necessarily the analytical outsider to the informant's insider experience. Part of ethnography requires that an analyst interrogates the effects of a ritual on him- or herself, as a participant in the group. Participation and observation go hand in hand—they oscillate—in order to establish the right balance between extrinsic and intrinsic knowledge, or between knowledge based on intellect and knowledge based on experience, or between a discursive or semantic understanding and an embodied one.

Bell's critique that incorporating performance theory into our understanding of ritual has meant a preponderance of distinctions drawn between observer and participant is nonetheless well taken, as is, even more incisively, her comment that such theories have tended to assume an integration rather than an exaggeration of the discursive and the practical spheres or modes of being. Her most compelling critique is that the anthropology of ritual has simply displaced the question of efficacy with that of (cognitive) meaning:

> [W]hen performance theory attempts to explain [ritual] communication it must fall back on ritual activity as depicting, modelling, enacting, or dramatizing what are seen as prior conceptual ideas and values. The meaningfulness of ritual that such interpretations attempt to explicate has nothing to do with the efficacy that the ritual acts are thought to have by those who perform them. The idiom of communication through symbolic acts may be a corrective to the notion of magic, but it does little to convey what these acts mean to those involved in them. (Bell 1992:43)

In a sense the answer to the mystery of ritual is contained in Bell's own critique: the efficacy of ritual lies in its evocation of (and capacity to display) meaning. In showing us—performers, participants, observers, audiences, anthropologists, and ritualists alike—who we are, by virtue of what we are doing, and by making us notice it, ritual can effect a shift in our consciousness, however deep and however long-lasting. Ritual effects may be superficial and may be temporary, but they also may be deepened or instantiated over time, with the practice that repeated performance implies. As we have seen, it is in this adjustment of collective meaning through practice or action that ritual achieves its efficacy.

Bell's worry is that the meaning analysists seek is preexistent not contested, or that it occurs in fixed boundaries or spheres, individually or collectively: "The interpretive endeavour requires, and assumes, that activity encodes something. . . . [T]he assumed existence of such a 'something,' the latent meaning of the act, once again devalues the action itself, making it a second-stage representation of prior values" (1992:45). But her fears may be unfounded. If the efficacy of ritual lies in its capacity for semantic shift—that is, if the action of the ritual is to direct us to a potential change in or even evacuation of meaning—the action of the ritual takes place at a symbolic level, and "the latent meaning" of the act is that which is the focus. Meaning takes center stage, and doesn't have to hide in the wings: a ritual is designed to play with—adjust, tweak—the meaning of whatever it is about, and in telling us of its intention, it exposes its fluidity. The action succeeds.

The oscillation of Southwark as it has battled the city—a taunting or teasing invitation to participate in its service economies as it refuses to hand over control—chimes with this oscillation of ritual and performance, where we recognize ourselves as individuals and in the other. Both are places where we know we have to do a double act. We are ourselves and each other at once: we understand—in our beings, if not conceptually (although perhaps that too)—that we are both unique and distinguished from one another, on one hand, and just another manifestation of humanity, equivalent, on the other. Southwark is across the river, but in the same boat, aligned with the city or in opposition as is appropriate for the case. We are the outcasts and also striving to fit in, all at once.

All these constructions assume that the dialogical relationship in cognition is between self and other. But the shaman reminds us that this dialogue can also take place between two poles of the self: between the Goose and the Crow, for example, the outcast and the popular activist. Just as performance invokes repetition and unique presence at once, it represents ourselves in all our capacities and everyone else, in all their capacities, in the same breath. John's ritual reminds us that we have qualities that others in history have had, and that are in some sense perennial; this perspective allows us to gain some distance from our own ego-bound emotions, even as we are drawn in because something is touched within.

The Winchester Goose is a Shakespearean innovation. But did he mean the whore (as we do now), or the churchman—the bishop himself? Is not one implicated in the other—the Shakespearean epithet meaning the Goose who is shown to live in a paradox of hierarchy? They are both part of the history of the Geese, or a diachronic genealogy and a longitudinal etymology for our collective consciousness as the ground of culture. Ritual is the making explicit, rendering literal—bringing to public awareness what is there already—the currents that form us as if from beneath the ground.

John Constable

❀ *Conclusion*

MAKING THE PRESENT

> What sets the cockfight apart from the ordinary course of life, lifts it from the realm of everyday practical affairs, and surrounds it with an aura of enlarged importance is not, as functionalist sociology would have it, that it reinforces status discriminations (such reinforcement is hardly necessary in a society where every act proclaims them), but that it provides a metasocial commentary upon the whole matter of assorting human beings into fixed hierarchical ranks and then organizing the major part of collective existence around that assortment. Its function, if you want to call it that, is interpretive: it is a Balinese reading of Balinese experience; a story they tell themselves about themselves.
>
> Clifford Geertz, "Deep Play: Notes on the Balinese Cockfight" (1972)

The way people construct themselves—and are constructed by others—takes place against the larger discursive frame or backdrop that is culture. Or better, groups construct themselves and others against historical frames that produce culture in the present, and that simultaneously reconstruct the events of the past. That is to say: our narratives about the past explain the way we find ourselves circumscribed in the present. History is constructed to explain the present; historical trajectories determine the cultural or symbolic terms of engagement through which group identities are articulated and against which they are defined. These are fluid processes, as we have known since Weber, neither fixed in outcome nor random in occurrence nor overdetermined at any point. We are both ourselves as individuals and part of constellations that are historically charged and that constitute cultural flows deeper and longer than we tend to remember or imagine.

When we describe social change as a dynamic set of circumstances, we always consider both the roles of individuals and the human tendency toward sociality. Human action produces narrative, too, and narrative has its own effects—the combination of practice and discourse produces reality. That is, discourse and praxis each play a role, much as individuals and groups do. Ritual is the oscillation between these poles, the capacity to encompass dyads in the overall process of human social maneuvering. Here lies the pendulum theory of social change: if social processes are not fixed or static, but rather in motion and dynamic, both individual and group identities are articulated against a larger frame that casts light (and that is directed by the agents in question) on the particular story that needs to be told. The same events may be cast in different ways; origin myths are reconfigured to explain the trajectory or path that takes us to where we are now, and that reorients the group back toward the point from which it narrates its history.

Such is not the story of the analyst, however. Human beings are sometimes aware of these maneuverings, these machinations. Human consciousness is more than capable of—indeed, it is arguably uniquely capable of—seeing the paradox between acting as an individual agent at a particular moment in time for the sake of a specific end, and acting as a member of the human race, for the sake of a subgroup's particular ends and objectives, at a more or less random moment in time. These puzzles and paradoxes constitute the reflective capacity of human thought, the mystery of the human existence into which we are thrust, regardless of our culture or our historical moment. And yet it shall never be solved—and so we act as best we can, within the circumstances and the cultural frames in which we find ourselves. The best we can do is remember our past, and—perhaps more importantly still—recall our present. There is no pure history, much as there is no single view of the present. Remembering both aspects of this temporal axis—the oscillation between past and present, and the way they construct or reconstruct each other—is the very core of the human condition, the kernel of ritual, and it mirrors our alternation between a consciousness of ourselves as agents in the present and a consciousness of ourselves as human beings across time.

So what are our ritualists calling for? What do their actions invite, or request? In short, they call us back to a time—and to a kind of market—before the Reformation and before the era of global commercial expansionism began in earnest. As Max Weber, whose teachings on social process have guided this analytical enterprise, wrote at the beginning of the twentieth century in his analysis of the growth of capital, "Since asceticism undertook to remodel the world and to work out its ideals in the world [here he is referring to the Reformation], material goods have gained an increasing and finally an inexorable power over the lives of men as at no previous period in history" (1985 [1930]:181). We have moved further still, past even those commodities (which Weber, unaware, was right to put in gendered terms), into forms of capital that are not limited to either material bodies or material objects.

It is this trajectory that our ritualists resist. Without wanting to put "the spirit of religious asceticism" back into its Weberian cage, John Constable's flock wants to challenge the contemporary formation of "victorious capitalism" (Weber 1985 [1930]:181). Let us be present in local formations, they say. Let our forms of exchange take place with—even be constituted by—embodied transactions. Let the exchange of commodities in virtual, global, absent, and digitized modes take a back seat to real human presence, action, and vitality. Let us claim our neighborhoods, our alliances, our bodies, and our roles as active human beings, in defiance of corporate ideologies and interests. They invoke a human economy, not a commercial one, to use the distinction David Graeber offers (2011:158).[1] The medieval Bankside sex worker uncovers this past, this mode, this earlier way of considering bodies and exchange and money: even on the lowest social notch of all, she calls for a return to a more embodied era. She—her body, her livelihood—is our totem.

Anti-Capital

Resistance to capitalist structures is not the explicit message of our ritualists, but the job of the cultural analyst is to penetrate the narrative, and ask what is going on beneath the surface. What motivates the action? What unstated forces drive the pulse of the events and the stories we see and hear at the Memorial Gates every month?

First, capitalism and its discontents are integral to the world that is contemporary London, one of the financial centers of the globe. In the years during which this book was researched and written, the Shard skyscraper—eighty-seven stories high, the tallest building in Europe, and owned by a transnational board, including a British firm (which could not afford the cost of the building in recession era London) and the Qatari government (which could)—was being constructed above the Crossbones Graveyard site, to our collective astonishment.[2] Started in 2009 and completed in 2012, the gleaming glass building stands (quite literally) in stark opposition to the centuries of raw poverty in this part of the metropolis. A beautiful structure, it symbolizes a city that had no real jurisdiction over Southwark until a century ago, effectively swallowing in its shadow a radical—and local—history that claimed its down-at-the-heels strength and creativity with pride. Just as Qatar paid for and now owns most of London's architectural triumph (upstaging the Eiffel Tower, of course, according to the building's English sponsor; Booth 2011), London has claimed its south-of-the-river opposition as its own. Migrant workers were supposedly the biggest public fear in the England of 2015, if election rhetorics were anything to go by, but transnational capital was, by contrast, welcomed with open arms. This structure of local, national, and international financing—and what goes down where, with whose approval—is part of the neighborhood considerations that are at the heart of our ritual.

The London of 2012 and 2013 was peppered with anti-capitalist movements, including Occupy, outside St. Paul's Cathedral, and a protest again the G8 summit known as the Carnival against Capitalism. (The G20 summit in 2009, too, saw street theater protests against bankers, even on the part of anthropologists.) Our ritual is not a radical activist movement in this way, although individual participants might well have joined in these explicitly political marches or demonstrations. It is rather a subtle call to reclaim the past, and the styles, issues, and modalities of old. The history it recounts—factual or not, literal or metaphorical, based on visions or on court records—is designed to resonate with the truth of this present.

Second, in the context of our particular investigation, John Constable's position also questions the unabated takeover of virtual and transnational finance. *The Southwark Mysteries* hints at a defiance of the city's economic values and financial priorities. In a combined finger to the establishment and claim for a new way of living—which is also a tried-and-true, old way of living—"The Book of the New South Bank" begins:

> We splish
> in the splash
> of the New Bankside Power
>
> We clash
> in the flash
> of the OXO Tower
>
> We Hole in the Wall
> to the Ministry Ball
> and We know how to pack
> a punch
>
> We Clink and Red-
> Cross Wicca and Dread
> the Original Real
> Wild Bunch. (Constable 1999:77)

In person, too, John is candid about his suspicions of the finances of the city. Asked about a new sculpture outside of London Bridge station, John waved his hand, and dejectedly said he barely recognized the neighborhood any longer. Anyone who shows up at the ritual after a hard day's work in a shirt and tie would certainly be welcome, but might also be the butt of a snide comment about bankers. And the campaign for the memorial garden is precisely about reclaiming the land of John's (spiritual) ancestors from a London corporation (with which he has developed increasingly positive relations). To offer a green and growing space in the heart of an area that is inundated with expensive redevelopment plans is at the core of the guerrilla garden movement in many great cities of capital, which Southwark, contrary to all expectations of the past thousand years, is rapidly becoming.

John's resistance to capitalist forces is apparent outside of Southwark as well. At a gathering of the Radical Anthropology Group on Fleet Street in London, in the heart of the financial district, John volunteered that, although he enjoyed camaraderie with this countercultural group—and supported the collective action of normally dispersed pockets of free-thinkers—"this is as far north as I'm willing to go." And as much as John has enjoyed the recognition he has received for his poems, his plays, and the ritual, when he received the 2011 Erotic Campaigner of the Year Award, which he was happy to accept, he warned that he was suspicious of any honors that were too mainstream. To do the job of being a thorn in the side, one cannot be co-opted.

"Englishmen are a practical race," wrote the jurist Harold Laski in 1917, "and they had discovered the benefits of fellowship long before they speculated about its nature" (562).[3] Writing about the parallels between medieval administrative structures—which we know preoccupied the strained relationship between Southwark and the city (Johnson 1969)—and modern corporations, Laski argues that the present form of the corporation as we know it dates to Elizabeth I's reign, through the monopolies she granted, first to individuals, but slowly to corporate groups (1917:582).[4] "A mercantile centre the borough is to become, with its gilds and fraternities. It will send twelve men to the assize and two to the Parliament. It has a power of self-direction that is earlier and more real than that of all other communities in England. But in these areas it is an administrative area rather than a corporate personality" (Laski 1917:567–568). Multiple processes of centralization contributed to the process of producing corporate bodies (including the possibility that Elizabeth was personally invested in finding a way to materialize transnational relations through commodity trade); Laski argues that England sports a long history of collective life that must be acknowledged if we are to chart the rise of corporations—and, now, a century on, corporate finance—with any theoretical longevity.

If Southwark has a legitimate (even if, in this case, its legitimacy rests upon a public flaunting of the rules of legitimacy) history of administrative independence at the level of the Borough, what John and his ritual call for is a similarly unique kind of corporation, in the era of the transnational. For so many centuries, Southwark flouted convention; why may it not do the same now, and claim a local mode of being, still embodied and not abstracted, here in the material present? If the exchange of money is that which transforms a collective body into a corporation, as Laski suggests, our ritual simultaneously critiques a denigration of prostitution as an exchange of intimacy that asks for a transfer of cash and, in an inverse but parallel case, questions the selling out of the independence of Southwark to the financial imperatives of the global market, so well housed in and represented by the corporate city. Therein lies the hypocrisy.

In Defense of Symbols: The Hooker as Hook

Sex work—and the particular Bankside sex workers of the medieval Borough—are thus the core of this story at the symbolic level. Naturally, sex workers' rights and solidarity with sex workers' unions across the world (and through space and time) are part of the explicit message of the Crossbones ritual; sex workers' advocates are welcome and willing conspirators and participants in the gatherings and events of our graveyard. But the prostitutes here—living and dead—are the beginning of the story, not the end. They are the way into the larger tale, one that is about local history, and local power, and the importance of material engagement in resisting the transnational corporate forces of capital that would threaten community, particularity, and embodied modes of exchange.

Geertzian symbolic frames are not as passive as his critics would have it: symbols are the stuff wars are made of. Symbols do not act independently: any given symbol—a church, the state, a woman, the whore—depends on the networks it elicits in an engaged, active, and always socially embedded mind. Definitions of particular religions—churches, constituencies, practices—and the rituals they depend upon ask for a specific configuration of symbols that tells participants that they belong, or are doing it right, or are having the experience intended, by their society or by God. This is what MacCulloch means when he writes of the Reformation being about changing "patterns of mind" (1990:22): theological history tells us as much about the way people thought things should be as about how they were. The particular conjunctions of a hotly contested symbol—in doctrine, in policy, and in practice—will determine the paths of social and political human history, as well as that of a victorious theology.

"Mind" here does not mean brain in opposition to body. Bodily experience is equally important to mind; the intention at this juncture is not to take up a debate with Descartes but to insist that physical, emotional, conceptual, and political experiences interact with each other in such a way that what people fight for—and the symbols they use to do so—will rely upon all these aspects of human experience. Ritual has the ability to symbolically represent—and convey, and be—all of these elements at one go, and to present these multiple dimensions of reality in such a way that an astute observer will note their congruity, and the ways they line up and reinforce each other, in ritual action (and perhaps also in everyday experience). In other cases, a ritual may impress this point in participants' minds in alternative ways—such as through their bodies, ironically enough, in Whitehouse's (2004) rendering.

It is not, then, that symbols are imprinted in people's minds and just sit there, as Asad (1983) wrongly critiques Geertz for suggesting. As we have seen, symbols are actively created and re-created by social conduct: this is what Geertz (1973) means when he writes that culture is public. One symbol is invoked by another, each upon the next; they form dense networks—think of grammar and its evolution—that are constantly open to manipulation and reframing. The famous Weberian "webs of significance" refer precisely to the layers of meaning that symbols and their contexts give rise to. These are the Durkheimian layers of representation.

Peeling the layers of history and culture back, to establish what the source of the current trouble is, what action or constellation has given rise to the concern—so both the issue at its surface and what it refers to in meaning and history—are questions that are contained in ritual. A particular occasion of ritual conduct may be a single linear event, even as it insists on its circularity and cyclicality, but the point is that it may contain a multitude of symbolic frames—and times—within itself. A ritual may represent the faith, or the people, or the church. In some cases it may create a sense of solidarity physiologically, in its effervescence (Durkheim 1995 [1912]). But it can also instantiate a sense of worth or symbolic continuity, as in our Crossbones gathering, and this is sufficient, too.[5]

Durkheim's effervescence—although he is cast as an evolutionist in his adherence to the colonialist construction that certain cultures are more primitive than others, placing nations like individuals in models of the life course—acknowledges flux, as does Weber's social process and, in both of their lineages, Geertz's symbolic system. All these great theorists of religion knew that human action takes place in time, and in history. But we need to recall that consciousness *about* time is historically grounded, too: the symbolic networks that make people function will likely determine—as well as constrain—the form their actions will take. People know ritual is about timelessness, and that is why they engage in it. In some instances, ritual will occasion mystical experiences; in others, false or hollow performances will expose a lack of faith, or cynicism, or resentment. These stories cannot always be gleaned from the historical record, nor from the clinical one. Human motivation is complex, no less human action. Neither can be reduced to the other. And as observers and analysts of these processes, we never know if we have a truly objective or clean slate: fate, or chance, always has a role in the construction of human history. Whether these slips of the pen or releases of the tongue are the hand of God, no one can tell.

Lévi-Strauss's brilliance was to argue that the nodes of connection in the structures of the human mind do not need to have content: they are empty, to use a Buddhist metaphor. Or rather, they inevitably have content, in the form of symbols—here is where Geertz comes in—and these symbolic forms vary across culture, invariably. The invariable—that is, cross-cultural—constant is the structure of the relationship. One can think about it as a series of nuggets, or nodes, in a wide complex web. Where Lévi-Strauss fell down in this superb—unmatched, many would say—analysis of the human mind is the default stasis of the system; like Durkheim before him, he was interested in the deep structures of the human mind, and the ways they play out in the world. Of course the historical moment will have an impact. But to insist too heavily on this absence in the work of Lévi-Strauss is to misunderstand his emphasis on the perennial nature of the relationships between the symbolic nodes or clusters that comprise human thought: his point was that symbolic content will inevitably be filled in, and presumably this is true both geographically and historically. But he also appears to have missed, or at least to have vastly underestimated, the fluid process of the dialogues between clusters. Fluid process, or flux, is temporal, diachronic. In the time taken by internal symbolic dialogues, interactions with the outside world are also occurring; it is through this coeval process, at individual and collective levels, that the relations between the two—and also within each individual's symbolic set, itself in flux—take form. Lest we forget, culture is public, and dynamic—because history is.

Geertz was not interested in stasis at all, although he was interested in symbols, and in the ways that what goes on in one person's head is both a product of and a contributor to what goes on in public culture. Public culture, of course, is performance, which is what a ritual is and also what a play is. Is ritual to religion as drama is to secular society? Not necessarily: we know we can have religious plays, and many world theaters developed as a way to express religious ideas or staged performances that were inspired by them. Can we have secular ritual, by the same token?

The Question of Secularism: Social Performance

Is the ritual on the twenty-third of every month a secular event, then, if it is not a religious one? John is amenable to that idea (as he is to the idea that social connectedness, in a Durkheimian mode, is itself religion). To be fixed on the ritual's categorization as any one kind of phenomenon would be to miss its fundamental flexibility. And to ignore that religion was an important influence on John as he was inspired to develop the ritual would be to misattribute both Anglicanism and Zen in his own history, or indeed the culture of the Church of England in which Southwark's history is implicated, as well as the multiple great and small traditions—including Brazilian, Côte d'Ivoirean, Egyptian, Indian, Indonesian, and Japanese—that have inspired and influenced the participants of the monthly gathering, and the teachers, friends, and fellow artists that John has met over the years. Transnational religious influences are alive and well in the context of this ritual—as long as they are expressed in the ritual predilections of those gathered, and not in the corporate boardrooms of the city.

Still, if John's inclination is to align the ritual with art or with politics in its intention, and even in its form, it is also a deliberately secular act. But is it possible for a play that focuses on the power of Jesus to vanquish Satan and the worth of Mary Magdalene, once she is redeemed through the love (literal in this instance) of Christ, to be a secular one? If a ritual with all the form and function of a religion is not religious, can a play similarly defy such expectations? Certainly one of John's successes is that he has questioned the distinction between secular and religious through the ritual, or at least he has reminded us that these categories are heuristic devices, not ontological realities. We human beings are specialists in crossing heuristic borders, and therein lies the talent, but also the downfall, of our species: lives, performances, actions, and intentions rarely fit into the conceptual categories we use to understand them.

At the same time, it is clear upon closer inspection that religion does play a part both in John's ritual and in his play. The figure of Mary appears as a guiding light, as does that of Kuan Yin. It may be syncretic religion, but it is religion nonetheless; that John was exposed to Anglicanism as a child and to Japanese Buddhism as a young man traveling the world is apparent in both performances. (He is open to the appearance of other spiritual forms, too—and one could argue that such ecumenicism is a kind of religion.) But in some senses he does as every artist before him has done, and he would argue that it is his prerogative to use the cultural (and religious) influences in his life to create the story he wishes to tell. Whether this personal history means his work is correctly cast as religious is clearly a matter of interpretation.

John Constable the writer joins a long line in England—and he would not want to challenge the fundamental construction that is England. But he would remind England to "let in, let in" (Constable 1999:88), to not become too fixed in its ways or exclusivist in its outlook. He is deliberately a pest to the Church of England, in the sense that it is an establishment institution, and he sees his role as being an antagonist of structures and conventions, especially when they are confined or restricted. But his irreverence is welcomed by the institution he challenges, which is itself an English dynamic. And so he is able to be a follower, too, in duty and in love, in loyalty and in faith, as the English and their church—or churches, in the Durkheimian sense—would have it.

Gender and religion are the operative terms of this culture—any culture, really: they are both the primary symbols and the main social ground through which those symbols are interpreted, as well as the institutional framework through which codes of ethical conduct tend to be developed and maintained or taught (formally, or through myth, or vernacular culture). In this case, we have looked at England as nation, literally and as understood—produced—by its people, over the course of the last half millennium. We might look at any culture on the globe, but one thing we know for sure: to be human is to contend with our bodies, our passions, our social settings, and our moment in time, in history, which we come to know all too well.

Ritual makes sure we see our moment in timelessness, too: our sheer humanity. As enduring as the human condition may be, however, and as perennial as ritual is as a way to help us see it, we are not culture-free—for, as we learned painfully in the case of the Wolf Boy in the seventeenth century, and as Geertz reminded us in the twentieth, there is no such thing: we are all encultured, acculturated, embodied, impassioned people in time. We are so much more than our biological beings, and indeed we cannot function at the level only of evolutionary or cognitive modeling, contrary to the neuro-imaging that is all the rage. Freud was right: religion is the institution through which our bodies and our passions are socialized, if not civilized; something has to try and get our unruly human selves into shape. But, as Durkheim would remind us, that is not the same as asking us to become automatons: we make our way in the world, just as the world makes its way in us, as full human beings—because of that structure called culture.

Ritual Action

This book has taken a loosely *longue durée* approach to history: it has looked at a place over the course of a thousand years, and traced how the conscious knowledge of that history plays a role in the contemporary representation of its identity. More than history, the deployment of history creates the present. That is what this ritual—and arguably every other human ritual—does.

Not all rituals consciously deploy historical narrative. But all ritual is designed to create the present, however history is construed. Sometimes ritual creates the present through manipulation of a different kind of time—deep time, timelessness, transcendent time—to mark it, in space, and thus in consciousness.

Here, then, at last, we arrive at our definition of ritual: ritual is human action to create the present, in place, through the manipulation or deployment of time and its passage. Thus does it bring about greater consciousness, or a potentially heightened awareness in and of the present. Whether the manipulation of time takes place through a historical, mythical, or deep time rendering, or is understood to be outside of time altogether (which nonetheless incorporates a consciousness of time), a reckoning of humanity's dependence upon—and any culture's emergence from—the seas or winds or sands of time is what ritual marks.

History and myth thus blur in ritual, as many commentators have noted, but so does a stance within and a stance outside time. Leach's famous oscillation between cyclical and linear time, or between ongoing and enduring time, on one hand, and time with finitude, on the other, is more about time that is counted, in the latter—tick tock, two hundred years, five hundred years, one thousand years—and time that isn't, in the former. It is not so much a matter of scale—although that is relevant—as a matter of consciousness: all times merge into one in the context of ritual or, indeed, in the context of the present. Ritual, in any time, in any place, is about making the present out of time past and time future, from a stance both outside of time and within it. The layers of time fold in upon each other, assuring both their relevance and their erasure, like a sandwich of human consciousness.

Ritual makes the present by claiming the past, rather than being made by either. To participate in ritual is ideally to be an actor, rather than a passive subject, in the flow of time (which is not to say that one cannot stand passively by or be distractedly present, which may have its own effects). The active, mindful aspect of ritual is what makes it stand apart from everyday life and action. Thus we have the weight and meaning of ritual performance, or why ritual is frequently understood and written about as performative: at its best, it is active, and it is conscious.

Scholars of ritual—and practitioners, too, sometimes—have been so focused on the way ritual links us and ties us to the past that the true object of ritual action as the present has dropped out of the forefront of our consciousness. We make ourselves through ritual, as we know, and the past is a way of situating who we are, as is our place, in location and in station. But what all these places and memories and identities and acts of empowerment, individual and collective, are about is the present, the discovery and articulation of who we are now. That is the transformative power of ritual: by claiming the present, we bring ourselves to the moment that matters, with full consciousness, thus allowing whatever shifts need to take place in order no longer to be burdened or held back by the past. At the same time, the very repeated or handed-down quality of ritual, not to mention those narratives that explicitly invoke history, acknowledges the effects of its traces and the importance of knowing (and sometimes even honoring) the way it has played a role in constituting our present selves.

Sexuality and modes of exchange—bodily, sensorily, commodity-based, or cash-based—constitute all human societies and in some sense are at the base of human encounter. Acknowledging the particular cultural and historical modes of production, as anthropologists like to say, is part of knowing who we are, in the formation of any given contemporary society or social group. Doing so through the act of ritual is a way of saying: here is who we are now, such that we may move forward in the way that we choose, rather than in the way that has seemingly been chosen for us. Ritual is, again, the way we move forward in time, the cosmic version of growing up, by acknowledging our current age and state of consciousness.

Making the present usually involves marking the present. Here is the aspect of ritual that requires and brings about action or practice, and certainly performance, requiring sesame seeds and ghee in Vedic rituals, *churingas* in aboriginal rituals, and lace and ribbons at the Crossbones Gates in Southwark. Even the invocation of Southwark and its history marks the present here, in place: we remember where we are and reclaim our location, and ourselves. This active aspect is the performative piece of ritual: we mark the present, as it is, and as we are, which is as open to change as it is tied to tradition and repetition. The present is necessarily open-ended.

Emile Durkheim's (1995 [1912]) understanding of ritual has often been critiqued as too static: by emphasizing a group identity, the critics say, we do not allow for rebellion, resistance, a call for social change. Ah, but we do. Ritual reclaims the group, but does so in a way that, without negating the past (on the contrary, we precisely remember it), we claim our potential. We assert who we are—with all due knowledge of our past (historically accurate or mythically embellished, a distinction that is for all intents and purposes irrelevant in the context of ritual)—in action, in word, in thought, or in some conscious or unconscious combination of the three. In so doing, we make and mark ourselves not only as we were but as we are, anew. Ritual is a re-creation of ourselves, a reminder of who we were, to be sure, but also a statement of who we are such that we may also move forward, possibly in a different cast or on an altered trajectory. Claiming the present means the future does not have to mimic the past.

This book has taken a Durkheimian approach to the analysis of ritual in the first instance: it is about the consolidation of a social group through shared—and furthered—reference to a set of symbolic representations (see Hausner 2013). But it does not accept that such an understanding of ritual reflects a static or unchanging society (nor did Durkheim, although he is unfairly accused of such often). What the pages of this book—or, rather, the ritualists who are its protaganists—have done is take a classic approach to ritual, showing how a society is created and strengthened through repeated actions. Certain classic elements are directly referred to in the ritual: the honoring of the ancestors, for example, is a central theme, and the engaging of the senses, with cymbals and incense. But it is not an exclusively synchronic event. By virtue of re-creating our social world, and by virtue of honoring our past, we perpetuate not the same society, but a subtly differentiated one. We cannot break from what has come before, but we can adjust what is to come, by noting where—and who—we might become. By claiming the synchronic aspect of ritual, then—the acknowledgment of what takes place as it is enacted—we do not deny the diachronic aspects of culture. On the contrary: we are in a better position to move forward. Such is the power of ritual, and the reason for its endurance.

Most of the literature on ritual emphasizes its capacity to establish continuity in the face of change for humans who wish to reassure themselves of stability and meaning in a world that causes suffering and death. This book has argued that ritual is as much about bringing about or embracing change, or reminding ourselves of our capacity to act, and to be agents in the construction of our own history over time. By remembering how defiant Southwark's own history is, our ritualists have a constant pillar around which to rally for change. A long history of alterity means that active and dynamic opposition is always in the cards.

This book tries to do for practice what Paul Ricoeur (1984 [1983]) did for narrative: show how the doing, or enactment, of ritual creates the temporal frame that is the present. Theories of ritual have tended to focus on whether thought or action dominate in these forms of human behavior, and to ascertain which types of thought or action are most instrumental in social cohesion and movement; they also elaborate upon the extent to which thought must underscore action, and debate which is more meaningful. This text moves the lengthy scholarly discussion about ritual along a different axis and in a different direction. Ritual necessarily involves both thought and action, transitively and in both directions. But it may be more productive for us to think about the way ritual mediates not only between thought and action, and individual and collective, but between past and present. By redirecting our theories of ritual to the uses (and effects) of time, deliberately or not, we move back to classic works on temporal cycles—regeneration and repetition—as the intention of ritual, and the human insistence on reckoning with mortality and finitude, alongside a consciousness of enduring humanity. It is this last part of the equation with which this book is most concerned: not the past or the future, neither the repetition nor the finitude, but the present. Ritual is the literal form, or vehicle, of human thought and intention and action, not empty of meaning but replete with it. Ritual is the medium of human capacity—as well as, extraordinarily, the human consciousness of that capacity—and the intention to transform our conditions and circumstances through deliberate or mindful action. This action, this book suggests, is what constitutes the heart of ritual.

Coda: Time and Truth

The bones at Crossbones did not belong to medieval prostitutes; the graveyard on Redcross Way is very likely not that referred to by Stow; and no one was called a Winchester Goose with any regularity until long after the Bankside brothels were shut. And yet none of these caveats means that the stories told in our ritual gatherings are untrue. They are rather features of an ever-unfolding history of people, places, names, and meanings; they are understood to be true, and like any good myth, all renderings together make up the whole. It is a story about now as much as about the past. The details are all, but they are also the trees that distract us from a broader vision of the forest that is the present. Historically particular as this tale is, the universal elements are as significant to us: sexuality, exchange (of cash or goods, emotions or bodily senses), and ritual, multiply constituted over space and time, form us. This story about medieval Southwark is one of many manifestations of human culture as it confronts gender, love, sex, money, poverty, inequity, and law—and it brings our attention to the way we think about these matters and their configurations now, in 2015 at the time of this writing, or in the year that it is at the time of your reading. Such is the power of myths, and narratives, and symbolic representations: they carry meaning at the time of the telling and at the time of the hearing and the feeling and the thinking. Such is the reason for contest and contingency.

The call here to reclaim and put right medieval inequities is of course a call to reclaim and put right contemporary inequities, and ironically it valorizes certain parts of medieval culture that we have subsequently lost. The world looked different then, and although we do not want to return there per se—it is good to be able to drink pure water, wear condoms, have real sewers—we may miss the kinds of human communication and certain messy freedoms that were part of a nontechnological life. We still want to be human beings, even with all that our science, our culture, and yes, our money, when we have it, offer us. Indeed, that is the definition of culture: the capacity to use our consciousness to make new meanings again and again, layer upon layer, discriminating, if we can, between those representations that distort or destroy and those that enhance and nourish ourselves and our bodies, and others and others' bodies. Money does not make the world go around, but our minds do.

It turns out that to do an anthropology of England requires an engagement with the history of England, and this is so for at least two reasons. First, much of contemporary English culture is owed to the historical processes that have produced it, as anywhere, and England has a long, complex, and formidable history. But second, partly as a result of this thick link with the past and partly responsible for (or itself engendering) it, contemporary England is fascinated with its past. To do justice to the popular or cultural interest in English history, we who study that interest have to study that history. Perhaps more than in most places, England's history is a "model of" and a "model for" its present, which in turn shapes and is shaped by its own understandings of its past, in Geertz's (1973:95) famous rendering. We are constructed by that which we construct, and formed by that which we have narrated—and the English love to narrate, as well as to stage, their history. They have done so for a long time.

The highly debated issues in the climate in which this book was written speak to and derive from the stories in this book (as it should be if the anthropologist has done her homework). For example, the fight about whether women can be bishops in the Church of England was finally won in the summer of 2014, and Bishop Libby Lane was formally installed in March 2015. In the same month, Richard III's bones (found under a parking garage a few years earlier) were laid to rest in Leicester with great pomp and circumstance. The worry about migrant workers in the buildup to an election, such that promises were forthcoming from all parties to keep English jobs for English workers, reflected a seemingly perennial public concern to keep the economic opportunities of the nation consolidated, and impervious to foreigners taking advantage of it. The Radio 4 announcement that more and more young women were turning to sex work to fund their educations and lifestyles was followed a few days later with one on a public reduction of corporate tax. The discovery of Henry VII's marital bed (in which, it was said in tittering tones of great importance, Prince Arthur and King Henry VIII were conceived!) was national news. The list goes on. The excavation of bones (and of beds); the uses of rituals; the structuring of economies and corporations; and the taint of sex work all strike at the very core of English life and culture—and history. Our ritual, as local and as particular as its focus may be, tells its story through universal themes at the heart of humanity, as it would have to be.

Shrine in Crossbones Garden

❀ *Epilogue*

CROSSBONES GARDEN

> A representation is not merely an image of reality, an inert shadow projected on us by things, but a force which raises up around itself a whirlwind of organic and psychic phenomena.
>
> Emile Durkheim, *The Division of Labor in Society* (1893)

Ten years of activism do not go unnoticed when they touch a cultural chord. In the spring of 2015, one of John's lobbying goals—to open a garden for Crossbones—came to fruition. Some years earlier, Bankside Open Spaces Trust, a neighborhood charity that works to create "precious patches of green amongst the concrete and glass of Bankside"[1] had been easily won over to the campaign to create a memorial garden. That it would be dedicated to the sex workers of old was less important, perhaps, than that it would offer another grassy corner in the steely metropolis. And with a devoted community organization on board, the tide seemingly turned, and what started as a somewhat defiant mobilization campaign became a collaborative neighborhood effort to reclaim local space. Early in 2015, Transport for London agreed to lease the land behind the Memorial Gates for three years to the local charity, and Bankside Open Spaces Trust began working in earnest with John and his crew to create the long-desired Garden of Remembrance.

By March it was done: the space was open. Precious land with new flowers and trees, scattered with incense pots and triptychs, already laid with bridges and walkways, stretched out behind the cramped street on which we had been gathering for so many years. Gone were the wooden boards keeping the area fenced off; rather than crouching to see the greenery between the slats of the fence, we could stroll across the earth and witness it for ourselves, from the other side. One participant estimated the land was worth £25 million; a large square block in the middle of a cityscape at the height of a booming real estate market is like gold dust. Leasing this land was an enormous gesture of goodwill to the green spaces of Bankside on the part of the government corporation that is Transport for London—the decision was notably covered by the *Financial Times*—but it would not have happened without John's shamanic efforts.

On June 23, 2015, the Crossbones Garden celebrated its official opening. Nigel of Bermondsey sang his Crossbones hymn. Katy brought carrot sticks and dips. The afternoon was given over to poetry readings, performances, and songs. Around seventy or eighty people came to the event in the new garden, and most stayed to participate in our regular evening ritual on the other side of the fence. The vast majority were residents of Southwark, enjoying their newest local common.

It is a new phase—one that is markedly about the present, rather than the past. No one is asking the Museum of London to dig deeper or excavate further; the motivation of Crossbones lobbyists is not to find out how old this graveyard really is. The quest is for organic life of a different kind: a guerrilla garden is just as good—better, really, for our lives now—than determining whether older bones might be lying under the ground, or drawing precise lines between what is history and what is myth. At the same time, the history of this patch of ground is not far from the consciousness of the participants. When asked about the plans, an official from Bankside Open Spaces Trust (who now also attends the ritual to commemorate the dead, usually wearing a suit) said straightforwardly, "Obviously we are not digging in this garden. So we're doing raised beds."

Those raised beds—and every other feature of the growing, living Crossbones Garden—will be the result of volunteer efforts. Already, a large wooden walkway with a sweeping arched roof, handcrafted by a local resident and called the Goose's Wing, marks the entrance to this small park. The London School of Dry Stone Walling will offer the rims of the flower beds for free. A crowd-funding campaign is under way for a small pond and a woodland garden. A sensory garden is in the plans.

In some sense, this garden marks the success of John's ritual actions: it is the result of effective activism. Telling a story of truth—well, of something akin to the truth, and with good narrative punch—works. Or rather, touching the heart of human relationships is perhaps more important than semantic historical details. If one purpose of the ritual gathering was to create a memorial garden, the commemorative act is done. This story of attempted appropriation, and dogged resistance, refracting out from local to global and back again, is complete. The capacity to mobilize us in the present, for the health of the contemporary world, is the reason for telling this tale. All that remains is to watch the grass grow.

Fin

PANDARUS A goodly medicine for my aching bones! O world!
world! world! thus is the poor agent despised!
O traitors and bawds, how earnestly are you set
a-work, and how ill requited! why should our
endeavour be so loved and the performance so loathed?
what verse for it? what instance for it? Let me see:
Full merrily the humble-bee doth sing,
Till he hath lost his honey and his sting;
And being once subdued in armed tail,
Sweet honey and sweet notes together fail.
Good traders in the flesh, set this in your
painted cloths.
As many as be here of pander's hall,
Your eyes, half out, weep out at Pandar's fall;
Or if you cannot weep, yet give some groans,
Though not for me, yet for your aching bones.
Brethren and sisters of the hold-door trade,
Some two months hence my will shall here be made:
It should be now, but that my fear is this,
Some galled goose of Winchester would hiss:
Till then I'll sweat and seek about for eases,
And at that time bequeathe you my diseases.

William Shakespeare, *Troilus and Cressida* (1602)

PERMISSIONS FOR TEXT AND PHOTOGRAPHS

The epigraph for the introduction, *Mind Games*, written by John Lennon © 1973 Lenono Music, is reprinted here with the kind permission of Downtown Music Publishing.

Excerpts from *The Southwark Mysteries* are reprinted with the kind permission of Oberon Books (www.oberonbooks.com).

The frontispiece, London and the Borough of Southwark, 1720, © The British Library Board, is reprinted with the kind permission of the British Library.

The illustration in chapter 2, of MS e. Mus. 229, folio 17r, is published with the kind permission of the Bodleian Libraries, The University of Oxford.

The illustration in chapter 4, of Queen Elizabeth I ("The Ditchley portrait"), by Marcus Gheeraerts the Younger, © National Portrait Gallery, London, is reprinted by kind permission.

All other photographs are © Sondra L. Hausner.

Ritual at Crossbones

NOTES

Introduction

1. “Get thee to a nunnery,” Hamlet directs Ophelia: some say it is a snide way of telling her to go become a prostitute.

2. See the International Union of Sex Workers website: http://www.iusw.org/campaigns/cross-bones-graveyard.

3. See the Tate Modern website: http://www.tate.org.uk/about/press-office/press-releases/tate-modern-most-popular-modern-art-museum-world.

1. The Myth of the Winchester Goose

1. The phenomenological study of religion has focused on this aspect of human experience since the early twentieth century, looking at the way that bodies (and their muscles, hormones, neurons, as well as the memories and senses they give rise to) may offer a ground of knowledge that far surpasses intellectual understanding, if only we know how to read them. Not all schools of thought agree that bodily experience is the most reliable form of knowledge, however: early phenomenologists thought that the external world had to be controlled before one could locate the true inner sense that could be rightfully heeded. And Indic sages have long argued, not unlike Christian ones, that bodily experiences can lead one down a path of highly misleading and inappropriate knowledge.

2. See also Moore 1990 [1987]:95, developing her idea: “Prostitution at all carefully defined is not only essentially an urban phenomenon, but necessarily a cash-based one; indeed the relationship between the prostitute and her client could serve as a paradigm of the anxiety so widely expressed in these centuries that money dissolved traditional personal ties and obligations and substituted for them impersonal one-way transactions which contributed nothing to the maintenance and renewal of the social fabric.”

2. Medieval Bankside

1. On prohibitions on owning boats, see clause B21 of the customary ordinances discussed below; on prohibitions on selling food and drink—specifically "that any man keeping a stewhouse neither sell nor retail out of the same house bread, ale, flesh, fish, wood, coal, candle or any other victual, upon pain of a fine"—see clause B29 (Karras 1989:132).

2. The Dutch were also named as perpetrators in two other areas designated for brothels, Yarmouth and East Smithfield (Karras 1989:116).

3. The text of the ordinances in modern English is cited in Karras 1989:128–134; the text in Middle English is cited in Post 1977:422–428. In what follows, the passages are cited by their clause numbers in the customary.

4. "[T]ime out of mind" is a phrase that is dated etymologically to the fifteenth century, which goes along with Post's dating of the manuscript. See http://www.etymonline.com/index.php?term=mind.

5. The later dating of the treatise than it claims for itself probably reflects a need to produce standing orders, as it were, for a practice that was thriving and yet was understood to have long-held roots: the inclination of the scribe to antedate the manuscript may indicate an intention to index the institutions as having been around for a long while, as he believed, and as the lore of Southwark foretold, in a gesture that Post calls "enthusiastic anachronism" (1977:420). Representing the acts that took place in Bankside as lascivious or sinful ones that were necessary for expedient purposes may thus itself be a Southwark practice that has lasted many centuries, and in reappropriating the city's denigration of the Borough, Southwark has consistently claimed an identity all its own.

6. In a wonderful example of "things set apart," we can see in the ordinances a classic Durkheimian social binary (1995 [1912]): that which is profane, namely the practices of prostitution, by being placed in opposition, engender a healthy social life, or that which is "sacred." Prostitution cannot take place on holy days; at other times, it is a free social practice.

7. It cost a stewholder twenty shillings if he had "women at board contrary to the custom" (B10); officers were supposed to ensure that he did not "keep any of the women to board against the ordinance" (B41).

8. A different clause specifies the opening hours as from noon to 2:00 PM (B15), which—along with the contradictory edicts that stews were meant to close altogether in the first part of the document but that specify legal opening hours in the second—indicates that multiple versions of the customary were amalgamated into the fifteenth-century version we have (see Post 1977).

9. The references to Parliament are another giveaway that the manuscript's self-ascribed date is much too early. As Post notes, "The idea of enactment in parliament by the commons, with confirmation by the king and the lords, was barely formed in the fifteenth century, let alone operative in the twelfth" (1977:420n28).

10. Officers were instructed to make sure that stewholders were not what we, in contemporary parlance, would call madams; they were to ask of "common women" themselves: "Is she single and does she keep a stewhouse?" (B55); it cost "a single woman . . . twenty shillings" if she did so. It is not clear whether the concern was the financial power a female stewholder would have or the low moral standard that would be incumbent in a house that was both leased and used by prostitutes, or both. Either way, it appears to have been a rule that was not much upheld, as we have seen, insofar

as women were often on the books as stewholders and as "frows." There is also evidence that married couples were joint stewholders, as listed in the 1381 poll tax record (McIntosh 2005:76). Certainly in today's brothels in South Asia, it is not uncommon for women who were former sex workers to become the managers of younger women arrivals; the danger in matters of liberty—medieval and otherwise—may be when women managers are in cahoots with "procurers" (B64), presumably agents or "traffickers," in contemporary language.

11. There was certainly one of those in the manor, too—known as the Clink, or Clink Prison—as would have been logical for a socially peripheral area like Southwark. The bishop's estate as a whole was itself sometimes known as the Clink, or the Manor of Clink, or Clink Liberty (Johnson 1969:57), and this late fifteenth-century name appears to antedate the colloquial name of the prison (see Carlin 1996:36n63, who suggests that the prison took the name of the manor, not the other way around).

12. They were in fact prohibited from taking in women "who want to be kept secretly as though unknown" (B5).

13. See Carlin 1996:224–226 for details of the increased association of prostitution and criminality in the years building up to 1546, and the attendant clamping down that began at the beginning of the sixteenth century.

14. My thanks to Diarmaid MacCulloch for suggesting this clear route of thinking about the expediency of Henry's actions.

15. See http://archive.museumoflondon.org.uk/Centre-for-Human-Bioarchaeology/Database/Post-medieval+cemeteries/Cross+bones.htm.

16. My thanks to Martha Carlin for directing me to these sources, and to Caroline Barron for facilitating the introduction. Errors of interpretation are mine alone.

3. Shamanism and the Ritual Oscillation of Time

1. See, for example, "Twisted Language" by Townsley and "Climbing the Twisted Ladder to Initiation" by Métraux, both in Narby and Huxley's compendium (2001).

4. The Virgin Queen and the English Nation

1. See Salgado 1977 for an account of all manner of illicit or underground activities in Elizabethan England. My thanks to Tamsin Lewis for bringing my attention to this well-known and entertaining text and for many engaging discussions about the period. Underground life was a world unto itself, it would seem, with a sizeable population and entire subcultures that are somewhat well documented—or at least it was represented as such. See also Judges 1965 [1930].

2. See Carlin 1996 for a discussion on how the number of prostitutes in Southwark may well have increased, rather than decreased, after the decisive mid-sixteenth-century ban on brothels.

3. Personal prayers also use whoredom as the very paragon of sin, as evidenced by at least one prominent religious activist's (Lancelot Andrewes) entreaty: "thou didnst not repel even the harlot like me, the sinner, coming to thee and touching thee" (cited in Tyacke 2001:213).

4. Warner goes on to suggest that this equation between virginity and unassimilable strength and power is the less frequent symbolic association in Christian history, which far more often glorifies "wholeness and purity" (1990 [1976]:74) without the resonance of power. The independence indicated in the ascetic stance is a liberation, Warner argues, but one that denies womanhood as gender.

5. On the difference between religious category and religious practice, based on a contemporary South Asian case, see Hausner and Gellner 2012; this distinction seems to be one the Queen adhered to in full.

6. This is not to say that all were welcome or that all practices were tolerated: consider the Queen's edicts against the Anabaptists (who were most often punished) and the Family of Love (whom the Queen rather surprisingly tolerated; see MacCulloch 2013), not to mention that "the Jesuits were banned from the realm, together with all Catholic clergy trained abroad, facing execution if they arrived in England and were captured" (MacCulloch 2009:670).

7. King Arthur was said to have founded the British Empire for the first time with the conquest of Rome; Henry VIII, too, insisted that "it is manifestly declared and expressed that the realm of England is an empire" (Hamilton 1990:64–66). My thanks to Mark Edwards, as ever, for bringing this reference to my attention, and for many conversations about the complex symbolic web connecting St. George to his English referents.

8. See both Red Crosse Street (today's Redcross Way) and Red Crosse Alley in the 1720 map of Bankside (Strype 1720:bk.4, 27).

9. It was not always straightforward to write about international law at a time when the Queen was pursuing it so vigorously, in all directions, with sometimes competing ends. For Gentili, it was "awkward . . . that, by the time he was writing, the use of the Turks to counterbalance the Habsburgs had started to be an element of a specifically protestant foreign policy. In 1579 Queen Elizabeth had sent a friendly letter to the Sultan, in support of efforts by English merchants to obtain special trading privileges in Istanbul, and part of the attraction of this trade to the Sultan was that the English were willing to send iron and steel for the Ottoman armaments industry" (Malcolm 2010:140).

10. For a wonderful, exhaustive, and engaging account, see MacCulloch 2009.

11. Tudor policies came in many forms; royal proclamations are but one, and are offered here in the spirit of a broad comparison. All proclamations in this section are given by number as printed in Hughes and Larkin 1969.

12. It seems that David Graeber's claim of a "baseline date of 1700" for "the dawn of modern capitalism" is about a hundred years too late (2011:346).

13. See Hastings 1997:8ff. for a discussion of why English nationalism as such must be dated prior to the Reformation.

5. Southwark, Then and Now

1. See the Southwark Council website: http://www.southwark.gov.uk/info/200223/census_2011/2723/census_2011_briefing.

2. Lepers were kept "just outside of Southwark" at St. Leonard's hospital, also known as "the Lock" (Johnson 1969:30).

3. See Salgado 1977 and Judges 1965 [1930] for some descriptions of prurience at the time.

4. My thanks to Mark Chapman for first pointing me to this reference.

5. St. Mary Overie is still the name of the riverside dock in Bankside.

6. It also has a strong record of religious participation, which is noticeably high: for example, 93 percent of mothers in Southwark accepted baptism in the 1630s (see Crawford 1993:55).

7. See http://cathedral.southwark.anglican.org.

8. Otis 1985 also notes that the argument of preventing plague was used to close down brothels in Languedoc.

9. See Dyce 1844:124 for a full debate among nineteenth-century Shakespearean commentators as to whether the epithet is "an allusion to the 'consequence of love' for the inhabitants of the stews" or "merely used as a term of abuse" toward a bishop who would countenance such acts in his manor. See Wabuda 2002:127 and Murphy 2012:68 for early references to Winchester Geese, or to Geese meaning prostitutes in general. Significantly, there do not seem to be attested uses before the sixteenth century, or before Stephen Gardiner was Bishop of Winchester.

10. Henry Bolingbroke, who speaks in the epigraph of this book, went on to become King Henry IV; the dissolute son of whom he speaks, but for whom he has hopes nonetheless, went on to become King Henry V.

11. See http://cms.oldvictheatre.com/about-us/history-of-the-old-vic-2.

12. See Ward 1979 for a Chinese case where theatrical performers are the outcasts.

13. This is why meditation is a sticking point in the study of ritual: a deity may not be invoked, but there is nonetheless a dialogue or dialectic at work. Conscious thought is directed toward consciousness: the ritual, if it is that, of the meditator is to parse the workings of the active mind. See Hausner 2016 on the distinction between ritual practice and ritual performance in this regard.

Conclusion

1. In a surprising omission, Graeber 2011 leaves the question of sex work almost entirely to the side, referring only in the most general terms to "sacred prostitutes" and "female slaves."

2. Architect Renzo Piano is said to have wanted the higher levels of the building to be available for meditation suites, rather than having it "become a playground only for the super-rich and powerful" (Booth 2011:n.p.).

3. My thanks to Carol Greenhouse for directing me to this important and wonderful reference, and for helpful thoughts about the book as a whole.

4. See Laski 1917:584 for debates in Elizabeth's time about the distinction between the two.

5. Whitehouse 2004 is right that doctrine is well placed in these high-frequency, low-arousal contexts, but this construction may not adequately consider the simple bodily nature of participation: collectivity—sociality—is the thing that needs repeating, even if it relies upon semantic memory. To parse into binary terms how a ritual effects solidarity recreates the old distinction between primitive and modern religion.

Epilogue

1. See the BOST website: http://www.bost.org.uk/about-bost.

BIBLIOGRAPHY

Allen, N. J. 1987. "Thulung Weddings: The Hinduization of a Ritual Cycle in East Nepal." *L'Ethnographie* 83(100–101):15–33.

Asad, Talal. 1983. "Anthropological Conceptions of Religion: Reflections on Geertz." *Man: The Journal of the Royal Anthropological Society* 18(2):237–259.

———. 1993. *Genealogies of Religion: Discipline and Reasons of Power in Christianity and Islam.* Baltimore, Md.: Johns Hopkins University Press.

Barron, Caroline. 2004. *London in the Later Middle Ages.* Oxford: Oxford University Press.

Bate, Jonathan. 1997. *The Genius of Shakespeare.* London: Picador.

Bell, Catherine. 1992. *Ritual Theory, Ritual Practice.* Oxford: Oxford University Press.

Bennett, Judith M. 1996. *Ale, Beer, and Brewsters in England: Women's Work in a Changing World 1300–1600.* Oxford: Oxford University Press.

———. 2002. *Queens, Whores and Maidens: Women in Chaucer's England.* Hayes Robinson Lecture Series No. 6. London: Royal Holloway, University of London.

Bennett, Judith, and Amy Froide, eds. 1999. *Singlewomen in the European Past 1250–1800.* Philadelphia: University of Pennsylvania Press.

Blumenfeld-Kosinski, Renate. 1999. "Marginalization in Medieval Culture: Christine de Pizan's Advice to Prostitutes." *Medieval Feminist Newsletter* 27 (Spring):9–13.

Booth, Robert. 2011. "London's Shard: 'A Tower of Power and Riches' Looking Down on Poverty." *Guardian*, December 30. http://www.theguardian.com/artanddesign/2011/dec/30/shard-of-glass-london.

Brickley, Megan, and Adrian Miles. 1999. *The Crossbones Burial Ground, Redcross Way, Southwark, London: Archaeological Excavations (1991–1998) for the London Underground Limited Jubilee Line Extension Project.* London: Museum of London Archaeology Service and Jubilee Line Extension Project.

Brundage, James A. 1987. *Law, Sex, and Christian Society in Medieval Europe.* Chicago: University of Chicago Press.

———. 1989 [1976]. "Prostitution in the Medieval Canon Law." In *Sisters and Workers in the Middle Ages*, ed. Judith M. Bennett, Elizabeth A. Clark, Jean

F. O'Barr, B. Anne Vilen, and Sarah Westphal-Wihl, pp. 79–99. Chicago: University of Chicago Press.

Burghart, Richard. 1983. "Renunciation in the Religious Traditions of South Asia." *Man*, n.s., 18(4) (December):635–653.

Butler, Judith. 1993. *Bodies That Matter: On the Discursive Limits of "Sex."* New York: Routledge.

Cannell, Fenella, ed. 2006. *The Anthropology of Christianity.* Durham, N.C.: Duke University Press.

Carlin, Martha. 1996. *Medieval Southwark.* London: Hambledon.

Collinson, Patrick. 1994. *Elizabethan Essays.* London: Hambledon.

Constable, John. 1999. *The Southwark Mysteries.* London: Oberon. www.oberonbooks.com.

Crawford, Patricia. 1993. *Women and Religion in England 1520–1700.* London: Routledge.

Csordas, Thomas, ed. 1994. *Embodiment and Experience: The Existential Ground of Culture and Self.* Cambridge: Cambridge University Press.

Czaplicka, Marie Antoinette. 1914. *Aboriginal Siberia: A Study in Social Anthropology.* Oxford: Clarendon.

Das, Veena, and Deborah Poole, eds. 2004. *Anthropology in the Margins of the State.* Delhi: Oxford University Press.

Davis, Natalie Zemon. 1995. *Women on the Margins: Three Seventeenth-Century Lives.* Cambridge, Mass.: Harvard University Press.

Delacoste, Frédérique, and Priscilla Alexander. 1987. *Sex Work: Writings by Women in the Sex Industry.* London: Virago.

Doran, Susan. 2003. "Virginity, Divinity and Power: The Portraits of Elizabeth I." In *The Myth of Elizabeth*, ed. Susan Doran and Thomas S. Freeman, pp. 171–199. Basingstoke, England: Palgrave Macmillan.

Douglas, Mary. 1966. *Purity and Danger: An Analysis of the Concepts of Pollution and Taboo.* London: Routledge.

Dunbar, Robin I. M. 2012. "On the Evolutionary Function of Song and Dance." In *Music, Language, and Human Evolution*, ed. Nicholas Bannan, pp. 201–214. Oxford: Oxford University Press.

Duncan-Jones, Katherine. 2010 [2001]. *Shakespeare: An Ungentle Life.* London: Methuen Drama.

Durkheim, Emile. 1989 [1897]. *Suicide: A Study in Sociology.* George Simpson, trans. London: Routledge.

———. 1995 [1912]. *The Elementary Forms of Religious Life.* Karen E. Fields, trans. New York: Free Press.

Dworkin, Andrea. 1981. *Pornography: Men Possessing Women.* London: Women's Press.

Dyce, Alexander. 1844. *Remarks on Mr. J. C. Collier and Mr. C. Knight's Editions of Shakespeare.* London: Edward Moxon.

Eliade, Mircea. 1954. *The Myth of the Eternal Return; or, Cosmos and History.* Princeton, N.J.: Princeton University Press.

———. 1970 [1951]. *Shamanism: Archaic Techniques of Ecstasy.* Willard Trask, trans. London: Routledge and Kegan Paul.

Elton, G. R. 1991 [1955]. *England under the Tudors.* 3rd ed. Abingdon: Routledge.

Evans-Pritchard, Edward E. 1953. "The Nuer Concept of Spirit in Its Relation to the Social Order." *American Anthropologist* 55(2):201–214.

Fabian, Johannes. 1983. *Time and the Other: How Anthropology Makes Its Object.* New York: Columbia University Press.

Fanon, Frantz. 1968 [1961]. *The Wretched of the Earth.* Constance Farrington, trans. New York: Grove Weidenfeld.

Foucault, Michel. 1980 [1976]. *The History of Sexuality,* vol. 1: *An Introduction.* Robert Hurley, trans. New York: Vintage.

Geertz, Clifford. 1973. *The Interpretation of Cultures.* New York: Basic.

Gellner, Ernest. 1983. *Nations and Nationalism.* Oxford: Basil Blackwell.

Goffman, Erving. 1963. *Stigma: Notes on the Management of Spoiled Identity.* Englewood Cliffs, N.J.: Prentice Hall.

Graeber, David. 2011. *Debt: The First 5,000 Years.* Brooklyn, N.Y.: Melville House.

Gunn, Steven. 2015. "Trade and Tillage." 2015 James Ford Lectures: The English People at War in the Age of Henry VIII. February 20. Examination Schools, University of Oxford.

Haigh, Christopher. 1993. *English Reformations: Religion, Politics, and Society under the Tudors.* Oxford: Clarendon.

———. 1995 [1982]. "The Recent Historiography of the English Reformation." In *Reformation to Revolution: Politics and Religion in Early Modern England,* ed. Margo Todd, pp. 13–32. London: Routledge.

———. 1998 [1988]. *Elizabeth I.* 2nd ed. New York: Longman.

Hamilton, A. C., ed. 1990. *The Spenser Encyclopaedia.* Toronto: University of Toronto Press.

Hastings, Adrian. 1997. *The Construction of Nationhood: Ethnicity, Religion, and Nationalism.* Cambridge: Cambridge University Press.

Hausner, Sondra L. 2005. *The Movement of Women: Migration, Trafficking, and Prostitution in the Context of Nepal's Armed Conflict.* Kathmandu: Save the Children USA.

———. 2007. *Wandering with Sadhus: Ascetics in the Hindu Himalayas.* Bloomington: Indiana University Press.

———, ed. 2013. *Durkheim in Dialogue: A Centenary Celebration of "The Elementary Forms of Religious Life."* Oxford: Berghahn.

———. 2016. "The Performance of Ritual Identity among Gurungs in Europe." *Journal of Ritual Studies* 30(1):95–104.

Hausner, Sondra L., and David N. Gellner. 2012. "Category and Practice as Two Aspects of Religion: The Case of Nepalis in Britain." *Journal of the American Academy of Religion* 80(4) (December):971–997.

Heesterman, J. C. 1993. *The Broken World of Sacrifice: An Essay in Ancient Indian Ritual.* Chicago: University of Chicago Press.

Hobsbawm, Eric J. 1990. *Nations and Nationalism since 1780.* Cambridge: Cambridge University Press.

Hobsbawm, Eric J., and Terence Ranger, eds. 1983. *The Invention of Tradition.* Cambridge: Cambridge University Press.

Hughes, Paul L., and James F. Larkin, eds. 1969. *Tudor Royal Proclamations.* Vols. 1–3. New Haven, Conn.: Yale University Press.

Humphrey, Caroline, and James Laidlaw. 1994. *The Archetypal Actions of Ritual: A Theory of Ritual Illustrated by the Jain Rite of Worship.* Oxford: Clarendon.

Hunt, Lynn. 1993. *The Invention of Pornography: Obscenity and the Origins of Modernity 1500–1800.* New York: Zone.

Jenkins, Simon. 2012. *A Short History of England.* London: Profile Books, in association with the National Trust.

Johnson, David J. 1969. *Southwark and the City.* London: Published for the Corporation of London by Oxford University Press.

Judges, A. V. 1965 [1930]. *The Elizabethan Underworld: A Collection of Tudor and Early Stuart Tracts and Ballads.* London: Routledge and Kegan Paul.

Karras, Ruth Mazo. 1989. "The Regulation of Brothels in Later Medieval England." In *Sisters and Workers in the Middle Ages*, ed. Judith M. Bennett, Elizabeth A. Clark, Jean F. O'Barr, B. Anne Vilen, and Sarah Westphal-Wihl, pp. 100–134. Chicago: University of Chicago Press.

———. 1996. *Common Women: Prostitution and Sexuality in Medieval England.* New York: Oxford University Press.

———. 1999. "Sex and the Singlewoman." In *Singlewomen in the European Past 1250–1800*, ed. Judith Bennett and Amy Froide, pp. 127–145. Philadelphia: University of Pennsylvania Press.

Kelly, Patty. 2008. *Lydia's Open Door: Inside Mexico's Most Modern Brothel.* Berkeley: University of California Press.

Kempadoo, Kamala, and Jo Doezma, eds. 1998. *Global Sex Workers: Rights, Resistance, and Redefinition.* London: Routledge.

Kertzer, David I. 1988. *Ritual, Politics, and Power.* New Haven, Conn.: Yale University Press.

Khare, R. S. 1984. *The Untouchable as Himself: Ideology, Identity, and Pragmatism among the Lucknow Chamars.* Cambridge: Cambridge University Press.

Kingsbury, Benedict, and and Benjamin Straumann, eds. 2010. *The Roman Foundations of the Law of Nations: Alberico Gentili and the Justice of Empire.* Oxford: Oxford University Press.

Kirsch, A. Thomas. 1973. *Feasting and Social Oscillation: A Working Paper on Religion and Society in Upland Southeast Asia.* Ithaca, N.Y.: Southeast Asia Program, Cornell University.

Kuper, Hilda. 1947. *An African Aristocracy: Rank among the Swazi.* London: International African Institute and Oxford University Press.

Laski, Harold Joseph. 1917. "The Early History of the Corporation in England." *Harvard Law Review* 30(6):561–588.

Leach, Edmund. 1954. *Political Systems of Highland Burma: A Study of Kachin Social Structure.* Cambridge, Mass.: Harvard University Press.

———. 1961. "Two Essays Concerning the Symbolic Representation of Time: Cronus and False Noses." In his *Rethinking Anthropology*, pp. 124–137. London: Athlone.

Leinhardt, R. Godfrey. 1961. *Divinity and Experience: The Religion of the Dinka.* Oxford: Clarendon.

Lévi-Strauss, Claude. 1963. *Structural Anthropology.* Claire Jacobson and Brooke Grundfest Schoepf, trans. New York: Basic.

———. 1969 [1949]. *The Elementary Structures of Kinship.* Boston: Beacon.
Lewis, I. M. 1971. *Ecstatic Religion: An Anthropological Study of Spirit Possession and Shamanism.* Harmondsworth, England: Penguin.
Lincoln, Bruce. 1987. "Ritual, Rebellion, Resistance: Once More the Swazi Ncwala." *Man,* n.s., 22(1) (March):132–156.
Lindholm, Charles. 2000. *Charisma.* Oxford: Basil Blackwell.
Loizos, Peter. 1988. "The Virgin Mary and Marina Warner's Feminism." *London School of Economics Quarterly* 2(2):175–193.
MacCulloch, Diarmaid. 1990. *The Later Reformation in England 1547–1603.* London: Macmillan.
———. 2009. *A History of Christianity: The First Three Thousand Years.* London: Penguin.
———. 2013. *Silence: A Christian History.* London: Allen Lane.
Macfarlane, Alan. 1986. *Marriage and Love in England: Modes of Reproduction 1300–1840.* Oxford: Basil Blackwell.
———. 1987. *The Culture of Capitalism.* Oxford: Basil Blackwell.
MacKinnon, Catharine, and Andrea Dworkin. 1997. *In Harm's Way: The Pornography Civil Rights Hearings.* Cambridge, Mass.: Harvard University Press.
Malcolm, Noel. 2010. "Alberico Gentili and the Ottomans." In *The Roman Foundations of the Law of Nations: Alberico Gentili and the Justice of Empire,* ed. Benedict Kingsbury and Benjamin Straumann, pp. 127–145. Oxford: Oxford University Press.
Malinowski, Bronislaw. 1948 [1925]. *Magic, Science, and Religion and Other Essays.* Garden City, N.Y.: Doubleday.
Mauss, Marcel. 1973 [1935]. "Techniques of the Body." *Economy and Society* 2(1):70–88.
McCauley, Robert N., and E. Thomas Lawson. 2002. *Bringing Ritual to Mind: Psychological Foundations of Cultural Forms.* Cambridge: Cambridge University Press.
McIntosh, Marjorie Keniston. 2005. *Working Women in English Society 1300–1620.* Cambridge: Cambridge University Press.
Mendelson, Sara, and Patricia Crawford. 1998. *Women in Early Modern England 1550–1720.* Oxford: Clarendon.
Miller, Alice M., and Carole S. Vance. 2004. "Sexuality, Human Rights, and Health." *Health and Human Rights* 7(2):5–15.
Moore, Helen, and Julian Reid. 2011. *Manifold Greatness: The Making of the King James Bible.* Oxford: Bodleian Library.
Moore, R. I. 1990 [1987]. *The Formation of a Persecuting Society: Power and Deviance in Western Europe, 950–1250.* Oxford: Blackwell.
Morgan, Giles. 2006. *St. George.* Edison, N.J.: Chartwell.
Murphy, Donna. 2012. *The Mysterious Connection between Thomas Nashe, Thomas Dekker, and T. M.: An English Renaissance Deception?* Newcastle-upon-Tyne, England: Cambridge Scholars.
Myerhoff, Barbara. 1974. *Peyote Hunt: The Sacred Journey of the Huichol Indians.* Ithaca, N.Y.: Cornell University Press.
Narby, Jeremy, and Francis Huxley, eds. 2001. *Shamans through Time: 500 Years on the Path to Knowledge.* London: Thames and Hudson.

Obeyesekere, Gananath. 1981. *Medusa's Hair: An Essay on Personal Symbols and Religious Experience.* Chicago: University of Chicago Press.

Ortner, Sherry B. 1974. "Is Female to Male as Nature Is to Culture?" In *Woman, Culture, and Society*, ed. Michelle Zimbalist Rosaldo and Louise Lamphere, pp. 68–87. Stanford, Calif.: Stanford University Press.

Otis, Leah Lydia. 1985. *Prostitution in Medieval Society: The History of an Urban Institution in Languedoc.* Chicago: University of Chicago Press.

Pocock, D. F. 1964. "The Anthropology of Time Reckoning." *Contributions to Indian Sociology* 7 (March):18–29.

Post, J. B. 1977. "A Fifteenth-Century Customary of the Southwark Stews." *Journal of Society of Archivists* 5(7) (April):418–426.

Radcliffe-Brown, A. R. 1952. *Structure and Function in Primitive Society: Essays and Addresses.* London: Routledge and Kegan Paul.

Reilly, Leonard, and Geoff Marshall. 2001. *The Story of Bankside: From the River Thames to St. George's Circus.* Neighbourhood History No. 7. London: London Borough of Southwark.

Ricoeur, Paul. 1984 [1983]. *Time and Narrative.* Vol. 1. Kathleen McLaughlin and David Pellauer, trans. Chicago: University of Chicago Press.

Roper, Lyndal. 1989. *The Holy Household: Women and Morals in Reformation Augsburg.* Oxford: Clarendon.

Rubin, Gayle. 1975. "The Traffic in Women: Notes on the Political Economy of Sex." In *Toward an Anthropology of Women*, ed. Rayna Reiter, pp. 157–210. New York: Monthly Review Press.

———. 1994. "The Valley of the Kings: Leathermen in San Francisco 1960–1990." PhD diss., University of Michigan, Department of Anthropology.

Salgado, Gamini. 1977. *The Elizabethan Underworld.* London: Dent.

Saussure, Ferdinand de. 2013 [1916]. *Course in General Linguistics.* Roy Harris, trans. London: Bloomsbury Academic.

Schaefer, Donovan. 2015. *Religious Affects: Animality, Evolution, and Power.* Durham, N.C.: Duke University Press.

Schröder, Peter. 2010. "Vitoria, Gentili, Bodin: Sovereignty and the Law of Nations." In *The Roman Foundations of the Law of Nations: Alberico Gentili and the Justice of Empire*, ed. Benedict Kingsbury and Benjamin Straumann, pp. 163–186. Oxford: Oxford University Press.

Sheldon, Harvey. 2000. "Roman Southwark." In *London under Ground: The Archaeology of a City*, ed. Ian Haynes, Harvey Sheldon, and Lesley Hannigan, pp. 182–209. Oxford: Oxbow.

Shilham, P. R., comp. n.d. *St. George the Martyr: Southwark Brothel Prosecutions 1887.* SLHL 837. London: Southwark Local History Library.

Spenser, Edmund. 1976 [1590–1596]. *The Faerie Queene: A Selection.* London: Dent.

Spenser, Edmund, and H. M. Percival. 1893 [1590]. *Spenser: The Faerie Queene: Book I, with Introduction and Notes.* London: Macmillan.

Staal, Frits. 1982. *The Science of Ritual.* Poona, India: Bhandarkar Oriental Research Institute.

———. 1989. *Rules without Meaning: Ritual, Mantras, and the Human Sciences.* New York: Peter Lang.

Stoller, Paul. 1989. *The Taste in Ethnographic Things: The Senses in Anthropology.* Philadelphia: University of Pennyslvania Press.
Strachey, Lytton. 1928. *Elizabeth and Essex: A Tragic History.* London: Chatto and Windus.
Strenski, Ivan. 2004. "The Religion in Globalization." *Journal of the American Academy of Religion* 72(3) (September):631–652.
Strype, John. 1720. *A Survey of the Cities of London and Westminster: An Electronic Edition.* http://www.hrionline.ac.uk/strype/index.jsp.
Taussig, Michael. 1987. *Shamanism, Colonialism, and the Wild Man: A Study in Terror and Healing.* Chicago: University of Chicago Press.
Thomas, Keith. 1971. *Religion and the Decline of Magic: Studies in Popular Beliefs in Sixteenth and Seventeenth Century England.* London: Weidenfeld and Nicolson.
Thomas, Nicholas, and Caroline Humphrey, eds. 1994. *Shamanism, History, and the State.* Ann Arbor: University of Michigan Press.
Thompson, Sharon. 1992. *Going All the Way: Narratives about Adolescent Sexuality.* New York: Farrar, Straus and Giroux.
Toffin, Gérard. 2010. *La Fête Spectacle: Théâtre et Rite au Népal.* Paris: Maison des Sciences de l'Hommes.
Townsley, Graham. 1993. "Song Paths: The Ways and Means of Yaminahua Shamanic Knowledge." *L'Homme* 33(126–128) (April–December):449–468.
Turner, Victor. 1969. *The Ritual Process: Structure and Anti-Structure.* New York: Aldine.
Tyacke, Nicholas. 2001. *Aspects of English Protestantism c. 1530–1700.* Manchester, England: Manchester University Press.
Vance, Carole S. 1984. *Pleasure and Danger: Exploring Women's Sexuality.* Boston: Routledge and Kegan Paul.
———. 1990. "Negotiating Sex and Gender in the Attorney General's Commission on Pornography." In *Uncertain Terms: Negotiating Gender in American Culture*, ed. Faye Ginsburg and Anna Lowenhaupt Tsing, pp. 118–134. Boston: Beacon.
———, chair. 2005. "Ethnography and Public Policy: What Do We Know about Trafficking?" School for Advanced Research seminar, Santa Fe, N.M., April 17–21.
van Gennep, Arnold. 1960 [1909]. *The Rites of Passage.* Monika B. Vizedom and Gabrielle L. Caffee, trans. London: Routledge and Kegan Paul.
Wabuda, Susan. 2002. *Preaching during the English Reformation.* Cambridge: Cambridge University Press.
Walkowitz, Judith. 1980. *Prostitution in Victorian Society: Women, Class, and the State.* Cambridge: Cambridge University Press.
Ward, Barbara E. 1966. "Sociological Self-Awareness: Some Uses of the Conscious Models." *Man*, n.s., 1(2) (June):201–215.
———. 1979. "Not Merely Players: Drama, Art and Ritual in Traditional China." *Man*, n.s., 14(1) (March):18–39.
Warner, Marina. 1990 [1976]. *Alone of All Her Sex: The Myth and the Cult of the Virgin Mary.* London: Picador.

Weber, Max. 1985 [1930]. *The Protestant Ethic and the Spirit of Capitalism.* Talcott Parsons, trans. London: Unwin.
Weeks, Jeffrey. 1986. *Sexuality.* London: Routledge.
Weitzer, Ronald. 2011. *Legalizing Prostitution: From Illicit Vice to Legal Business.* New York: New York University Press.
Whitehouse, Harvey. 2004. *Modes of Religiosity: A Cognitive Theory of Religious Transmission.* Walnut Creek, Calif.: AltaMira.
"Winchester House and Park." 1950. In *Survey of London*, vol. 22, *Bankside (The Parishes of St. Saviour and Christchurch Southwark)*, ed. Howard Roberts and Walter H. Godfrey, pp. 45–56. London: London County Council. http://www.british-history.ac.uk/survey-london/vol22/pp45–56.
Woodhead, Linda. 2002. "Christianity." In *Religions in the Modern World: Traditions and Transformations*, ed. Linda Woodhead, Paul Fletcher, Hiroko Kawanami, and David Smith, pp. 153–181. New York: Routledge.
Wunderli, Richard M. 1981. *London Church Courts and Society on the Eve of the Reformation.* Cambridge, Mass: Medieval Academy of America.
Žižek, Slavoj. 1989. *The Sublime Object of Ideology.* London: Verso.

INDEX

Page numbers in italics refer to figures and tables.

SONDRA L. HAUSNER is Associate Professor in the Study of Religion at the University of Oxford and a Fellow and Tutor at St. Peter's College. She is the author of *Wandering with Sadhus: Ascetics in the Hindu Himalayas* (IUP, 2007), the editor of *Durkheim in Dialogue: A Centenary Celebration of "The Elementary Forms of Religious Life,"* and the co-editor of *Women's Renunciation in South Asia: Nuns, Yoginis, Saints, and Singers* and *Religion in Diaspora: Cultures of Citizenship*. She has published widely on the religions of South Asia, gender, and migration.